Reconciliation

After

Violent Conflict

A Handbook

Handbook Series

Reconciliation
After
Violent Conflict
A Handbook

Editors:

*David Bloomfield, Teresa Barnes
and Luc Huyse*

Contributors:

*David Bloomfield, Noreen Callaghan, Vannath
Chea, Mark Freeman, Brandon Hamber,
Priscilla B. Hayner, Luc Huyse, Peter Uvin,
Stef Vandeginste, and Ian White.*

Handbook Series.

The International IDEA Handbook Series seeks to present comparative analysis, information and insights on a range of democratic institutions and processes. Handbooks are aimed primarily at policy-makers, politicians, civil society actors and practitioners in the field. They are also of interest to academia, the deomocracy assistance community and other bodies.

© International Institute for Democracy and Electoral Assistance 2003
Reprinted: October 2005

Applications for permission to reproduce or translate all or any part of this publication should be made to:
Information Unit
International IDEA
SE -103 34 Stockholm
Sweden

International IDEA encourages dissemination of its work and will promptly respond to requests for permission to reproduce or translate its publications.

Graphic design by: Holmberg & Holmberg Design AB, Stockholm, Sweden
Front cover photos sourced from: CORBIS/SCANPIX
Printed by: Bulls Tryckeri AB Halmstad, Sweden
ISBN: 91-89098-91-9

Foreword

There is no handy roadmap for reconciliation. There is no short cut or simple prescription for healing the wounds and divisions of a society in the aftermath of sustained violence. Creating trust and understanding between former enemies is a supremely difficult challenge. It is, however, an essential one to address in the process of building a lasting peace. Examining the painful past, acknowledging it and understanding it, and above all transcending it together, is the best way to guarantee that it does not – and cannot – happen again.

As our experience in South Africa has taught us, each society must discover its own route to reconciliation. Reconciliation cannot be imposed from outside, nor can someone else's map get us to our destination: it must be our own solution. This involves a very long and painful journey, addressing the pain and suffering of the victims, understanding the motivations of offenders, bringing together estranged communities, trying to find a path to justice, truth and, ultimately, peace. Faced with each new instance of violent conflict, new solutions must be devised that are appropriate to the particular context, history and culture in question.

And yet, despite the differences between Cape Town and Kigali, between Belgrade and Belfast, there are also similarities in each situation. The authors of this Handbook are not proposing simple solutions, but they are offering a range of options, built on expertise and experience drawn from around the world. They provide a solid basis for constructing, adapting and adopting ideas and tools – new and old, foreign and domestic, but above all practical and effective – to design a reconciliation process appropriate to a particular set of circumstances.

In South Africa we have travelled a long way down the road of reconciliation, but our journey is not yet over. Reconciliation is a long-term process and it must – and will – continue for many years to come. And yet, we have made a good start. For us, truth was at the heart of reconciliation: the need to find out the truth about the horrors of the past, the better to ensure that they never happen again. And that is the central significance of reconciliation. Without it people have no sense of safety, no trust, no confidence in the future. The aim must be, as the Handbook's authors say, 'to build a shared future from a divided past'. There is no alternative way to lasting peace.

As we continue our own journey towards peace in South Africa, I commend this Handbook to those who struggle for reconciliation in other contexts around the world. I hope that the practical tools and lessons from experience presented here will inspire, assist and support them in their supremely important task.

DESMOND TUTU
Archbishop Emeritus

Preface

IDEA's vocation is to promote sustainable democracy around the world. This includes attention to the specific challenges of democratization after violent conflict. This may involve the reconstruction of politics and society by national actors, or the temporary stewardship of democracy-building by the United Nations or others. In either context, the subject of reconciliation – the process of addressing the legacy of past violence and rebuilding the broken relationships it has caused – is a focus of increasing interest. There is also an urgent demand for better tools to address this most difficult of post-violence issues. This Handbook is a response to such demand.

For IDEA, democratic processes and structures are in themselves the most effective means for the peaceful prevention and management of conflict, especially in post-conflict contexts, where the most urgent need is for mechanisms that will, first and foremost, ensure that there will be no return to the violence of the past. More specifically, an appropriate reconciliation process – designed to fit the context, and owned by all stakeholders concerned – is a vital measure in order to address adequately the legacy of the past, to develop working relationships in the present, to build a shared vision of the future, and thus to support and sustain nascent democratic structures. We do not offer universal models of reconciliation in this handbook. Rather, we offer general advice and specific options to policy-makers and practitioners, to assist them in designing the most suitable reconciliation process for their particular needs. These options are based on actual experience from post-conflict situations around the world. This book contains accumulated wisdom from acknowledged experts, politicians, civil society leaders, all of whom speak from their own personal experience of tackling the challenges of reconciliation in their own situations.

Reconciliation has only recently been recognized as a necessary component of post-violence reconstruction. Evidence and experience are still being accumulated. Consequently, this Handbook does not pretend to be a definitive statement on the subject, but rather a practically-oriented survey of the knowledge to date. Indeed, we invite critical comment and further inputs. We know that reconciliation can never be a quick fix. It requires time and patience, an incremental approach and a capacity to evolve and adapt to challenges and opportunities.

The topic is huge, but the need is great since reconciliation is among the most difficult challenges facing new or restored democracies. We hope that the contents can be of practical assistance in stimulating the design and implementation of appropriate reconciliation processes which will, in turn, support and strengthen appropriate democratic structures. This Handbook, which is produced as part of IDEA's work on democracy building and conflict management, will also be used in training, discussion and co-operation with colleagues and partner bodies around the world and we invite interested organizations to make contact.

We owe a huge debt of thanks to Prof. Luc Huyse, who shouldered the onerous task of lead writer on this project. We could not have chosen a more able, more knowledgeable or more co-operative colleague. We also thank the many experts of world renown who have contributed to the text, including Birgitte Soerensen, our adviser on gender issues. We are very grateful to our member state, the Netherlands and observer country, Switzerland, which contributed towards the cost of the project. Last but not least, credit also goes to our own staff in the Democracy, Dialogue and Conflict Management Programme and the Publications Section, who have seen the Handbook through from start to finish.

KAREN FOGG
Secretary-General, International IDEA

Reconciliation After Violent Conflict
A Handbook

PART IV THE INTERNATIONAL COMMUNITY

ANNEXES

BOXES, FIGURES AND TABLES

ACRONYMS

ANC	African National Congress
CCF	Christian Children's Fund
CEH	Comisión para el Esclarecimiento Histórico
	(Commission for Historical Clarification, Guatemala)
CPP	Cambodian People's Party
ICC	International Criminal Court
ICTR	International Criminal Tribunal for Rwanda
ICTY	International Criminal Tribunal for the former Yugoslavia
IRA	Irish Republican Army
LIVE	Let's Involve the Victims' Experience
LTTE	Liberation Tigers of Tamil Eelam
MSF	Médecins Sans Frontières
NGO	Non-governmental organization
OAU	Organization of African Unity
REMHI	Proyecto Interdiocesano para la Recuperación de la Memoria Histórica
	(Inter-Diocesan Project for the Recovery of the Historical Memory)
RRC	Reparation and Rehabilitation Committee (of the South African TRC)
RUC	Royal Ulster Constabulary
SERPAJ	Servicio Paz y Justicia en América Latina
	(Service for Peace and Justice in Latin America)
TRC	Truth and Reconciliation Commission (South Africa)
UNCC	United Nations Compensation Commission
UNDP	United Nations Development Programme
UNCHR	United Nations Commission for Human Rights
UNHCHR	United Nations High Commission for Human Rights
UNHCR	United Nations High Commission for Refugees
URNG	Unidad Revolucionaria Nacional Guatemalteca
	(Guatemalan National Revolutionary Unit)
WHO	World Health Organization
ZANU	Zimbabwe African National Union
ZANU-PF	Zimbabwe African National Union-Patriotic Front
ZAPU	Zimbabwe African People's Union
ZIPRA	Zimbabwe People's Revolutionary Army

CHAPTER 1

Reconciliation: an Introduction

DAVID BLOOMFIELD

1.1 Democracy and Reconciliation

Our starting point for this Handbook is a conviction that the best form of post-conflict government is a democratic one. This is not so much a principled stand as a pragmatic one. Winston Churchill famously expressed a similar pragmatism when he remarked: "Democracy is the worst form of government except all those other forms that have been tried from time to time". It may not be perfect, but in an imperfect world it is the best option available. As universal human rights become increasingly accepted as the core principles of governance, democracy becomes more and more clearly the most effective way of implementing those principles - equality, representation, participation, accountability and so on. Quite rightly, every democracy is unique in some aspects, depending on context, culture and values. But each has those principles at its heart.

Additionally, though, democracy is unique among forms of governance in its capacity to manage conflict. And this is a key attribute in a post-violence context. Democracy is a system for managing difference without recourse to violence. Differences (of opinion, belief, ideology, culture etc.) are a natural part of every society. And conflict arises from such differences. Rather than eradicating or removing differences, or excluding some groups who differ within society, democracy functions as a process through which differences are brought out, acknowledged and dealt with in a way that permits them to exist without threatening the whole system. It is, in other words, a system for managing conflict. This process of conflict management involves debate, argument, disagreement, compromise and cooperation, all within a system that permits opposing points of view to coexist fairly without recourse to violence. Of course, sometimes democracy fails, but evidence from around the world suggests that it succeeds more often than the alternatives.

This makes democracy particularly relevant given the changes in the nature of violent conflict since the end of the cold war. Most violent conflicts in the world now originate as intra-state conflict, that is, they begin as internal struggles within a state - civil wars, internal oppression of minorities, uprisings, ethnic or religious rivalry, perceived resource inequities and so on - as opposed to the previously prevalent pattern where they originated most often between separate states. In general, the resolution of intra-state conflict requires not new or reformed government structures that have not eradicated the difference(s) over which the conflict was fought, but rather structures that are designed, through a negotiation process, to manage those differences peacefully. And the most popular way to construct such a system nowadays is to base it on the principle of respect for human rights in the form of democratic structures. As we move away from either–or, win–lose solutions to conflict, democracies become the practical manifestation of cooperative, win–win solutions.

> Democracy is a system for managing difference without recourse to violence.

A functioning democracy, then, is built on a dual foundation: a set of fair procedures for peacefully handling the issues that divide a society (the political and social structures of governance) and a set of working relationships between the groups involved. A society will not develop those working relationships if the structures are not fair and, conversely, the structures will not function properly, however fair and just they are, if there is not the minimum degree of cooperation in the interrelationships of those involved.

This realization has in recent years been absorbed and assimilated by the international community. Thus, for example, the United Nations (UN) now speaks of democracy as being not only the holding of regular elections but the development of a "democratic culture" within a society, so that the patterns of democratic discourse, of conflict management, filter through to all levels of political and civil society and manifest themselves in constructive relationships between society's differing constituencies and opinion groupings. There is still considerable debate on exactly what a democratic culture means and how to promote it, but clearly it suggests the need for cooperative relationships to implement the structures of democracy.

The conclusion to all this is that relationships matter. And that is where reconciliation comes in.

In what are nowadays termed "post-conflict" societies, the pattern is generally that the warring sides negotiate a settlement in the form of new structures for governance. Almost always, these structures are democratic. So former enemies - often with a long history of violence between them - find themselves faced with the challenge of implementing the new negotiated structures for the future management of their differences on a minimally cooperative basis. One of the biggest obstacles to such cooperation is that, because of the violence of the past, their relations are based on antagonism, distrust, disrespect and, quite possibly, hurt and hatred. It is hardly a recipe for optimism, no matter how effective or perfect those new structures may be.

So there is a pressing need to address that negative relationship. Not to make enemies love each other, by any means, but to engender a minimum basis of trust so that there can be a degree of cooperation and mutual reliance between them. To achieve this, they need to examine and address their previous relationship and their violent past. Reconciliation is the process for doing exactly that.

While democratic compromise produces the solutions regarding the *issues* in conflict, then, reconciliation addresses the *relationships* between those who will have to implement those solutions. It is important to point out, though, that this applies not simply to the politicians and the deal-makers who are engaged in the compromise. It applies to the entire population. The relationship which must be addressed is not simply that between parliamentarians or leaders, but between whole communities. It is entire communities who have to begin to reorient themselves from the adversarial, antagonistic relations of war to more respect-based relations of cooperation. The very best democratic system in the world produced by the most able democrats will not survive if the general populations to which it applies are not minimally prepared to trust the system and each other and at least try it out. A key element of that process of developing a democratic culture is to engender the relationships necessary for good democracy between communities, neighbours, constituencies, individuals and so on.

In a very important sense, then, reconciliation underpins democracy by developing the working relationships necessary for its successful implementation. Likewise, of course, democracy also underpins reconciliation: at many points in this Handbook, the authors repeatedly point out that reconciliation - the healing of relationships - needs the underpinnings of economic justice, of political and social power-sharing, and so on. Democracy and reconciliation are intertwined, indeed, interdependent.

Again, we return to the point made above: we promote democracy and reconciliation for pragmatic reasons. There is a moral case to be made that reconciliation is the right thing to do. But there is also a powerful pragmatic argument to be made: positive working relationships generate the atmosphere within which governance can thrive, while negative relations will work to undermine even the best system of governance. Reconciliation, though not easy, is the most effective way to address those relations. (Indeed, the case study of Cambodia that follows chapter 3 warns against trying to deal with reconciliation purely through politics. Issues and relationships are separate, though intertwined, elements; and politics and reconciliation are separate but interdependent processes.) As this Handbook demonstrates, all the experience around the world teaches the importance of this point. Reconciliation is not a luxury, or an add-on to democracy. Reconciliation is an absolute necessity.

> While democratic compromise produces solutions regarding issues in conflict, reconciliation addresses the relationships between those who will have to implement those solutions.

1.2 The Process of Reconciliation
1.2.1 What is Reconciliation?

Reconciliation is a complex term, and there is little agreement on its definition.

This is mainly because reconciliation is both a *goal* - something to achieve - and a *process* - a means to achieve that goal. A great deal of controversy arises from confusing these two ideas. This Handbook focuses very firmly on the process. The goal of reconciliation is a future aspiration, something important to aim towards, perhaps even an ideal state to hope for. But the process is very much a present-tense way of dealing with how things are - building a reconciliation process is the means to work, effectively and practically, towards that final goal - and is invaluable in itself.

A second source of complexity is that the process of reconciliation happens in many contexts - between wife and husband, for example, between offender and victim, between friends who have argued or between nations or communities that have fought. The focus of this Handbook is on reconciliation after sustained and widespread violent conflict. Typically, we have in mind what is often called a post-conflict situation: war has ended, a settlement has been reached, and a new regime is struggling to construct a new society out of the ashes of the old. Part of that task of construction is to build better relationships between the previously warring factions. This Handbook concentrates on such specific situations, typically the aftermath of civil war or the end of a brutally oppressive regime, because those are the contexts around the world today where the need for reconciliation is most pressing. But we hope and believe that the tools offered here will be useful in other, different contexts.

> Reconciliation is both a goal and a process. This Handbook focuses very firmly on the process.

Reconciliation is an over-arching process which includes the search for truth, justice, forgiveness, healing and so on. At its simplest, it means finding a way to live alongside former enemies - not necessarily to love them, or forgive them, or forget the past in any way, but to coexist with them, to develop the degree of cooperation necessary to share our society with them, so that we all have better lives together than we have had separately. Politics is a process to deal with the *issues* that have divided us in the past. Reconciliation is a parallel process that redesigns the *relationship* between us. This is an immense challenge, and no one should think that it is quick or easy. But the effort carries a great reward: effective reconciliation is the best guarantee that the violence of the past will not return. If we can build a new relationship between us that is built on respect and a real understanding of each other's needs, fears and aspirations, the habits and patterns of cooperation that we then develop are the best safeguard against a return to violent division.

And so we reach our basic definition of reconciliation: it is a process through which a society moves from a divided past to a shared future.

1.2.2 The Process

We can make three simple, but very profound, observations about this process, which underpin most of what follows in this Handbook:

• It is not only a process: unfortunately, it is a long-term process. There is no quick-fix to reconciliation. It takes time. And it takes its own time: its pace cannot be dictated.

• It is also a deep process: it involves a coming to terms with an imperfect reality which demands changes in our attitudes, our aspirations, our emotions and feelings, perhaps even our beliefs. Such profound change is a vast and often painful challenge, and cannot be rushed or imposed.

• As defined in this Handbook, reconciliation is also a very broad process. It applies to everyone. It is not just a process for those who suffered directly and those who inflicted the suffering, central though those people are. The attitudes and beliefs that underpin violent conflict spread much more generally through a community and must be addressed at that broad level. So, while there is a crucial individual element to reconciliation, there is also a community-wide element that demands a questioning of the attitudes, prejudices and negative stereotypes that we all develop about "the enemy" during violent conflict. This is because our definition of the enemy is rarely limited to a few politicians or fighters, but rather grows to encompass a whole community (e.g., "Palestinians", or "Irish Protestants" or "Tutsi") or a regime and all its supporters ("Sandinistas" or "the Taliban"). Even those who have suffered or benefited little from the past absorb the beliefs of their community and their culture, and those beliefs can effectively block the reconciliation process if they are left unaddressed. So reconciliation needs to be a broad, inclusive process.

> Reconciliation applies to everyone. It is not just a process for those who suffered directly and those who inflicted the suffering.

If it is to be a properly broad process, reconciliation must be inclusive of the many and various interests and experiences across a society.

Gender Aspects

The most obvious and pressing example of this need concerns gender perspectives. This requires an understanding of how violent conflict involves and affects different social groups beyond the most immediate impact, such as torture and displacement. A gender perspective illustrates some of the "small conflicts" that lie beneath the main conflict and which need to be addressed in order to create a sustainable peace and a democratic society. For example, women have experienced sexual abuse in the form of mass rape, forced marriages and prostitution, with social stigmatization and marginalization as a consequence. For such women reconciliation involves offences against them being recognized and punished, illegitimate children being recognized as legitimate with full rights, and resources being allocated to deal with the physical and psychological consequences. For war widows, reconciliation would be expected to include compensation and to address existing inheritance laws and practices that dispossess them or hinder them in fulfilling their new obligations as family providers.

A gender perspective also entails looking at how men are affected. In the context of reconciliation it is perhaps necessary to recognize that armed conflict encourages a "warrior identity" while at the same time doing damage to the male self-perception as provider and protector of a family. The frustration and anger this may give rise to can be a serious threat to a reconciliation process. Establishing trustful and respectful relations between men and women, and between particularly targeted groups of men and women, is essential for fashioning a democratic society. Such relations require full recognition of how a particular conflict has involved and affected men and women in different ways.

Gender is an indispensable dimension of reconciliation at the official and institutional levels. Most experience demonstrates that women (and often also other politically marginalized groups) have limited access to peace negotiation processes and little or no representation in government and other decision-making bodies. This lack of involvement in political processes seriously reduces their possibilities to voice their concerns and interests and ensure that these are recognized as political concerns at a crucial point. And this may again result in a certain alienation from the nation and the state.

1.2.3 Truth, Justice and Reconciliation

This Handbook recommends a wider view of the reconciliation process than is often used. For example, in many post-conflict contexts, people talk about "truth and reconciliation" and often establish commissions of enquiry with exactly that title. Seeking for accuracy about the past is a vital step in the reconciliation process, according to our wide definition, as is allowing victims to tell their stories. But "truth" in itself will not bring reconciliation. Truth-seeking is a key ingredient, but only one ingredient, in reconciliation. In the same way justice is a vital requirement for healing wounds, making offenders accountable and re-establishing relations of equity and respect. But justice alone does not bring reconciliation. Truth and justice are not separate to reconciliation: they are key parts of it.

Box 1.1: The Reconciliation Process

The process of reconciliation is not:

• an excuse for impunity;

• only an individual process;

• in opposition to/an alternative to truth or justice;

• a quick answer;

• a religious concept;

• perfect peace;

• an excuse to forget; nor

• a matter of merely forgiving.

The process of reconciliation is:

• finding a way to live that permits a vision of the future;

• the (re)building of relationships;

• coming to terms with past acts and enemies;

• a society-wide, long-term process of deep change;

• a process of acknowledging, remembering, and learning from the past; and

• voluntary and cannot be imposed.

Many people, especially the victims of great hurt, are suspicious of reconciliation and see it as an excuse to belittle or ignore their suffering. It can indeed be misused in that way. But this is the result of thinking of reconciliation as only a goal, not a process. These people often, and rightly, suspect that a fast move to a state where everyone is apparently reconciled to the past and to each other is a way of short-cutting proper processes of justice, truth-telling and punishment - that it means they must "forgive and forget". This is not the aim of this Handbook. That state of reconciliation is a very long-term objective, which can only be reached after all the important ingredients of justice, truth, healing and so on have been addressed. And the overall process in which all these and other issues combine is the reconciliation process.

Most of what follows in these pages is about examining the complex relationships between these issues as they make up the process.

1.3 The Necessity of Reconciliation

There is nothing simple about the reconciliation process. Especially in the immediate aftermath of a negotiated settlement to a violent conflict, it can appear to be an impediment to more important priorities. With the urgent political pressures to establish the newly agreed democratic structures, resource pressure and time pressure, it is in fact very tempting, especially to politicians, to concentrate on the political process. Indeed, they may genuinely not see how to include reconciliation in the mass of work ahead of them. Thus reconciliation can be delayed until other priorities are completed, or can be reduced to a quick commission of enquiry which will acknowledge the painful past and rapidly move on. Everyone wants to get on, to move fast, to get away from the past as quickly as possible.

It can seem as if slowing things down, dwelling on the painful past and the unfinished thoughts and feelings around past violence, would endanger the new political and social structures. The argument runs something like this: "How are we to expect our politicians to begin establishing the patterns of future cooperation in government if we spend time digging up and examining in public the very things that divided them in the past? That will surely just undermine the fragile cooperation that we are attempting, by holding on to the past instead of looking to the future. Would it not be better to concentrate for the time being on our similarities and leave our differences to a later, less tense time?"

This is understandable, but it is counterproductive. Such reflection on the past is as necessary as it is painful because a divided society can only build its shared future out of its divided past. It is not possible to forget the past and start completely fresh as if nothing had happened. Indeed, the motivation for building a future is precisely to ensure that the past does not return - and so a clear understanding of, and a coming to terms with, that past is the very best way to guarantee it will not come back to haunt a society. The past must be addressed in order to reach the future. Reconciliation, if it is designed and implemented in a genuine and meaningful way, is the means to do that. Throughout this Handbook, tools are offered for such examination of the past, the use of which will generate a more cooperative present in order to begin to develop a safer future of coexistence.

> The past must be addressed in order to reach the future. Reconciliation is the means to do that.

At the political level, failure to address the past through a reconciliation process - easier option though it might appear - will almost guarantee the failure of the future. Politicians reach agreement through negotiation over the issues in conflict. They find compromises, bargains or pragmatic ways to cooperate within the bounds of their self-interest. That is their job, and it is a vital part of transforming a situation of former conflict into one of future peace. But their best efforts will be totally undermined if they do not also address the broken relationship between the communities they represent, as well as the issues that broke it. The very best democratic system in the world will not endure if sections of its population do not have a modestly cooperative relationship underlying their agreement to work with the new structures.

This is the basic, pragmatic reason why every new post-conflict democracy has to reconcile. Where reconciliation, at first glance, may seem to be a hindrance to establishing working democracy, in fact it is a necessary requirement for the long-term survival of that democracy. This is not the easy answer, but it is the reality. Meaningful reconciliation is a difficult, painful and complex process, but it must be grasped, because ignoring it sows the seeds of later, greater failure. On the other hand, effectively reconciling the divided elements of a society will, with time, permit the development of truly cooperative patterns of working and envisioning the future, which will be among the strongest guarantors of successful democratization.

1.4 No Easy Answers

Reconciliation is never a theoretical matter, but always happens in a specific context.

There is therefore no simple recipe for success that can be described here and which may then be applied around the world. There is no single correct way to devise such a process. Reconciliation is not a problem with one solution. As every conflict is different, and every democratic settlement (indeed, every democratic system) is different, so a reconciliation process will differ from all others in important respects, even as it shares many similarities with them. That is why this Handbook does not prescribe a single solution for all contexts. The only thing which applies to every post-violence transition is the need to address the issue of reconciliation.

Beyond that, it is important to remain flexible and creative about designing a specific process to achieve reconciliation in a specific context. Since the experience of the South African peace process it has become almost automatic to emulate that example and establish a truth and reconciliation commission as part of a settlement. Clearly, for all its imperfections and limitations, the South African Truth and Reconciliation Commission (TRC) played a vital and very high-profile role in embedding new and peaceful patterns of interaction in that previously deeply divided society. Much can be learned from it. But one lesson that cannot be assumed is the absolute need for a TRC in all circumstances. (Northern Ireland, for example, continues along the rocky road of implementing and bedding down its new settlement structures without such a commission. Its settlement did, however, provide for a Minister for Victims to address the issues of the past violence in a way appropriate to the Northern Irish context and culture.)

Resources

The issue of resources, financial and human, is another element where there are no easy answers. It would be pointless to prescribe state-of-the-art ideal reconciliation processes that demand huge financial resources, since the sad reality is that most post-conflict societies are precisely those who have fewest resources to spare. Yet a reconciliation process is not necessarily a cheap option. So how can resources be found?

This is impossible to answer in general terms, but various options have been noted in different contexts.

Reparations schemes, in particular, tend to be hugely expensive. Following Iraq's 1990–1991 invasion of Kuwait, the United Nations Compensation Commission (UNCC) set up a system to pay compensation to victims of the invasion from money garnered through a tax on Iraqi oil exports. In South Africa, the possibility of levying a tax on the incomes of those who had indirectly benefited from the apartheid system was proposed, but never implemented. (See chapter 9 for a discussion of such issues.) In Rwanda, a public fund has been set up from which reparations payments will be drawn at a future date. (Of course, the challenge still remains for Rwanda to convince more international donors to actually put money into the fund.)

Comparatively, some aspects of reconciliation are not that expensive. The case study from Northern Ireland (following chapter 6) demonstrates that many reconciliation activities rely above all on one resource which is usually plentiful - ordinary people who are prepared to pay a personal, rather than a financial, price to achieve progress. Indeed, much reconciliation work is about small-scale human interaction. Symbolic forms of apology, reparation and restitution - public ceremonies, awards, memorials and so on - can also be effective and low-cost (though certainly not sufficient on their own). Reparations in the form of access to services - for instance, education or medical help on a free or subsidized basis - also reduce the real cost without reducing the value.

Some post-conflict societies tend to look within their own culture and traditions for existing, home-grown mechanisms for reconciliation and justice (see chapter 7). The fact that these are usually cheaper than importing huge Western-designed models is one reason to encourage this development. (Another reason is that, since such mechanisms are anchored in existing values and relationships, they are more likely to win broad support. But this does not mean that they are the perfect answers. Adaptation is still needed to ensure that such "local justice" tools function inclusively and fairly, particularly with regard to women and their interests, experiences and rights.)

While it may sound almost trite to say that the international community is a potential source of finance and expertise, there is a growing degree of truth in this. Increasingly, bilateral and multilateral donors, as well as multilateral and regional actors, are beginning to realize the importance of reconciliation as an ingredient in conflict prevention, human development, human security, the elimination of poverty and peace-building, as has been shown by recent declarations from the Organization for Economic Co-operation and Development (OECD) Development Assistance Committee (DAC), for example, or the literature produced by several development cooperation agencies in the West. Such donors are more prepared than before to see reconciliation as fitting their general parameters for assistance.

Above all, lack of resources must not become an excuse for not beginning the process of reconciliation. Some elements are low-cost; some elements will attract donors. Economic constraints can, and always will, impinge on the process design, but even economics is not a good enough reason to avoid completely the necessity of effective reconciliation.

Every attempt has been made to illustrate all assertions in this Handbook with a concrete example from the real world. This has not been straightforward, and it has not always been possible. Reconciliation as a concept is still a comparatively new element in peacemaking, and some of its ideas remain untested or unaddressed; others have only been applied in real situations once or twice. Consequently, it has sometimes been necessary to fall back on making general points without a specific example. Nonetheless, the generalizations made here are based on impressions gathered from close examination of many varied reconciliation initiatives, peace-building efforts and conflict management strategies.

> There is no universally applicable, perfect reconciliation method or model.

What is perhaps most important is to emphasize that no one has produced a perfect reconciliation method or model - indeed, of course, there is no such universally applicable thing - and therefore those who face the challenge of post-conflict peace-building should trust their own capacities to take what advice they can get from elsewhere but to be creative in developing their own original process.

What follows in this Handbook is a wealth of information and advice, tools and methods, to assist such a process. For now, in a brief conclusion to this introductory chapter, we simply offer the following very basic general principles which should underpin the design of every reconciliation process, and which may assist readers as they work through this Handbook:

• Begin early, when attitudes are most receptive to change and challenge.
• Stick to the commitment, and deal with the hard issues: they will only get harder with time.
• Give it sufficient time: it cannot be rushed.
• Be transparent about the goals, the difficulties, the time span and the resources.

1.5 How to Use This Handbook

The pages that follow present an array of the various tools that can be, and have been, employed in the design and implementation of a reconciliation process. There are some practical ideas borrowed from academics and practitioners. (In the interests of readability, full reference details of individual citations are provided in the "References and Further Reading" sections at the end of each chapter.) Most of the tools, however, come from the experience of others grappling with the issues of reconciliation in various contexts.

There is no "right answer" to the challenge of reconciliation, and so we do not try to prescribe a one-size-fits-all solution. Instead, we present the tools, with their strengths and weaknesses: they are to be adopted and adapted, changed or replaced, as they suit the specific context to which a reader applies them. Some will be appropriate, while some will not. The business of carefully thinking through their relevance or otherwise (including asking the question, "Why won't that work here?") should be an illuminating one and a positive step towards providing the most suitable process for the context to hand.

Part I examines the basic concepts and general principles of the process of reconciliation (chapter 2) and the context within which it takes place (chapter 3). The points it makes are illustrated by case studies from Zimbabwe and Cambodia. Part II looks in depth at the people involved at the core of the process - the victims (chapter 4) and the offenders (chapter 5). Part III examines the key instruments - healing (chapter 6), justice (chapter 7), truth-telling (chapter 8) and reparation (chapter 9). It is illustrated by case studies from Northern Ireland, Rwanda, South Africa and Guatemala. Part IV looks briefly at the supportive role of the international community (chapter 10), followed by a brief summary and conclusion to the entire Handbook (chapter 11).

Annexes at the end provide information on relevant organizations and useful internet sites.

CHAPTER 2

The Process of Reconciliation

LUC HUYSE

Reconciliation means different things to different people. Its significance varies from culture to culture, and changes with the passage of time. To get a grip on the concept, the Handbook poses four basic questions:

- What?
- Who?
- How?
- When?

2.1 What is Reconciliation?

2.1.1 Ideally

Ideally reconciliation prevents, once and for all, the use of the past as the seed of renewed conflict. It consolidates peace, breaks the cycle of violence and strengthens newly established or reintroduced democratic institutions.

As a backward-looking operation, reconciliation brings about the personal healing of survivors, the reparation of past injustices, the building or rebuilding of non-violent relationships between individuals and communities, and the acceptance by the former parties to a conflict of a common vision and understanding of the past. In its forward-looking dimension, reconciliation means enabling victims and perpetrators to get on with life and, at the level of society, the establishment of a civilized political dialogue and an adequate sharing of power.

2.1.2 In Practice

In practice such all-encompassing reconciliation is not easy to realize. The experience of a brutal past makes the search for peaceful coexistence a delicate and intricate operation. Reconciliation is not an isolated act, but a constant readiness to leave the tyranny of violence and fear behind. It is not an event but a process, and as such usually a difficult, long and unpredictable one, involving various steps and stages. Each move demands changes in attitudes (e.g., tolerance instead of revenge), in conduct (e.g., joint commemoration of all the dead instead of separate, partisan memorials) and in the institutional environment (e.g., integrating the war veterans of both sides into one national army instead of keeping ex-combatants in quasi-private militias). Above all, the approach must be that every step counts, that every effort has value, and that in this delicate domain even a small improvement is significant progress.

There is a certain danger in talking about reconciliation in terms of strict sequences. The process is not a linear one. At each stage a relapse back into more violent means of dealing with conflicts is always a real possibility. And the stages do not always follow logically after each other in any set order. Nonetheless, they remain essential ingredients for lasting reconciliation.

Three Stages
Stage 1. Replacing Fear by Non-Violent Coexistence

When the shooting stops, the first step away from hatred, hostility and bitterness is the achievement of non-violent coexistence between the antagonist individuals and groups.

This means at a minimum looking for alternatives to revenge. A South African observer, Charles Villa-Vicencio, writes: "At the lowest level coexistence implies no more than a willingness not to kill one another - a case of walking by on the other side of the street". For some the basis for this step will be war-weariness or the simple but realistic conclusion that killing does not bring the dead back to life, or it may be based on the belief that, as Martin Luther King said, those who do not learn to live together as brothers [SIC] are all going to perish together as fools. An encouraging thought here is that, even in the midst of the most cruel conflicts, small islands of tolerance and civility always continue to exist - men and women who, through acts of extreme courage, save the lives of people "from the other side".

The move towards such coexistence requires first of all that victims and perpetrators be freed from the paralyzing isolation and all-consuming self-pity in which they often live. This involves the building or renewal of communication inside the communities of victims and offenders and between them. Political and community leaders, non-governmental organizations (NGOs) and religious institutions have a serious responsibility here. They can initiate or sustain programmes for such liberating communication. Or, as symbolic representatives of victims and offenders, they can initiate dialogue if those directly involved are not yet ready to talk. (Chapter 6 concludes with a case study of a Northern Irish initiative for victim-to-victim and victim-to-offender dialogue.)

A second condition is a safe environment. Without a minimum of physical security there is no prospect of any progress along the path to reconciliation. Local and/or international political decision-makers have a crucial role to play at this point. Serious effort must be directed towards establishing the rule of law on equitable and accepted terms.

Conflicts do not disappear with this step in the reconciliation process. Individuals, groups and communities continue to be adversaries, but they agree to disagree and to use less violent means to accommodate old (and new) disputes. One possible way is to exchange private vengeance for retribution by an institution (e.g., a criminal court) which is bound by agreed rules (see chapter 7).

Stage 2. When Fear No Longer Rules: Building Confidence and Trust

Then, in due course, coexistence evolves towards a relation of trust. This second stage in the process requires that each party, both the victim and the offender, gains renewed confidence in himself or herself and in each other. It also entails believing that humanity is present in every man and woman: an acknowledgement of the humanity of others is the basis of mutual trust and opens the door for the gradual arrival of a sustainable culture of non-violence. In the context of Kosovo, Howard Clark writes: "One can counsel distinguishing between a person and his actions, hating the sin while trying not to hate the sinner; one can also attempt to understand the human weakness of those who were swept away by the tide. However, even when one cannot forgive, there are some minimum standards below which one should not sink: social reconstruction demands respecting the rights of those one detests. This respect is in itself an assertion of one's own humanity".

Another product of stage 2 is the victim's capacity to distinguish degrees of guilt among the perpetrators - to disaggregate individual and community. This is an important move in destroying atrocity myths, which keep alive the idea that all the members of a rival group are actual or potential perpetrators. Courts of law can make a difference here: their mission is precisely to individualize guilt. Traditional justice mechanisms often create similar opportunities. In October 2001 the population of Rwanda elected more than 200,000 lay judges who oversee some 10,000 gacaca tribunals, a society-rooted institution where individual guilt in the 1994 genocide will be publicly discussed (see the case study at the end of chapter 7).

For trust and confidence to truly develop, a post-conflict society has to put in place a minimum of functioning institutions - a non-partisan judiciary, an effective civil service and an appropriate legislative structure. It is this condition that links a reconciliation policy to the many other tasks of a transition from violent conflict to durable peace.

Stage 3. Towards Empathy

Empathy comes with the victims' willingness to listen to the reasons for the hatred of those who caused their pain and with the offenders' understanding of the anger and bitterness of those who suffered.

One way to make this possible is the work of truth commissions, sifting fact from fiction, truth from myth. In addition such commissions may lead to an official acknowledgement of the injustice inflicted (see chapters 7 and 8). Truth-telling is also a precondition of reconciliation because it creates objective opportunities for people to see the past in terms of shared suffering and collective responsibility. More important still is the recognition that victims and offenders share a common identity, as survivors and as human beings, and simply have to get on with each other. In some cases the parties in the conflict will seek and discover meeting points where partnership appears more sensible than sustained conflict. Common interests may be found in roles and identities that cross former lines of division, such as religion, gender and generation - or region, as in the case of the Burundian province of Ngozi, where Hutu and Tutsi are collaborating closely in an attempt to improve the prospects of their region, thus transcending the divisions of the past. Economic concerns too may inspire such bridging activities, as they do in Kosovo, where Albanian trade unionists and a Serbian workers' movement have established post-war contacts.

Empathy does not necessarily lead to a fully harmonious society or to national unity. Conflicts and controversy are part and parcel of all human communities. Moreover, empathy does not exclude the continuation of feelings of anger. Nor does it require that the victim be ready to forgive and forget. Pardoning the offenders will, of course, broaden the basis for empathy, but for many victims it may be too distant, or too sudden, a goal, and to pursue it relentlessly may result in an abrupt and early end to the entire reconciliation process. At this stage it may be unjust to ask victims to forgive if perpetrators refrain from expressing regret and remorse, as has been the case in Argentina, Chile and Guatemala.

Accompanying the Three Stages: Introduction of the Codes of Democracy and a Just Socio-Economic Order

Peaceful coexistence, trust and empathy do not develop in a sustainable way if structural injustices in the political, legal and economic domains remain. A reconciliation process must therefore be supported by a gradual sharing of power, an honouring of each other's political commitments, the creation of a climate conducive to human rights and economic justice, and a willingness among the population at large to accept responsibility for the past and for the future - in other words, reconciliation must be backed by the recognition of the essential codes of democracy.

There are many examples of societies where reconciliation has remained hollow or unfinished precisely because one side of a previous divide refused, consciously or unintentionally, to acknowledge this need for democracy. Zimbabwe's recent history is a frightening demonstration of what happens when this is the case. Zimbabwe was for many years acclaimed as a model of reconciliation between blacks and whites after long-lasting colonial rule and a bloody military conflict. But thorough going economic justice has not been achieved. It is widely believed that the end of the policy of reconciliation is partly based on and backed by a general disappointment among large sections of the black population who see that the economic disparities between Africans and white settlers have not disappeared. The experience of Zimbabwe is examined in the case study at the end of this chapter.

2.1.3 What Reconciliation Is Not

The use of the term "reconciliation" in dealing with past human injustice is not without its dangers. The interpretation of the concept is contested, and there are many erroneous notions of what reconciliation is. (See section 1.2 for clarification of the definitions of reconciliation.)

In a political context, those who want nothing done may cynically plan reconciliation merely as a smokescreen. Victims, on the other hand, may perceive and condemn it as a code word for simply forgetting. For those who have to live with their own pain and trauma, the term is indeed extremely sensitive. As a victim of apartheid told the South African Truth and Reconciliation Commission (TRC), "Reconciliation is only in the vocabulary of those who can afford it. It is non-existent to a person whose self-respect has been stripped away and poverty is a festering wound that consumes his soul". A general feeling among black and coloured South Africans is that the discourse on reconciliation has pressured them towards a premature closure with the past.

> Reconciliation must be seen as a long-term process that may take decades or generations.

A second source of misunderstandings is that the people of a post-conflict society are sometimes forced to be impatient, as if coexistence, trust and empathy can come swiftly. Such timing, expecting too much too soon - especially if it is proclaimed as official policy - is doomed to fail. Reconciliation must be seen as a long-term process that may take decades or generations. Reconciliation based on ambiguity will not last. The notion and its interpretation must be publicly discussed. Here lies a task for the authorities, the media, schools and civil society in its broadest shape - NGOs, advocacy groups, religious institutions and so on. The need for peaceful coexistence, trust and empathy must be internalized before any effective policy can be set in motion. Such society-wide debate will have to take into account that genuine reconciliation is much more than rebuilding relationships between former enemies, or between victims and perpetrators.

2.2 Reconciliation: Who is Involved?

Coexistence, trust and empathy develop between individuals who are connected as victims, beneficiaries and perpetrators. This is reconciliation at the interpersonal level. That is, for example, what happens when the victim is willing to shake hands with the torturer who inflicted their pain. Many initiatives in the area of healing (for example, counselling victims and offenders together) and restorative justice (for example, mediation) take this route towards reconciliation. However, all the steps in the process also entail the reconciling of groups and communities as a whole. Each perspective, the interpersonal and the collective, has its own chemistry but they are equally important in the process.

> All the steps in the process entail the reconciling of not only individuals, but also groups and communities as a whole.

Individual victims and perpetrators are at the heart of all reconciliation activities. However, both categories embrace many more persons and groups than those who are directly involved in acts of political, ethnic or religious violence. The definition of victimhood, as it is used in chapter 4, includes family members, neighbours and even friends of direct victims, all of whom may have been traumatized by what they have experienced or witnessed. Accountability must be understood in similarly broad terms. For example, beneficiaries of the South African apartheid system are guilty in a moral sense. Indifference, incompetence or neglect may be at the origin of the complicity of the international community (see chapter 5). Special attention should be given to the victims and offenders who fled their country and are living as refugees in neighbouring countries or as asylum seekers around the world. The tendency to forget these people is often the source of persistent problems in the search for reconciliation. The question is particularly delicate in cases where refugees return to areas and communities that remain unhealed and are consequently unprepared to receive men and women who are either victims or perpetrators. As a former head of the United Nations High Commission for Refugees (UNHCR) wrote, "Returnees can indeed be an obstacle to coexistence and reconciliation. Their return inevitably raises issues of property, compensation, unpunished crimes".

There are various types of collective victims and offenders (see chapters 4 and 5). Religious institutions may be both victims (for example, in East Timor) and co-responsible for grave violations of human rights (as was the case in apartheid South Africa). Churches can act as facilitators - in Northern Ireland members of the Protestant clergy held meetings with Catholic paramilitary and political leaders - organize victim support, provide safe places for victim/offender dialogue and deliver a spiritual contribution to healing programmes. Hate media, like Radio Milles Collines in Rwanda, which helped incite the geno-cide, may be extremely culpable, but the media can be an invaluable tool in disseminating information to increase trust and empathy.

Lasting reconciliation must be home-grown.

The role of the international community is important, too, but it must take a cautious and restrained approach. Respect for the specific historical and cultural context of a conflict and of a domestic reconciliation process is essential. Lasting reconciliation must be home-grown because in the end it is the survivors who assign meaning to the term and the process. The credibility of official institutions like the UN and of NGOs is often damaged because of an explicit disregard for this central rule that a post-conflict society must "own" its reconciliation process. However, even within such a context of caution and restraint, the international community can be very useful in supporting and monitoring local reconciliation programmes, giving advice and train-ing, and providing material resources. For example, the UN has constructively sponsored truth-telling in El Salvador and Guatemala.

2.3 Reconciliation: How?

Burying the past in a reconciliatory way requires the mobilization of a variety of techniques (see figure 2.1). Most of them have to be activated in the short run:
- healing the wounds of the survivors;
- some form of retributive or restorative justice;
- historical accounting via truth-telling; and
- reparation of the material and psychological damage inflicted on the victims.

There are close links between these four mechanisms. Without reparation there can be no healing. Restorative justice, if adequately organized, can heal the wounds of both victim and perpetrator. Telling his or her story also can have a healing effect on the victim and the offender ("revealing is healing" was the slogan of the South African TRC). In addition, the acknowledgement of what happened is a way of breaking the vicious circle of impunity: silence and amnesia are the enemies of justice.

Much has been written about the influence of these four instruments in the reconciliation process. Some believe that truth-telling, for example, leads directly to trust, empathy and even forgiveness. This conviction is clearly present in the label "truth and reconciliation commission". It is an accurate name insofar as seeking for accuracy about the past is a vital step in the reconciliation process, according to our wide definition. But "truth" in itself will not bring reconciliation. Truth-seeking is a key ingredient, but only one ingredient, in reconciliation. In the same way, justice is a vital requirement for healing wounds, making offenders accountable, and re-establishing a relationship of equity and respect. But justice alone does not produce full reconciliation. Truth and justice are not separate from reconciliation: they are key parts of it.

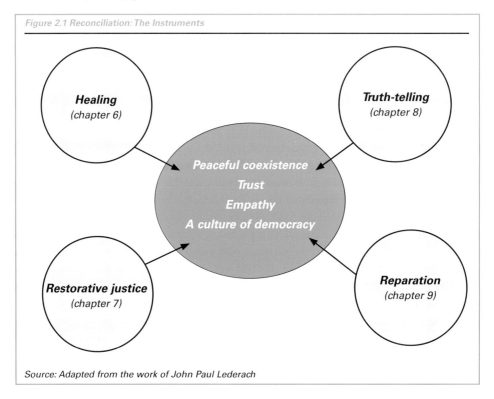

Figure 2.1 Reconciliation: The Instruments

Healing
(chapter 6)

Truth-telling
(chapter 8)

Peaceful coexistence
Trust
Empathy
A culture of democracy

Restorative justice
(chapter 7)

Reparation
(chapter 9)

Source: Adapted from the work of John Paul Lederach

Healing, truth-seeking, justice and reparation lay the foundations for the gradual creation of the various outcomes of the reconciliation process. They create favourable conditions and generate opportunities. But other, often long-term, investments are also needed, such as educational programmes and human rights awareness activities.

Decisions to be Taken, Choices to be Made

Political and civil society leaders are faced with a variety of strategic and structural choices. The identification of critical factors and potential solutions is crucial. Many of these choices are dealt with in other chapters, but the following is a brief presentation of some of the more general problems.

The Question of Whether to Address Reconciliation

It seems self-evident to see reconciliation as a vital requirement in societies that are emerging from a terrifying past, but there are post-conflict countries where the notion of reconciliation is simply rejected in public discourse. A UNHCR memorandum notes: "In Rwanda, for example, the attitude of the government in the years that followed the genocide was to insist on the need for justice. The word 'reconciliation' was taboo for those who had survived genocide, and was never publicly used.... In Kosovo, the very word 'reconciliation' is so charged for the Albanian community, that it is simply not used".

The place reconciliation receives on the agenda of a transitional society depends on the particular conjunction of political, cultural and historical forces. Demands for a reconciliation policy tend to be widespread following a negotiated shift from the old to the new order, for example, but largely non-existent in the wake of a military victory. Where religion is a predominant feature of the culture, as in South Africa, calls for reconciliation programmes can be numerous and explicit. History, too, may have an effect, depending on previous experience with reconciliation initiatives. In post-World War II Belgium, the idea of eventual reconciliation with those who had collaborated with the Nazis was greatly affected by memories of what had happened in the aftermath of World War I: many of the Belgians who had collaborated with the German occupiers in World War I and were granted amnesty afterwards simply repeated the offence in 1940. Their opponents felt that the repetition was encouraged by this leniency, and they consequently rejected as unthinkable calls for speedy reconciliation after World War II.

> Any reconciliation process is a very delicate operation. But not to address the issue is by far the worst response.

Any reconciliation policy, as we have seen, is a very delicate operation, and failures do happen. This may encourage post-conflict societies to choose a minimalist approach or to avoid the venture altogether. But all one can say is that not to address the question of reconciliation is by far the worst response.

No "One-Size-Fits-All" Policy

This Handbook presents a conceptual framework, but it is up to the local decision-makers to translate the concepts into concrete, systematic programmes. This "reality check" is one of the most difficult challenges in putting together a reconciliation policy, above all because the particular requirements of each post-conflict context require politically and culturally rooted responses.

Moreover, one tool alone will not achieve reconciliation against a background of accumulated feelings of hostility. A combination of measures and instruments is called for. Such a mixture will have to be innovative, again because of the uniqueness of each society that emerges from a violent conflict.

Who "Owns" the Process?

The role of the public authorities in planning and setting up reconciliation programmes is crucial, but opinions differ as to the direction such official policies should take.

The bottom–up approach is one that sees improved interpersonal relations among community members as the primary area for reconciliation work. Local, home-grown reconciliation and grass-roots initiatives are viewed as the key to success. "In contrast", writes Hugo van der Merwe, a South African scholar, "the top-down approach is characterized by a perception that ... for local dynamics to change, national intervention must first take place. This will then filter down, or create the conditions (and incentives) within which local actors can pursue reconciliation processes".

The South African TRC took the top–down approach. Many observers have commented that this strategy led to some of its neglect of the perceptions of reconciliation in local communities and insufficient mobilization of NGOs. As a result many opportunities have not been taken - the educational potential of the NGOs in informing the population at large on the TRC, the databases they built up over the course of time, and the networks through which evidence could be collected.

It is also an illusion to believe that reconciliation imposed from the top will automatically engender individual steps towards reconciliation. The authorities cannot impose trust and empathy by decree. Nor can they forgive in the name of the victims. (Former President Nelson Mandela's rhetoric about forgiveness is still a source of considerable frustration in parts of South Africa's black community.) The history of amnesty legislation delivers the same lesson. Shortly after World War II, France and the Netherlands issued amnesty laws for those who had collaborated with the Germans in a move to bury the past and speed up reconciliation and national unity, but this proved to be little more than a "legal forgetting". It did not touch the hearts and the souls of many citizens. The amnesty policies of several Latin American countries in the 1980s were even less successful. They did not, for example, discourage the families of the disappeared from demanding, again and again, justice and retribution.

> Authorities cannot impose trust and empathy by decree. Nevertheless, they can create a climate that encourages private steps towards reconciliation.

Nevertheless, what occurs at the official level is not entirely without effect on individual attitudes and behaviour. The authorities can create a climate that encourages private steps towards reconciliation. A public apology by a president, the establishment of a memorial day or the construction of a museum can have a considerable impact on individual victims and perpetrators.

One conclusion might be that, in the words of van der Merwe: "Top-down and bottom-up processes are both essential for a more sustainable long-term reconciliation process. They should, however, be pursued in a complementary fashion rather than at the expense of one another".

Balancing Reconciliation and Retributive Justice

Restoring the moral order that has broken down requires that "justice be done". A successor government owes it, above all, as a moral obligation to the victims of the repressive system. Post-conflict justice serves to heal the wounds and to repair the private and public damage done by the antecedent regime. As a sort of ritual cleansing process, it also paves the way for a moral and political renaissance. On the other hand, judicial operations may thwart and stifle efforts for the lasting reconciliation on which the new regime depends in order to function.

The need to "close the history books" is one of the main arguments of advocates of amnesty laws: they claim that reconciliation can only be produced if the successor elites refrain from prosecuting the officials of the previous regime. Such was Uruguayan President Sanguinetti's justification of an amnesty law pardoning abuses of a previous military regime: "The Uruguayan government has decided to take measures of magnanimity or clemency using a mechanism provided for in the Constitution of the Republic. The 12 years of dictatorship have left scars that will need a long time to heal and it is good to begin to do so. The country needs reconciliation to face a difficult but promising future". The same argument has been used by Nelson Mandela in defence of the amnesty clauses in the South African provisional constitution and in the mandate of the TRC. Others argue that the absence of judicial actions precludes reconciliation.

Tina Rosenberg, a journalist who has written extensively on this topic, says: "If the victims in a society do not feel that their suffering has been acknowledged, then they . . . are not ready to put the past behind them. If they know that the horrible crimes carried out in secret will always remain buried . . . then they are not ready for reconciliation". She adds: "The kind of reconciliation that lets bygones be bygones is not true reconciliation. It is reconciliation at gunpoint and should not be confused with the real thing". To strike a balance between the demands of repressive justice and of reconciliation is no easy enterprise. It entails a difficult and, on occasion, tortuous cost–benefit analysis. All costs and gains must be balanced against each other. (See chapter 7 for a more detailed discussion.)

2.4 Reconciliation: When, in What Order and How Fast?

Given the volatility of an immediate post-conflict context, time management in processing reconciliation is an extremely important but difficult dimension in the search for a shared future. Policies must not come too soon or too late. Questions and challenges abound.
• When to develop reconciliation activities?
• What is the proper sequencing?
• What is the appropriate pace?

2.4.1 Time

The end of a violent conflict creates a complex agenda - rebuilding the political machinery and the civil service, holding free elections, drafting a national constitution, guaranteeing a minimum of physical security, establishing a non-partisan judiciary, prosecuting human rights abusers, stabilizing the currency, rebuilding the economic infrastructure, and so on. More often than not it will be impossible to tackle all tasks simultaneously. As reconciliation is only one of the many challenges, short-term political or economic interests may lead to reconciliation measures being postponed. Or a post-conflict society may be forced to direct its efforts in several directions at once, ultimately allocating insufficient attention to the building of coexistence, trust and empathy.

The decision as to when to develop reconciliation processes will inevitably impact seriously on the final outcome. Difficult decisions have to be taken. To get the time as right as possible, policy makers must:
• "Understand the times", that is, make an adequate reading of the forces that exert an influence on the transition agenda.
• Be conscious of the importance of measures for the long term.
• Be aware that the mere passage of time will not ultimately generate reconciliation.

Understanding the Times

Some of the factors affecting a society's dealings with a violent past, such as the nature of the peace settlement, also shape the ranking of problems that appear on the transition agenda. Past experience shows that this has often led to politics and economics being put first, at the expense of reconciliation programmes. International financial institutions (particularly the World Bank and the International Monetary Fund) tend to encourage that approach. If political and economic reforms receive priority then, since improvement in socio-economic conditions for victims is a key step to reconciliation, care must be taken not to damage the prospects of long-term reconciliation by establishing inappropriate political and economic structures. (See chapter 3 for further discussion of factors affecting a society's dealing with a violent past.)

However, reconciliation efforts cannot be put off indefinitely. Experience with past truth commissions suggests that the quality of witness statements diminishes quite fast. Healing also has to start soon, as with time victims become further trapped in their pain and isolation. If the context prevents an early start, at least interim measures should be taken. Recent developments can help facilitate an early start of reconciliation-oriented activities:

- Reconciliation is now clearly seen as a crucial dimension of conflict prevention - hence the more prominent place given to it in the policies of post-conflict states, of the UN and of many donor countries.
- In some post-conflict countries mobilization and empowerment of victims have reached a point where demands for progress in the area of healing and truth-seeking can no longer be denied.
- The amount of information available on healing, truth-telling, justice and reparation programmes has grown considerably. The experience of the South African and Guatemalan truth commissions has led to the dissemination of quasi-models. Information networks now exist - for example, the New York-based International Center for Transitional Justice, and the Institute for Justice and Reconciliation in Cape Town - which offer professional expertise in the domain of reconciliation. Several international NGOs support local activities. Avocats sans Frontières, for example, has produced the manual that is being used in Rwanda to train the gacaca judges.

> Reconciliation is now clearly seen as a crucial dimension of conflict prevention.

The Importance of Long-Term Measures

Healing, truth-telling and reparation will deliver important short-term benefits but generally they will not eliminate altogether the underlying causes of the past violence. They serve as an invaluable starting point and lay the foundations for more durable reconciliation processes, but long-term tools are also required. Three such tools are education, memory and retrospective apologies.

Education for reconciliation *

Education - described in the Oxford English Dictionary as "systematic training and instruction designed to impart knowledge and develop skill" - has too often been manipulated in the pursuit of domination and oppression. Denial of access to basic education has been used to maintain political, economic and social imbalances and injustice, to separate and subjugate, to engender prejudice and to fuel the animosity and antagonism upon which violent conflict is based.

Education systems segregated along ethnic or religious lines - such as those in Northern Ireland, Israel and Palestine and the former Yugoslavia - help to perpetuate dramatically divergent views of both history and current events. A segregated education system can hinder the development of meaningful relations across ethnic or religious divides. When the knowledge imparted and the skills developed are those that separate us, or further separate us, should we not ask more of our education systems? If we consider that one of the basic tenets of reconciliation is the building - or rebuilding - of relationships after conflict, then what would education for reconciliation entail?

A 1996 report from the UNESCO Commission on Education puts great emphasis on a type of education called "Learning to Live Together". The report demonstrates the contribution this approach can make to a more peaceful world "by developing an understanding of others and their history, traditions and spiritual values and, on this basis, creating a new spirit which, guided by recognition of our growing interdependence and a common analysis of the risks and challenges of the future, would induce people to implement common projects or to manage the inevitable conflict in an intelligent and peaceful way".

Programmes designed to educate in "an intelligent and peaceful way" have been developed globally and are encompassed in a number of different educational models. One of them is "Education for

---

* This sub-section was contributed by Noreen Callaghan.

Reconciliation", in Ireland. Basically it is an educational framework designed to assist the recovery of post-conflict societies. Inasmuch as every conflict arises in a unique context, programmes need to be devised - or adapted - to meet the specific psychological, political, social and cultural circumstances in which the conflict, and therefore the recovery process, occurs.

However it is structured, there are a number of basic elements fundamental to an education for reconciliation programme. The themes of justice, tolerance and peace need to be woven into the education system. Education for reconciliation should therefore:

Education for reconciliation must be rooted in fundamental values such as respect and equality, be concerned with issues of pluralism, and address specific issues of culture, identity, class and gender.

• Promote an understanding of the causes, consequences and possible resolutions of conflict and estrangement on the personal, social, institutional and global levels.

• Introduce and develop the skills necessary to rebuild relationships torn apart by violent conflict.

• Develop an understanding and accommodation for the differences that may exist in experience, ethnicity, religion, political beliefs and so on. It must be rooted in fundamental values such as respect, dignity and equality, be concerned with issues of pluralism in general, and address specific issues of culture, identity, class and gender.

We must ensure that education for reconciliation is not only a utopian idea but also a realistic and responsible praxis. In Ireland, for example, consideration is being given to the development of reconciliation-oriented curricula, textbooks and other educational materials across a broad range of subjects within the formal education system. The potential of education for reconciliation is being explored in history, geography and science, in the Irish and English languages, in religious education and in civic, social and political education courses.

Education for reconciliation needs also to be a fundamental part of non-formal education systems, particularly in situations where the education system is still strongly divided along ethnic and political lines. For example, education for reconciliation in Croatia and Bosnia and Herzegovina takes place not within the school system but within the NGO and youth sectors. Projects are practical and creative, and often need to be quite simple in the face of complex, devastating conflict. They offer an opportunity for people who have been divided by violent conflict to come together and discover their common humanity, to help rebuild their own lives and the fabric of society, and to find ways to ensure that the cycle of violence ends.

Development assistance agencies can encourage and support such efforts by:

• Providing funding for conflict transformation, peace and reconciliation-related education and training projects.

• Facilitating opportunities by which communities emerging from conflict can share their experience and learn from others who have tackled similar issues.

• Encouraging and supporting education ministries to analyse and examine how education systems need to change and expand in order to promote sustainable peace.

The Role of Memory

Post-conflict countries sometimes choose to ignore the past completely. This may arise from a desire not to reopen wounds for fear of endangering a fragile peace: Cambodia is often cited as a case in point (see the case study at the end of chapter 3). In other societies, forced amnesia is part of a conscious strategy on the part of those who committed violence, as happened in the 1980s in some Latin American countries.

History teaches that, in the long run, such a policy is a serious obstacle on the road from a divided past to a shared future. Amnesia is the enemy of reconciliation because:
- It refuses victims the public acknowledgement of their pain.
- It invites offenders to take the path of denial.
- It deprives future generations of the opportunity to understand and learn from the past and to participate in the building of a lasting reconciliation.

However, memory is a two-edged sword. It can play a crucial role in making reconciliation sustainable. But it also has the capacity to hinder reconciliation processes.

There is the danger of too much memory. As Andrew Rigby writes: "Too great a concern with remembering the past can mean that the divisions and conflicts of old never die, the wounds are never healed. In such circumstances the past continues to dominate the present, and hence to some degree determines the future". Memory is often selective and, worse, it can be manipulated and abused.

Memory naturally tends to be selective. This is the case in everyday life, even in situations that are not haunted by conflict. Selectivity produces real risks in the context of prolonged violence. Most Albanians and Serbs in Kosovo, or Muslims and Serbs in Bosnia, for example, have developed completely different recollections of their common past. If they are not corrected through mechanisms such as an independent truth commission, then selective memories are handed down from generation to generation.

Memory can be manipulated. Policy makers in post-conflict societies often tend to impose a version of the past that increases the chances of much-needed unity being achieved. This happened in post-World War II France, where the German occupation had deeply divided the population into resisters and collaborators. After the war a well-planned operation of public discourse and academic research minimized the importance of collaboration and maximized the role of the Resistance. A glorious past was invented. Only in the 1960s did cracks begin to appear in this official self-image, and the old divisions rose again to challenge it.

Wholesale abuse of memory is not uncommon. Some leaders of parties in a brutal conflict may deliberately keep alive a memory that fuels the fires of hatred - Northern Ireland over many years is just one example.

Yet memory can also be a powerful instrument for achieving reconciliation.

It may provide early warning signals, teaching future generations how to identify the first signs of renewed and potentially dangerous distrust. In the context of this argument the words of philosopher George Santayana carry their full weight: "Those who cannot remember the past are condemned to repeat it".

It can be cast in forms that are conducive to reconciliation - permanent monuments to commemorate the fate of victims, places of remembrance (for instance, Robben Island in South Africa), memorial days or plays and poems. These give a collective dimension to private pain, creating a long-lasting healing mechanism. An appropriate use of memory is considerably facilitated if a truth-seeking institution - independent, official or civil society-based - has prepared the ground. A publicly acknowledged reconstruction of the past might even allow for competing memories to coexist. Given the dangers of too much memory, a society must try to attain the right delicate mixture of remembering and forgetting.

> *Society must try to attain the right delicate mixture of remembering and forgetting.*

The Relevance of Delayed Apologies

Recent times have been characterized by a wave of apologies for injustices that happened in the distant past. Slavery, the atrocities committed in the context of colonialism, the Holocaust, the inhuman internment of American-Japanese during World War II, stealing aboriginal children in Australia, apartheid, the Rwandan genocide - all have recently been the subject of apologies by the political heirs of these acts. In some cases official expressions of regret and admissions of accountability have been accompanied by the full or partial payment of an old and still unpaid debt.

Are such apologies part of a final reconciliation-oriented gesture? Do they really contribute to reconciliation? Who is entitled to offer, and who to accept, apologies? Opinions differ. Some say that the politics of apologizing is a cheap and easy way of getting rid of a bad conscience, or that it is completely meaningless because it is rarely followed by compensatory measures. Others argue that such acts can have an important effect - if certain conditions are met:

• The sincerity of the gesture must be clearly demonstrated.
• There must be full and unqualified acceptance of responsibility.
• Any justification of the original action (or inaction in the case of bystanders) must be avoided.
• If the events of the past still produce grief or inequalities, those who apologize in the name of their ancestors must express a clear commitment to change.

Time Does Not Heal All Wounds

It is unwise to believe that the mere passage of time will ultimately produce reconciliation. All the evidence today shows that the quest for truth, justice and reparation - essential stages on the way to reconciliation - does not simply disappear with time.

In the case of Cambodia, a more pronounced search for justice and truth has only recently become a realistic possibility, many years after the end of the violence. In Latin America, the political and cultural imposition of "forgiving and forgetting" failed completely to stifle demands for the prosecution of the Pinochets of the continent. South African members of the TRC have been asked by Native Americans to help them set up a commission to examine the treatment of their ancestors in the 1800s and early 1900s. And the 2001 UN Conference on Racism raised the question of reparation and compensation for the pain and damage inflicted during the times of slavery and colonialism. A violent past, particularly if not dealt with in an adequate manner, is like a fire that intermittently flares up. Years of silence alternate with periods of unrest and deep emotion.

2.4.2 Timing

Any reconciliation policy needs a "flight plan" to control the proper sequencing of the steps and dimensions of the process. What should come first - healing initiatives, positive discrimination in favour of the victims in housing and education, locking up leading offenders, or saving vital documents for the future search for truth? Improper sequencing may have undesirable effects. The threat of trials may incite suspects to destroy evidence. Giving priority to truth-telling may frustrate victims who are in urgent need of housing or medical care.

The problem is that historical analogies from which firm, unequivocal lessons can be drawn are scarce. It is well known that certain measures are more urgent than others, for instance, facilitating communication between the former warring parties, taking provisional disciplinary action against the primary offenders, and repairing the most grave physical and material damage inflicted on the victims. Flexibility is the watchword that should guide policy makers and civil society leaders. They also must be aware of the fact that authorities and victims have different timescales, and that community and individual needs tend to change fast in the immediate post-conflict period.

2.4.3 Tempo

What is the appropriate cadence of reconciliation activities? Again, there is no standard approach. The appropriate time frame of the various stages in the process (achieving peaceful coexistence, trust and empathy) depends on each context. So does the amount of time needed to implement the four pillars of reconciliation policy (healing, justice, truth-telling and reparation).

Experience suggests that a rushed approach, as regularly advocated by national and international peacemakers and facilitators, will almost certainly be counter-productive. In the immediate aftermath of a civil war or of an inhuman regime, victims are too preoccupied with their own distress to develop trust and empathy in a hurry. In addition, coming to terms with human injustice is a deeply personal process. It touches the cognitive and the emotional, the rational and the non-rational in human beings. It is culturally determined and gender-based. How people view the tempo of a reconciliation process is also intimately linked with their position and experiences during the conflict. All this results in individuals and groups finding themselves at different levels and stages on the continuum that leads from open hostility to trustful relations.

> *A rushed approach to reconciliation will almost certainly be counterproductive.*

References and Further Reading

Main Sources

Mani, Rama. *Beyond Retribution: Seeking Justice in the Shadows of War.* Cambridge and Malden, Mass: Polity Press and Blackwell, 2002.

Rigby, Andrew. *Justice and Reconciliation after the Violence.* London: Lynne Rienner, 2001.

Schmitter, Philippe and Javier Santiso. "Three Temporal Dimensions to the Consolidation of Democracy." *International Political Science Review* 19(1) 1998:69–92.

Theissen, Gunnar. *Supporting Justice, Co-Existence and Reconciliation after Armed Conflict: Strategies for Dealing with the Past.* Berghof Handbook for Conflict Transformation. Berlin: Berghof Research Center for Constructive Conflict Management, 2001.

Other References

Curriculum Development Unit of the Vocational Educational Centres and the Area Development Management/Combat Poverty Agency. *Education for Reconciliation: A Curriculum Investigation.* Dublin, 1999.

Clark, Howard. *Kosovo: Closing the Cycle of Violence.* Coventry: Centre for the Study of Forgiveness and Reconciliation, 2002.

ENCORE (European Network for Conflict Resolution in Education). *Transforming Conflict: The Role of Education.* Belfast: ENCORE, 2001.

Lederach, John Paul. *Building Peace: Sustainable Reconciliation in Divided Societies.* Washington, DC: United States Institute of Peace, 1997.

UNESCO. *Learning: The Treasure Within. Report to UNESCO of the International Commission on Education for the Twenty-first Century.* Paris: UNESCO Publishing, 1996.

Rosenberg, Tina. *The Haunted Land: Facing Europe's Ghosts after Communism.* New York: Vintage Books, 1996.

van der Merwe, Hugo. *The South African Truth and Reconciliation Commission and Community Reconciliation: A Case Study of Duduza.* Johannesburg: Centre for the Study of Violence and Reconciliation, 1998.

Villa-Vicencio, Charles. "Getting On with Life: A Move towards Reconciliation." In *Looking Back, Reaching Forward: Reflections on the Truth and Reconciliation Commission of South Africa*, edited by Charles Villa-Vicencio and Willem Verwoerd. Cape Town: University of Cape Town Press, 2000:199–209.

Zimbabwe: Why Reconciliation Failed

LUC HUYSE

Introduction

"If yesterday I fought you as an enemy, today you have become a friend and ally with the same national interest, loyalty, rights and duties as myself. If yesterday you hated me, today you cannot avoid the love that binds you to me and me to you. The wrongs of the past must now stand forgiven and forgotten." The words are those of Robert Mugabe, Zimbabwe's first post-colonial leader, and the time 17 April 1980, a few months after white Rhodesian rule ended. They mark the beginning of the so-called Politics of Reconciliation. Victor de Waal has called Mugabe's attitude a "miracle" and "a demonstration of human maturity so far rarely equalled in our world". It put him, many observers said, in the company of other African reconciliation-minded statesmen - Léopold Senghor of Senegal, Julius Nyerere of Tanzania, Kenneth Kaunda of Zambia and Jomo Kenyatta of Kenya.

Mugabe was speaking about the future relationship between white and black citizens of his country. He wanted, he said, to draw a line through the past - a past of colonialism in general and of the liberation war of the 1970s in particular. He put much less emphasis on the question of reconciliation within the black community where two groups had fought bitter conflicts, both in the far past and as rivals in the liberation movement. This second conflict is based on three interrelated divisions:
• Ethnic -- majority Shona versus minority Ndebele.
• Regional -- North and South Matabeleland (predominantly Ndebele country), versus most of the other regions.
• Political -- diverging visions of how to build the country after independence.

The two dimensions of post-colonial inter-communal relationships - white-black and inter-black - have taken different courses. After a brief honeymoon period the officially declared reconciliation between the black and the white population has turned sour. In recent statements Mugabe has declared the Politics of Reconciliation completely dead. Within the black population reconciliation has remained, at best, politically motivated coexistence, all too regularly interrupted by violent confrontations.

This case study poses the following questions:
• Why did the relations between the (heirs of) the white settlers and the black Zimbabweans not become the success story they initially promised to be?
• What factors are responsible for the lack of inter-black reconciliation?

The Failure of White-Black Reconciliation

Since the late 1990s relations between the Mugabe government and the ruling Zimbabwe African National Union-Patriotic Front (ZANU-PF) on the one hand, and most of the white citizens on the other, have sunk to their lowest point since the coming of independence. The compulsory, often aggressive, government acquisition of white commercial farms is its most visible sign. It is clear enough that ZANU-PF's partisan and electoral strategies are a crucial factor in current developments.

The issue of land reform - giving the black population back the resources that were theirs before the white settlers came - is a crucial tool in the process of staying in power. But other, less recent, aspects of the Politics of Reconciliation are at least as important. This policy was from the very beginning built on sand: it was almost exclusively based on political and economic imperatives, weakened by the triple culture of amnesia, impunity and contentment (or easy satisfaction), and imposed from above.

The Context of the 1979 Peace Agreement

On 11 November 1965 a Unilateral Declaration of Independence (UDI) by the white rulers of Rhodesia disrupted 75 years of British colonial rule. The armed struggle of black liberation movements started less than six months later. The war that followed was cruel. The Rhodesian Army committed many human rights violations in the country itself and in the border zones with Mozambique and Zambia. The rebel movements, too, perpetrated atrocities, often during internal conflicts.

After two failed conferences convened by the United Kingdom in 1976 and 1977 in Geneva and Malta, increasing international pressure finally led to the 1979 "constitutional conference" at Lancaster House in London. By this time the white minority government had conceded nominal power to Bishop Abel Muzorewa, leading a black civilian government elected in a non-racial election in which the liberation movements did not participate as a result of a combination of self-denial and exclusion. This failed to end the war, but for the UK and the West it created a "recognizable" Rhodesia–Zimbabwe. In these circumstances a constitution was reluctantly accepted and a ceasefire concluded between the liberation movements and the Muzorewa regime on 28 December 1979. (Ironically the UK, under whose ultimate colonial legal authority most of the land had been alienated, was able to cast itself in the role of arbitrator and mediator at Lancaster House. Lord Carrington and his team earned much praise for their use of "dominant third-party mediation". This enabled Britain to avoid any further formal responsibility for reconciliation in Zimbabwe.)

The Lancaster House Agreement created a constitution for an independent Zimbabwe, based on majority rule. However, it granted the white Zimbabweans significant minority rights: 20 seats out of 100 in the first parliament and, even more important, a strict and detailed protection of commercial farmland. Rhodesian perpetrators of human rights violations were allowed to go unpunished. All this came in the name of reconciliation.

Essentially, political and economic considerations lay at the heart of the willingness of the liberation movement's leaders to accept and initially respect the peace agreement and the constitutional deal on which peace was to be based (although Mugabe did not disguise his disappointment at having to lose in the peace agreement that which he was convinced could be won by war - the land). But the power of the white Rhodesians had not completely disappeared. The UK and the United States put considerable pressure on, and made significant unwritten promises to, the black negotiators. There was also the weight of states such as Mozambique and Zambia, emphasizing the need for stability in the region and fearing that a radical, revolutionary or vengeful Zimbabwe would give South Africa's apartheid regime the ideal argument to destabilize the post-colonial states in the region. (The destruction of Mozambique by the South African-sponsored Mozambique National Resistance Movement (RENAMO) in the 1980s underlined this point.) Economic pragmatism also played a major role. The white community remained extremely important economically. The black leaders knew that a lack of flexibility had caused serious economic problems in Mozambique when, soon after independence, thousands of qualified white people fled the country, leaving a deliberately uneducated population to run it.

The Cultures of Amnesia, Impunity and Contentment

Pragmatism is not of itself necessarily a source of weakness in a policy of reconciliation, but it is never a sufficient foundation. Circumstances are likely to change and political and economic imperatives lose force, as they did in Zimbabwe. By the 1990s apartheid was at an end, and the constitutional barriers to parliament abolishing the clauses protecting the land expired. More urgently, the liberation government faced, for the first time, the prospect of electoral defeat in the wake of economic liberalization, which had brought unemployment, strikes and demonstrations against increasing signs of corruption. At this stage the reality of reconciliation faced its first real test.

Reconciliation has to be based on more than pragmatism and rhetoric. A public acknowledgement of what went wrong in the past, a minimum of retribution and redress and, above all, progress towards economic justice are needed. These crucial factors were not sufficiently developed in post-colonial Zimbabwe.

Amnesia

Amnesia, by which we mean here an officially imposed form of forgetting, was included as a constituent element in the Lancaster House Agreement. Silence about the past, it was argued, was what the newborn country needed. Searching for the truth would constantly reopen old wounds and damage the politics of reconciliation. This strategy drew a veil over the human rights violations of the Rhodesian secret service, army and police. It was, at the same time, appreciated by the leaders of the liberation movements because it meant also closing the books on their violence against civilians in Rhodesia and against their rivals in the training camps in Mozambique and Zambia.

Information about the colonial and liberation war atrocities was not completely lacking. Domestic NGOs such as the Catholic Commission for Justice and Peace in Rhodesia and the Catholic Institute for International Relations have documented torture, resettlement and eviction in the 1970s. Amnesty International has published reports on war crimes in Rhodesia. Women members of the liberation movements have spoken out about sexual assaults by their male companions in the camps. But any official acknowledgement of the horrors of the past has consistently failed to materialize.

Amnesia has its institutional expression in legal immunity and amnesty. It thrived in both Rhodesia and Zimbabwe, and the consequence is a culture of impunity.

Impunity

The pattern of impunity in pre-independence Rhodesia and post-colonial Zimbabwe consists of many elements: erosion of the independence of the judiciary; political manipulation of the police; and silencing independent media and human rights organizations. But by far the most forceful instrument is the recurrent use of indemnities, amnesties and pardons.

Granting an amnesty to the Rhodesian police and military personnel for human rights violations was a tradition long before the liberation war was at its height and the Indemnity and Compensation Act of 1975 sanctioned this tradition. The key provision of the Act was granting indemnity in advance: it proclaimed that members of the army, the police, the Central Intelligence Organization, the government or the civil service who had committed crimes "in good faith" could not be prosecuted. In accordance with the Lancaster House Agreement, Lord Soames, the British Governor for the transitional period, passed the Amnesty Ordinance of 1979 and another General Amnesty Ordinance in 1980, pardoning both sides of the liberation war. Initially the Mugabe government was confronted by an embarrassing situation when its Secretary General, charged with the murder of a white farmer, successfully used the 1975 Act to escape conviction. The Act was repealed, but the political utility of immunity was underlined and surfaced in the form of the repeated use of the executive's power of pardon and ad hoc clemency orders. Furthermore, the ZANU-PF government also retained, and has reinforced, most elements of the previous state of emergency (giving it, among others, the power to detain without trial).

Contentment

The white population gratefully believed Mugabe's promise in April 1980 of reconciliation. That there was no enforced redistribution of land in the first decade after independence was the ultimate proof to them of his reliability. Observers have noted that this belief lulled many Rhodesians into a false sense of economic security. The maintenance of their pre-independence privileges was seen as absolutely normal. Prejudices and the destructive social relations they generated were kept alive. Explicit acceptance of responsibility for the past and for the future was an exception, not the rule. This "culture of contentment" led to the persistence of serious economic and social inequality, most visible in the skewed distribution of land and in the wealth that is so obvious in the white suburbs of cities like Harare.

Reconciliation Imposed from Above

The various parties in the negotiations that led to Zimbabwe's independence imposed the Politics of Reconciliation on the black population. It was a project conceived and developed at the level of the elite. There was no society-wide debate or involvement. Victims and survivors were not consulted, but rather watched powerlessly as many perpetrators of human rights violations went unpunished and even took on key roles within the Zimbabwean Army and secret services. As a consequence the need to forgive and forget was not internalized by the general public. Such unaddressed resentment explains in part why Mugabe's actual "economic revolution", aimed primarily at taking over white commercial farms, attracts a popular following. Imposed reconciliation fed, rather than eased, the unresolved grudges.

The Failure of Inter-Black Reconciliation

Historians disagree about the origins of the antagonism between the Shona and the Ndebele. Some have argued that it goes back to the arrival of the Ndebele in what is now Matabeleland somewhere in the mid-nineteenth century. The Ndebele were feared because of their raids on Shona villages. Some observers also point to the deliberate fostering of their rivalry by the white settlers as an instrument of "divide and rule". Others believe that these ethnic identities were created more recently in the process that deepened the political and regional divides in the liberation movement of the 1960s.

In 1963, controversies led to a split within Joshua Nkomo's Zimbabwe African People's Union (ZAPU), then the main movement. A rival group, the Zimbabwe African National Union (ZANU), was set up by Ndabaningi Sithole. Robert Mugabe became its leader in 1966. Initially the split was not based on ethnic or regional differences or composition, but gradually it became significantly tribal in nature because ZANU and ZAPU campaigned and recruited in different areas - ZAPU mainly in Matabeleland, ZANU in the Shona-populated areas. The rift deepened into serious conflict between the armed wings of the two movements - the Zimbabwe People's Revolutionary Army (ZIPRA) linked with ZAPU whilst the Zimbabwe African National Liberation Army (ZANLA) was the armed wing of ZANU. ZIPRA and ZANLA differed in outlook, training and ideology: the former was Russian-trained, the latter Chinese-trained. Fighting between them occurred in training camps in Mozambique and Zambia, in certain combat zones and, shortly after independence, in the assembly points for former guerrillas.

The Matabeleland Atrocities

ZANU-PF obtained 57 of the 100 parliamentary seats in the February 1980 elections, and Nkomo's ZAPU 20 (including all 15 Matabele seats). Mugabe formed the new government, inviting Nkomo and two other ZAPU leaders to become ministers. This move towards black-black reconciliation was short-lived. Antagonism reached a new level in 1982 following allegations (partly fostered by apartheid South Africa) of a ZIPRA plot to overthrow the ZANU-PF government. ZAPU leaders in the government of national unity were dismissed. Conflict and mutiny in the new army broke out; ex-ZAPU commanders were arrested, and some charged with treason and detained without further trial after being cleared of the charges. Dissidence continued, predominantly in Matabeleland and parts of the Midlands, culminating in what could be called undeclared civil war between 1983 and 1985.

The government's reaction to incidents and unrest in these areas was harsh. The 5th Brigade, a North Korean-trained and Shona-composed part of the army, committed a multitude of human rights violations which it justified as revenge for the nineteenth-century Ndebele invasions. Thousands of civilians were killed, tortured or forcibly relocated. The events caused profound trauma in these regions and their predominant Ndebele population. They also increased ethnic awareness, hardening the divide between Ndebele and Shona.

From 1985 onwards the government's policy towards the people in the Ndebele regions took a less violent course: aggression was replaced with neglect and discrimination. This policy change is attributable mainly to the fact that ZAPU's leaders had yielded to military pressure and agreed to "unite" and become part of ZANU-PF. The Unity Accord, signed in December 1987, marked the start of a period of (uneasy) coexistence between the rival groups. But essential dimensions of a reconciliation process - trust and empathy, a democratic sharing of power and growing equality (other than at the elite level of the former ZAPU leadership) - failed to materialize.

The Effects of Amnesia and Impunity

After the Matabeleland events and in the face of widespread demands from civil society, the ZANU-PF government set up the Chihanibakwe Commission of Inquiry. Its report was never made public. There was and remains no official acknowledgement of guilt, no apology, and only extremely limited redress. Just as in colonial times, amnesia was now the preferred strategy. In the mid-1990s NGOs, like the Catholic Commission for Justice and Peace in Zimbabwe, tried to break the silence by collecting massive amounts of data on the events. The Catholic hierarchy, which had initially promised to publish the data, was so shaken by its findings that publication of the report was postponed and finally cancelled, resulting in an "unauthorized" publication.

The culture of impunity, originally conceived to deal with the human rights violations of the liberation war period, also became a driving force. A Clemency Order of 1988 pardoned all violations committed by all parties between 1982 and the end of 1987 - thus covering the Matabeleland atrocities. The Amnesty International report of 2002 on impunity in Zimbabwe notes that a 1995 presidential amnesty "officially excused the politically-motivated beatings, burning of homes and intimidation perpetrated by supporters of ZANU-PF during the 1995 elections, by granting amnesty to those liable to criminal prosecution for, or convicted of, these crimes. This set a further precedent for yet another presidential pardon for political violence, Clemency Order of 2000, which was declared after the June 2000 parliamentary elections. Once again, those involved in human rights violations - such as kidnapping and torture, but excluding murder, rape and fraud - were placed beyond the reach of the justice system".

Many of these acts of violence were perpetrated against men and women in Matabeleland and the

Midlands, but increasingly also against the "disloyal" urban-dwellers in central Mashonaland who voted against ZANU-PF.

Concluding Remarks

A stable democracy in Zimbabwe will remain a distant dream as long as the sad legacy of violence and discrimination against an ethnic/regional minority is not dealt with in a genuine and thorough process of reconciliation. This will need to be historically all-encompassing and deal with issues of justice across a range of political, social and economic acts, involving not only the communities and races in Zimbabwe, but also the global and colonial actors implicated in this drama over the past century.

There were, no doubt, very good reasons to avoid explicit retributive justice in the Zimbabwe of the early 1980s. However, other less menacing strategies were available to the new elites: a fair degree of truth-seeking, forms of restorative justice, reparation of the damage inflicted to the victims, and the fight against economic inequality. The white heirs of the Rhodesian regime and the black leaders preferred to impose a shallow, "cheap" form of reconciliation without historical, restorative or economic justice. Cheap, imposed and based (for whatever pragmatic reasons) on amnesia and impunity - in such a form, reconciliation can only damage fundamentally the prospect of a viable, peaceful and inclusive Zimbabwean democracy.

References and Further Reading

Amnesty International. *Zimbabwe: The Toll of Impunity*, 2002 (This report can be downloaded from the Amnesty International web site at http://www.amnesty.org).

Catholic Commission for Justice and Peace in Zimbabwe and Legal Resources Foundation. *Breaking the Silence, Building True Peace: A Report on the Disturbances in Matabeleland and the Midlands (1980 to 1988)*. Harare, 1997.

de Waal, Victor. *The Politics of Reconciliation: Zimbabwe's First Decade*. London: Hurst & Co., 2002.

CHAPTER 3

The Context of Reconciliation

DAVID BLOOMFIELD

Each context, like each country or each conflict, is different. In the immediate aftermath of a settlement after violent conflict - during the transition from violence to peace - there is usually a unique set of factors present that together affect the ease with which the necessary but painful issue of reconciliation can be tackled. In some cases they can produce dilemmas over apparently conflicting goals; in others they may ease the path to reconciliation. It is impossible to list them all, precisely because they depend on the specific context. However, we can suggest the themes that generate such factors. We examine some of these now.

3.1 The Legacy of the Past

One obvious set of key factors that affect the business of devising an effective reconciliation process derives from the history of the conflict and the history of relations between the divided communities. This does not only relate to what actually happened in the past (the history); equally important are people's perceptions of what happened in the past (the mythology).

There will always be what may be termed historical, "objective" issues (for example, who killed whom, who ruled unjustly, who organized human rights violations). But there will also be subjective perceptions, beliefs, mythologies and interpretations of that history - why someone acted as he or she did - which may or may not reflect actual events but will significantly shape people's readiness or room for manoeuvre in the present. Historical accuracy is always to be pursued. But the mythologies that we all build over our histories - our heroes and martyrs, our hate-figures and villains, our glorious victories and our proud suffering - are often as important. It is necessary to understand the past, and also to understand how people interpret their past. Often it is their beliefs about what happened, as much as what actually did happen, that will render the history more or less amenable to a reconciliation process. If there are opposing histories, opposing truths, then they too must be recognized and reconciled.

> It is necessary to understand the past, and also to understand how people interpret their past.

Other issues from the past will also have an effect on attempts to heal the current division. Have the alienated groups coexisted peacefully before? Were they initially "one people" before divisions set in, or have they always considered themselves as separate entities? Have there been previous reconciliation efforts? If so, what has their effect been? In particular, how well is their failure understood and in what ways can it inform the design of a better process this time around?

3.1.1 Longer-Term History

The past has many layers. This fact needs to be acknowledged before addressing the past through a reconciliation process. Many violent conflicts and wars are not simply the outcome of one particular set of recent circumstances which led to violence. For example, reconciliation processes in Latin America often focus quite naturally on the violence of a particular military regime, but a full understanding of many of those conflicts also requires an investigation of the much longer history of the treatment of indigenous people at the hands of settler cultures. In Croatia, the focus of reconciliation is on the violence of the war in the 1990s, but no reconciliation process could function properly without the understanding that there is a long history of violent episodes between the opposing sides, and that the oppressor side at one stage has also been the oppressed at other times. The same applies in Rwanda and Burundi, where the tables have been turned more than once over time, so that the victims of one outburst of violence have become the perpetrators of the next.

This clearly raises the question of the period of time the reconciliation process should cover. Does it refer only to the latest outbreak of civil war or violence? If it does, will that leave unresolved the atrocities committed at another time by another group? How far back in history should a reconciliation process reach? Is living memory the realistic limit? Or can, and should, amends be made for historic wrongs? There are no easy answers, and it is not the aim of this Handbook to prescribe neat responses. Our message, rather, is simply that such complexity must be thought through and resolved as well as possible, even if there are apparently logical arguments for reducing the problem to the least complex form, which seems most amenable to a solution. A realistic balance must be struck that takes into account all the conflicting claims on justice, all the differing demands for truth, and all the pain and suffering that may arise from the many layers of a complex social history.

More global factors may impact as well. For example, in some regions, especially in Africa, the pre-independence history of a country will have a vital role to play in explaining the dynamics of post-colonial conflict. In many situations the cold war will have been a factor. While the greater, global agenda of East–West ideology inflamed many violent conflicts, it also acted as a fire-blanket on others, keeping them "on hold" so that those involved were released only in the 1990s to continue their struggle on their own terms.

Conflict analysis is always complex and wide-ranging, and the analysis that underpins the reconciliation process must be no less nuanced and extensive.

3.1.2 The Nature, Scale and Degree of Past Violence

The intensity of the violence that has taken place directly affects the depth of response of those involved, and partly defines the scale of the problem to be addressed.

Without for a moment belittling the suffering of the victims of the conflict in Northern Ireland, the intensity of violence there (around 3,000 dead in around 30 years) is clearly different from that of the 1994 Rwandan genocide (about 1,000,000 dead in about 100 days). At the individual level there is little effective difference between the pain of a grieving family in Belfast and that of one in Kigali. Nonetheless, the effect of the intensity of the violence on Rwandan society is far more profound. In particular, this may dictate the degree of optimism or pessimism within a society when it looks at the challenge of reconciliation. Not only has the violence affected a far broader spectrum of the society in a direct way, because of its scale: additionally, at the communal level the wounds appear much deeper, the trauma and emotions involved much more profound. The worst strategy in such a case is to try to underestimate the size of the challenge. A wounded society cannot afford to underplay its tragedy and apply ineffectual remedies any more than it can afford to be overwhelmed by the trauma it has suffered.

The intensity of the previous violence may make the challenge appear even greater; but it also serves to increase the pressure for a process that will guarantee that there is no repetition. This may serve usefully to focus minds and commitment on the need for reconciliation. At the same time it also produces pressures and a great urgency to move fast: yet reconciliation, as we repeatedly point out in this Handbook, cannot be rushed.

One important consequence of intense and/or sustained violence will be the extent of the damage to a country's infrastructure, and in particular economic destruction. Logistical and resource capacities for implementing reconciliation (or any other) initiatives will depend on the economic state of the country, both present and projected. Planning must therefore be realistic in terms of what is feasible and deliverable.

3.1.3 The Depth of Division in Society

The depth of the divisions in a society will obviously dictate significantly how amenable it is to a healing process of reconciliation. Those divisions will be deepened, clearly, by prolonged and intense violence, but this may also be a matter of time.

The reconciliation process involves a society in questioning the confrontational attitudes and beliefs that have sustained it during conflict. The longer those attitudes have survived intact, the more resistant they will be to change. Northern Ireland was mentioned above as a conflict in which the intensity of violence was comparatively low; but the two communities who are currently striving to live together in Northern Ireland have been struggling to do so in the same territory for almost 400 years.

> The longer confrontational attitudes have survived, the more resistant they will be to change.

Even if the violence has usually remained at what one British military officer once cynically termed "an acceptable level", the sheer longevity of the conflict has entrenched deep and widespread attitudes and beliefs about one's own community and the other - indeed, complete mythologies and histories - which are now presenting great challenges to the process of building a cooperative social and political framework.

3.2 The Transition
3.2.1 Types of Transition

A previously all-powerful regime (for example, a long-standing dictatorship) will have been both able to use and quite possibly enthusiastic in using state violence to perpetuate itself. This increases the amount of hurt caused to the opposition, and thus the amount of trauma to be dealt with through reconciliation. But it also in a way simplifies the direction of the reconciliation dialogue: most of the hurt to be addressed will have flowed in one direction - from the regime to the population and the opposition - and it will be much easier to identify, and differentiate between, offenders and victims. Likewise, when such an all-powerful regime decides itself to dismantle the old order, its motivation to admit past wrongs may be greater and/or the degree of forgiveness from the oppressed may be greater given that an expression of guilt is implicit in the regime's self-dismantling.

In contrast, when both sides work in partnership to produce the transition - as was the case in South Africa - the potential for a similar partnership in the reconciliation process is greatest.

However, if a negotiated settlement arises, as it often does, from a stalemate after sustained violent struggle, the complexity of wrongs suffered and committed by both sides and the consequent difficulty of differentiating victims from offenders may be much greater. A system where a regime dealt with dissent by the summary killing of dissenters is appalling but at least straightforward. A system where state violence (characterized by its victims as "oppression") and rebel violence (interpreted by its victims as "terrorism") have intertwined over an extended time is much less clear. Guilt and culpability rest on both sides, albeit possibly to different extents. This, indeed, is the norm in the transitional phase.

One of the most determining factors of post-conflict reconciliation is the balance of power between the previous regime and its successor at the point of the transition. At least three different typical scenarios present themselves. Each will produce significantly and structurally different types of reconciliation processes:

• Where a formerly oppressive regime has been violently and completely overthrown, or where a civil war has ended through a decisive military victory for one side (for example, the end of the Mengistu regime in Ethiopia in 1991).
• Where transition arrives at the initiative of reformers within the previous regime and those in power take the initiative and play the decisive role in ending the regime (for example, the former Soviet Union).
• Where transition may result from joint action, including the negotiation of a settlement, between the former government and opposition groups. The forces of the previous regime have not lost all power; nor have the former insurgents gained absolute control. Instead, in the new context, every aspect of life must be negotiated between them (for example, South Africa and many Latin American countries).

Each of these types of transition will facilitate a reconciliation process to a different degree. Each will produce a different way of dealing with the legacy of the past. The first scenario - the overthrow of an oppressive regime - may more strongly encourage punitive structures for retributive justice (see chapter 7). The second, reform from within, may encourage self-protecting moves towards amnesty (again, see chapter 7). The third, a negotiated peace, may open up the possibility of a process designed through negotiation between equals. In this case, though, one side may pursue amnesty for its members and supporters as the price of its agreement to support coexistence while the other is pursuing justice and punishment as the price of its support. Lacking absolute control, neither side will achieve its goal in this. What is important is that the negotiated compromise on justice facilitates, or at least does not obstruct, the even deeper process of long-term reconciliation. If such a negotiation simply gives the victory to one side, the lingering resentments, however deeply they appear to be buried, will almost certainly come back to haunt and hinder reconciliation at a later stage - and ultimately that path leads back to conflict and to renewed violence.

Finally, if the transition produces a new, all-powerful regime, this will affect the reconciliation process too. On the one hand, the new state may find that it has great power to insist on reconciliation and to implement it by forcing the old powers to accept judicial punishment for their acts. On the other hand, such a one-sided process may simply stoke the former powers' perception that they have now become the victims - which will almost certainly guarantee problems of unreconciled resentments further down the road.

3.2.2 The Nature of the Peace Settlement

Clearly, the nature of the settlement reached by the conflicting sides dictates both the shape of the transitional arrangements and, to some degree, the future shape of the social and political order. Naturally, then, it has consequences for the reconciliation process.

Assuming, as this Handbook does, that the settlement consists of democratic structures designed to produce inclusive and fair governance, how will that improve the context for reconciliation? For example, a simple easing of the previously prevailing atmosphere of fear and distrust may be enough to enable victims to trust the new context and thus to speak out more confidently and with more tolerance of past acts. On the other hand, a new economic order which discriminates against one side in its share in the new hoped-for prosperity will have the opposite effect.

Where possible, it is important that the negotiators of the settlement recognize in advance the need (a) to address the issues of reconciliation in constructing the agreement, (b) to make sure that appropriate and meaningful reconciliation processes, formal or informal, are devised, and (c) to ensure that the necessary resources for those processes are available. To do otherwise, as noted earlier in this chapter, is to store up trouble in the form of a continuing dysfunctional relationship between the communities that will potentially undermine even the very best of democratic settlements.

3.3 The Post-Transition Context

In the first years after a transition, post-conflict societies usually have to operate in an unstable environment, trying desperately to grapple with the issues arising from the violence and from the settlement, while giving the fragile new democratic structures time to bed down into normality. This is the critical time for developing the habits of coexistence, for building the legitimacy of the new regime on its record of action and achievement, and for dealing with the general expectations of the new dispensation. It is the time when previous promises are measured by subsequent actions.

Most new dispensations have as their aim simply to uphold a minimal degree of peaceful coexistence during this critical period. More positive relationship-building will hopefully develop with time, but just the "negative peace" of an absence of overt violence between the previously warring communities may well be enough to hope for. It is also the minimally fertile ground in which the fragile reconciliation process, having been planted, must now be nurtured and maintained.

The various contextual factors working to enable or restrict this fragile growth do not only depend on the pre-transition period and the ingredients of the settlement and the transition discussed above. There are other factors which have much more to do with the current context than with any legacy from history. Some of these are reviewed below. Some work to enable reconciliation, some to constrain it, and some can work with either or both effects depending on the timing and/or the context. This Handbook can offer no definitive list, but examples of the kind of themes involved can be given. Some have an obvious relation to reconciliation. The relevance of others may be less apparent but they must be considered nonetheless, if only briefly, in process design.

3.3.1 Cross-Cutting Interests

Sometimes it is possible for conflicting sides to come together to support something of equal importance to both of them - a transcendent nationality, for example, such as adherence to the Soviet Union despite local differences. Segments of the Ethiopian population have drawn together as nationalist Ethiopians, despite their differences, to support the national war against Eritrea. Often people may come together in solidarity against an external threat: it is as easy to see Ethiopian nationalism simply as a logical response of pooling resources and following common interests when faced with the threat from Eritrea.

Realistically, though, such factors are fairly rare and, when they do appear, somewhat transitory. They are the result of chance and fortune, rather than strategies on which to base action. Indeed, they are a favourite, if obvious, tactic of desperate or unpopular leaders, who see fear of the external enemy as a way to quell internal unrest. Nevertheless, they can have an influence on the post-transition context.

What is much more typical of divided societies, and can be very effectively utilized in facilitating a reconciliation process, is the existence of the same self-interests among sub-groups on each side of the divide. Such interests can be developed, with care, into a basis for cross-community cooperation. A society that is at war usually sees every aspect of itself through the particular lens of the issue that has caused the conflict: ethnicity, for example, often becomes the single defining issue that places each person on one or other side of the war. No middle ground is permitted. But often there are other interests which, if allowed to have influence, would divide the society along different lines, moderate that all-powerful divide and develop that middle ground. In the fragile post-conflict peace, these issues begin to exert, or re-exert, their influence, and to encourage other non-traditional groupings among the population that will ignore, say, ethnic cleavages and concentrate on others based on class, gender, religion, economic interests or the rural-urban divide.

Women from both sides in a war may have very good reason to join together the better to pursue their demands for an equal share of social power with men. Labour groupings may find it much more effective to pursue their interests in combination, so forming a more significant pressure group in society, than

> *Self-interests that cut across the divide can be very effective in facilitating a reconciliation process.*

to do so as two divided camps. Business and industrial interests may be better served by a larger, combined market, by complementing each other's human, financial and natural resources. Where poverty affects people on both sides of the conflict, the poor can increase their resources by joining together to fight for more equitable resource sharing. There may be common religious or linguistic links that can act as bonds to bring people together across the original divide.

All these and many more such potential areas of cooperation tend to appear as delicate shoots in the transition period, and nurturing them can generate a subtle but significant momentum away from the simplistic, binary division that has fuelled the violence along one dimension in the past. When they are nurtured, they add a complexity to social life that makes it more difficult to return to the "them-and-us" rivalry of the war. And of course, in the process of such reaching out across the divide, these developing patterns of cooperation lead to the forming of real cross-community relationships. It is those new relationships which lie at the heart of lasting reconciliation.

3.3.2 The International Context

Were neighbouring or other countries or regions involved in the conflict? And will they need or demand involvement in the reconciliation process?

They may greatly complicate the design of the process, and/or they may be able to contribute resources to it. It must be admitted that where third-party states have had a long-term engagement in a conflict it has usually been to negative effect, for example, the role of the USA in sustaining and supporting violence in many Latin American contexts and in some cases obstructing peacemaking and reconciliation initiatives there also. On the other hand, powerful outside states may, through their self-interest in the region or the country, have the potential to add greatly to peacemaking and reconciliation: the supporting role of the US White House and Irish-Americans in developing the peace settlement in Northern Ireland in 1998 is an example.

There is also a regional dimension to most conflicts, so that regional actors may have to be a part of the reconciliation process. One example is Central Africa: not only is reconciliation in Burundi greatly influenced by events in Rwanda and the eastern Democratic Republic of the Congo, but regional African institutions, intergovernmental or non-governmental, can significantly help or hinder reconciliation initiatives.

The "international community" in the wider sense has the potential to contribute in two ways. First, it is a potential source of information, expertise and training on reconciliation - this Handbook, for example, is an attempt to gather advice, experience and good practice from many contexts around the world for use in handling specific problems. Second, the slow but inexorable development of international humanitarian and human rights law is having a growing effect by setting and supporting standards in the shape of an international legal order, and forming a supportive external consensus on issues such as impunity for serious human rights violations, the right to truth, the unacceptability of certain crimes and the need to bring perpetrators to justice irrespective of where their crimes were committed. (Chapter 10 reviews in more detail the potential role of the international community.)

> *Powerful outside states have the potential to add greatly to peacemaking and reconciliation.*

3.3.3 Culture

The way in which a community deals with a violent past is intimately linked to its more general customs and culture. One key element is the way in which the culture influences the system of collective memory. Some societies embody a natural urge to forgive the injustices inflicted on them in the past; others display a strong aversion to letting bygones be bygones.

Ali Mazrui cites several examples of an African tendency to forgiveness: Jomo Kenyatta, independent Kenya's first leader, became one of the country's most enthusiastic Anglophiles despite his years of imprisonment by the British; there was no acrimony in Nigeria at the end of the Biafran civil war; Ian Smith, the leader of Southern Rhodesia's white breakaway movement, entered the new parliament of Zimbabwe. Archbishop Desmond Tutu has considered this culture of forgiveness extensively. "What is it", he writes, "that constrained so many to choose to forgive rather than to demand retribution?" His answer is what Africans know as *ubuntu* in the Nguni group of languages (or *botho* in the Sotho languages). It is a difficult concept to render in a Western language. Tutu says that a person with the African world-view of *ubuntu* "is open and available to others, for he or she has a proper self-assurance that comes from knowing that he or she belongs in a greater whole and is diminished when others are humiliated or diminished". Such a cultural outlook, the argument runs, will predispose its members towards forgiveness and reconciliation.

But opposed to such cultural beliefs are others - for example, in Albania - which prize revenge and honour above forgiveness.

Since cultures provide the atmosphere in which social systems work, they can be powerful forces to help or to hinder the reconciliation process. It is necessary to be culturally sensitive, and to design or adapt the reconciliation process accordingly. Since reconciliation cannot be imposed from outside and must flourish or fail depending on how far the people in a society are able to embrace it as meaningful and in their interests, then it must be culturally appropriate. However, culture never supercedes the need for a reconciliation process: all the pragmatic arguments for the necessity of a reconciliation process to develop the relationships that will underpin a healthy new regime still apply, whatever the cultural context.

One increasingly acknowledged role that culture can play is to act as a rich resource for finding home-grown tools to use in the reconciliation process. Most cultures have developed, within their norms and customs, methods for dealing with conflict in various shapes and forms. There is still a tendency, especially among Western or Northern interveners, to export conflict management mechanisms from the developed world and try to impose them in novel contexts - Western models of mediation, for example, or Western justice mechanisms. One of many reasons for the subsequent failure of such exports is that the models are rarely culturally appropriate to the context - they do not fit the situation and are thus seen by the recipients as alien, irrelevant and imposed from outside. More and more, people are looking within their existing cultures and finding models and mechanisms that can be adapted or adopted to suit a home-grown reconciliation process.

The Rwandan gacaca tribunals process is a modernized form of a very traditional justice mechanism (see the case study following chapter 7). One of the great strengths of the gacaca system is precisely that it includes a healing element, so that it can serve reconciliation at the same time as it serves justice. Another strength is that it is culturally familiar to Rwandans. However, the Rwandan Government has come in for considerable international criticism for implementing gacaca precisely because it contradicts some of the norms of international (and especially Western) legal models. Other examples of home-grown healing and reparation tools include cleansing rituals in Sierra Leone and healing circles among Native Americans. Examples of home-grown justice and decision-making tools include the Afghan loya jirga; the "joking relationship" between tribes in Burkina Faso; and so on.

This trend of looking "within" for tools and solutions, rather than looking outside for ready-made answers, is a new and developing one. Whatever the country or the culture, decision-makers should be encouraged to examine their own cultural resources before, or at least as well as, looking for outside help. (Chapter 7 discusses various home-grown and indigenous methods of achieving restorative justice.)

> *Decision-makers should be encouraged to examine their own cultural resources before, or at least as well as, looking for outside help.*

3.3.4 Geography

Less obvious factors can have powerful effects. Sometimes ethnic differences are broadly reflected in geographical location, for instance, in the physical separation of the Yoruba and the Ibo to specific parts of Nigeria. Elsewhere, as in Northern Ireland, two communities may be living closely inter-linked in the same space.

It is difficult to generalize about the effect of geography on conflict, except to say that either situation can work positively or negatively in creating the space for reconciliation, and so must be taken into account when planning for a reconciliation process. Geographical separation can make it easier to coexist, or that very distance can make it more difficult to generate the interaction that could lead to cooperative relationship-building. On the one hand, "good fences make good neighbours". On the other hand, it is virtually impossible for people to challenge their negative images and stereotypes of a former enemy in order to engender better understanding and a minimum of respect if they do not encounter them as a human reality.

> *It is virtually impossible for people to challenge their negative images and stereotypes of a former enemy if they do not encounter them as a human reality.*

3.4 Concluding Remarks

A great many factors must be considered in the delicate work of designing and implementing the most appropriate reconciliation process for a particular context. Pressures for quick results must be resisted, since quick results will only scratch the surface and, while bringing temporarily the appearance of a reconciled society, will leave underlying resentments or emotions unaddressed and fail to address the relationship-building that is the basis of real reconciliation. Equally, however, too subtle or too invisible a process will discourage people from seeing progress and will breed scepticism.

This chapter has tried to give a sense of the kinds of issue that must be considered and to instil the importance of reviewing all relevant factors, including, and especially, the difficult ones. The presence of some or all of the positive, enabling factors will not guarantee success, any more than their absence will guarantee failure. And while there will always be negative, constraining factors, these must not be used as excuses for inaction when in fact what is missing is the political will to grasp the nettle of reconciliation.

Despite all the pressures and logical temptations, the other agendas and pressing needs, the worst decision is to postpone addressing the difficult issues - the pain, the guilt, the emotions - in an attempt to preserve stability and peace. The "right time" to deal with these matters never comes: they only become more difficult to deal with as time passes. Ignoring the divisive issues will only produce frustration and cynicism about the new dispensation, especially among those who see themselves as the victims of past violence, and who may initially be the new regime's strongest supporters.

References and Further Reading

Tutu, Desmond. *No Future Without Forgiveness.*
London: Rider, 1999.

Reconciliation in Cambodia: Politics, Culture and Religion

VANNATH CHEA

Historical Factors

For almost three decades of Cambodia's recent history, its people suffered ongoing wars and social upheaval. The period began in 1970 when General Lon Nol's Republican forces ousted then Prince Norodom Sihanouk. Since then, Cambodians have lived under a variety of political regimes as the country changed from a monarchy to a capitalist republic, to a communist republic, to a socialist republic and then to the current constitutional monarchy. The most traumatic years of this period were undoubtedly those of the "Killing Fields" from 1975 to 1979, when the Khmer Rouge established what they called Democratic Kampuchea and attempted to transform all aspects of society totally. In this endeavour, acts of unspeakable barbarism were committed against the people: out of an estimated population of eight million, some five million were displaced. Most scholars place the number of dead from murder, torture, disease and starvation at around 1.7 million. Unlike other experiences of genocide, where race or religion were key factors, the Khmer Rouge drew their lines in terms of social class: the killing and horror took place amongst Cambodians, a largely homogenous ethnic, linguistic, religious and cultural grouping. The violence occurred as Pol Pot and his followers sought to abolish utterly the existing culture and replace it with a newly invented one, which combined Maoist principles with mythical ideals of an Angkorean past. In so doing, they destroyed all the institutions of state - the education, financial and legal systems - as well as religious and other social institutions.

Prior to this Norodom Sihanouk had worked hard to steer a neutral path for the post-colonial nation, but the conflict was largely driven by cold war relations and the world's then superpowers were implicated in it. While local factors had been crucial in bringing the Khmer Rouge to power, China was Democratic Kampuchea's main supporter. Later the USSR financed Democratic Kampuchea's Vietnamese-backed opponents, while China, the USA and other Western and Association of South-East Asian Nations (ASEAN) powers provided support to the Khmer Rouge and two royalist anti-Vietnamese factions.

In December 1978 the Vietnamese Army entered Cambodia and, together with a group of Khmer Rouge defectors, mounted a decisive military campaign against Democratic Kampuchea forces, which resulted in a new Vietnamese-sponsored government being declared in January 1979. A mistrust of further socialist experimentation, along with deep-seated historical suspicion of Vietnamese intentions towards Cambodia, undermined support for the new regime. The conflict continued during the 1980s, as Khmer Rouge forces formed an alliance with the two royalist factions to drive out what they characterized as foreign control of Cambodian political and civil life. But, as the cold war drew to a close, international support for all four warring factions dried up. In the face of this lack of resources, and exhausted by years of conflict, all parties found the idea of a political settlement more appealing.

Although a political solution was probably the only acceptable way out of the deadlock, using this method to decide the war raised the political stakes very high. Not only did the Cambodian parties need to agree: so did all the international players who had involved themselves in one way or another. The stage was set for a lengthy and highly politicized peace process.

The Peace Agreements and the Politicization of Reconciliation Processes

The Paris Peace Agreements of October 1991 were meant to end the war in Cambodia. They were signed by 18 countries and the Cambodian parties, and were based on a "framework" agreement reached by the five permanent members of the UN Security Council the previous year. Within the agreements, the extent of the tragedy was formally recognized and respect for human rights enshrined. In their detail, however, they focused mainly on political issues related to the cessation of hostilities, the provision for national elections and the rehabilitation and reconstruction of Cambodia.

It seems that "reconciliation" was considered synonymous with the involvement of the four factions in a free and fair election. For the Cambodian people at that time, however, reconciliation was largely equated with the cessation of hostilities and the return of refugees. More complex questions of justice and reintegration were yet to become apparent.

Ironically, by proposing elections as the solution to the conflict, the Paris Peace Agreements had ensured that reconciliation was closely linked with a political contest that no party was prepared to lose. The three anti-Vietnamese resistance forces returned to Phnom Penh in preparation for the 1993 multiparty elections; but the Khmer Rouge ultimately withdrew from the electoral contest, which meant that the election process could only ever deliver a partial solution at best.

Peace was finally secured following a series of defections after 1993. These began with Khmer Rouge Foreign Minister Ieng Sary in 1996 and then, following the death of Pol Pot in 1998, other high-ranking Khmer Rouge cadres rallied to the government. The defectors were allowed to resettle in and around the semi-autonomous zone of Pailin, a gem- and timber-rich area near the Thai border. (The infamous Ta Mok, known as "the Khmer Rouge Butcher" for his cruelty, was captured, as was Duch, known for his role as the S-21 Prison Torturer. Both are now in prison awaiting trial for crimes against humanity while in power.)

The strong links between party politics and the peace process persist to this day. The Cambodian People's Party (CPP), the successor to the Vietnamese-backed regime, is still able to capitalize on its victory over the Khmer Rouge in current political campaigning, promoting itself as the liberator and patron of Cambodian society to whom the people remain indebted. In this way, issues of security and stability have also become politicized.

The Khmer Rouge Tribunal

Currently, the main focus of reconciliation efforts is the ongoing issue of the creation of an Extraordinary Chamber of the Criminal Courts of Cambodia. The UN–Cambodian Khmer Rouge Tribunal, as it is more popularly known, would seek to try key surviving high-ranking members of the Democratic Kampuchea regime.

In securing the defection of Ieng Sary and many others, a number of political deals were struck between the government and the former Khmer Rouge. Most notably, an amnesty was granted to Ieng Sary for a death sentence imposed under a widely discredited Vietnamese-convened war crimes tribunal held in August 1979. Whether he and others who formally defected will be tried under the new tribunal remains to be determined, and there are concerns that key figures will be shielded from prosecution by the mutually beneficial arrangements reached between the former Khmer Rouge and the CPP. Again, the pattern of partisan interests determining peace and reconciliation processes becomes apparent.

The People's Views on Reconciliation

The Center for Social Development (CSD) is an NGO in Phnom Penh which holds regular public forums on issues of national concern. In early 2000, the Center decided to hold a three-part series of debates to consider whether a trial of the former Democratic Kampuchea leaders should be held. At these forums, all sides, including the former Khmer Rouge, stated the need for truth, justice, healing and national reconciliation. Yet it was clear that there are widely different views on what these terms might mean in practical terms.

Each party has its own version of what happened: there is the truth according to the Khmer Rouge, the government, the international community and ordinary Cambodians. If a reconciliation process is to move forward and be seen to be trustworthy, each of these truths must be accommodated to the satisfaction of all parties. From the discussions it was also clear that a tribunal is only one part of a comprehensive process of reconciliation. In addition, there were almost no calls for reparation. It seemed that this was too abstract a concept to consider when the truth is not yet even known. Most people simply wish to be free of their suffering and return to the family life that was so cruelly interrupted through the refugee experience and policies of forced displacement. For them, real reconciliation will be found when trust returns between individuals: when "they can smile at and trust each other again".

The answer therefore relies on finding a vehicle for addressing these issues at a personal level, and in a manner consistent with the foundations of Khmer culture. One potential path for finding this reconciliation is that of the national religion, Buddhism, to which at least 90 per cent of Cambodians are said to subscribe and which has a powerful influence in daily life. Buddhism has at its heart messages of compassion and reconciliation.

Buddhism and Reconciliation

In dealing with the emotional and psychological scars left by so many years of war, many ordinary Cambodians have returned to the faith that had been so brutally attacked under the Democratic Kampuchea regime. Many Westerners perceive Buddhism as a doctrine of acceptance, which effectively hampers social change. A noted Khmer Buddhist monk, Yos Hut Khemacaro, explains that Khmer Buddhism in particular, arising as it does from an agrarian society that places high value on patron–client relationships and harmony, has provided "a strong disincentive among monks and the wider population to challenge the social order". Yet, despite these cultural constraints, he goes on to argue that the practice of the Dhamma (teachings of the Buddha) can lead to social action.

One practical example of this is the Dhammayietra, or annual "Pilgrimage of Truth" marches, which began in 1992. The first saw hundreds of refugees who had been living in camps along the Thai–Cambodian border return to their homeland as they marched for four weeks from Battambang in the north-west to Phnom Penh. The spiritual leader of the pilgrimages, Maha Ghosananda, nominated three times for the Nobel Peace Prize, also made explicit the idea that the adoption of a Buddhist process does not mean that justice will not be served. He argues that reconciliation "does not mean that we surrender our rights and conditions" but instead that "we use love" to address these questions.

If Buddhism is to prove a useful tool in the process of national reconciliation, we must therefore ensure that it does not become as politicized as other aspects of reconciliation have. King Sihanouk has suggested holding a cremation ceremony of victims' remains, but opposition to this from Prime Minister Hun Sen, who believes that the remains must serve as a historical legacy, also threatens to become polarized. While the Prime Minister's view is probably more pragmatic, both claim to be devout and manage to use religion to justify opposing positions. To avoid politicization Yos Hut Khemacaro advocates following the "Middle Path", the traditional metaphor for the Buddhist way - neither joining the fight nor hiding from it. The Middle Path of non-violence and compassion provides a model for solving undoubtedly political problems outside the adversarial framework implicit in partisanship. As these ideas arise from traditional Khmer concepts, they can help the Cambodian people to find their own peace instead of feeling that their problems can only be solved by outsiders.

Local Initiatives

The accumulated history of oppression, repression and ongoing trauma has had a profound, continuing effect. In responding to these, a range of very different organizations has been working on a variety of strategies that are an important part of Cambodian reconciliation and provide a useful complement to more formal processes.

Most closely linked to the question of the Khmer Rouge trial is the project of the Documentation Center of Cambodia. Originating in an academic programme of Yale University, USA, this now independent Cambodian-run centre serves as a permanent resource for providing information about the Khmer Rouge, both in order to support potential litigants and to prevent such a tragedy happening in the future. Its mission is perhaps best summed up in the title of its regular publication, *Searching for the Truth*. By stressing the importance of the truth above all else, this project has chosen the non-partisan Middle Path in dealing with these extremely sensitive issues.

Even as we move away from the fields of politics and history, we can see the continuing effects of the "Killing Fields" period in Cambodian daily life. There is a high prevalence of mental illness, including many chronic cases, which has reduced the ability of many people to cope with everyday problems. As children grow up with mentally ill parents, they are far more likely to become depressed and abusive themselves, creating a vicious cycle with consequent social implications. Until now, ordinary people have relied on their understanding of the law of karma and their instinct for survival as their means of healing, but many of these problems have undoubtedly been made worse by the lack of adequate treatment services or facilities. This problem has been acknowledged, and Cambodians are learning to deal with the question of mental illness in more constructive and healing ways. The work being done by some health sector organizations and emergent psychiatric facilities is another important step forward in facing up to the past.

Concluding Remarks

The messages of non-partisanship in reconciliation are fundamental to the proper practice of Buddhism. It is this type of leadership that is required of Cambodia's politicians, if they and the population are to move beyond their painful past. Cambodians need to overcome the deep-seated mistrust of, and animosity towards, each other that arose as the consequence of the Khmer Rouge and their aftermath. Open discussion, improvement in social justice and human rights, education and health care for all - these are all fundamental to a step-by-step process of building mutual trust and understanding.

There are many elements to this overall process of national reconciliation. The Paris Peace Agreements were one step and the proposed tribunal will be another. Negotiations over the running of the tribunal broke down in February 2002 because of what the UN saw as the failure of the current proposal to address concerns over potential political interference by the Cambodian Government. At the time of writing, it seems that this process is tentatively restarting. It is hoped that the key issues can be tackled and that the process will regain momentum. A tribunal is important as it will uncover the truth and thus educate people about the past, provide justice for the victims, and promote the return of the rule of law to Cambodia. There must also be a role for ordinary people to play in reaching reconciliation at the level of everyday life, where old wounds are still deeply felt. The forums were a step, as are the other grass-roots programmes described here. Above all, these steps should be taken along the Middle Path, in full consultation with the Cambodian people.

References and Further Reading

Agreements on a Comprehensive Political Settlement of the Cambodia Conflict, Paris, 23 October 1991.

Chea, Vannath. "Let Ieng Sary's Karma Decide His Future." *Phnom Penh Post* 6–19 September 1996:9.

Documentation Center of Cambodia, "Background Information", http://www.bigpond.com.kh/users/dccam.genocide.

"One Million Kilometres for Peace: Five Years of Peace Action Walks in Cambodia", http://www.igc.org/nonviolence/niseasia/dymwalk.

Yos Hut Khemacaro. "Steering the Middle Path: Buddhism, Non-Violence and Political Change in Cambodia." Safeguarding Peace: Cambodia's Constitutional Challenge, *Accord* 5 November 1998:71–76.

CHAPTER 4

Victims

LUC HUYSE

Violent conflict creates all sorts of victims: those killed and tortured, those bereaved and maimed, those assaulted and raped, those injured in battle and by mines, those abducted and detained, the banned and the homeless, those intimidated and humiliated. This chapter aims to clarify the factors and processes that lead to their identification (section 4.2) and mobilization (section 4.3). Starting with a presentation of the various types of victim (section 4.1), the chapter concludes with a discussion of cases where all rival groups have committed atrocities and where it is consequently impossible to draw a sharp line between victims and perpetrators (section 4.4).

4.1 The Many Faces of Victims

Victims are at the heart of all dimensions of the reconciliation process in societies emerging from years of violent conflict. It is crucially important that policy makers and civil society leaders are aware of the many faces of victimhood. This awareness must guide the search for adequate victim programmes, even if the means are insufficient to deal with all those who suffer - individually and/or collectively, directly or indirectly, today or in the future. There has to be a broad public debate about which individuals and communities should be acknowledged as victims. Such civic debate should ideally add to the development of guiding principles for all healing, truth-telling and reparation work.

> There has to be a broad public debate about which individuals and communities should be acknowledged as victims.

Victims can be classified on the basis of three broad distinctions. Two of these, individual/collective and direct/indirect, are constitutive parts of the various definitions of victims issued by the UN (see box 4.1). A third distinction, between first- and second-generation victims, is based on the dimension of time. It is also important to bear in mind the fate of children and the implications gender has for victimization.

4.1.1 Individual and Collective Victims

All brutal conflicts inflict severe harm on individual men and women but most, in particular genocide and civil war, also cause collective victims. Collective victims are created when violent actions are directed at a specific population, for example, an ethnic, ideological or religious group. In such cases, individuals are targeted because of their connection to an identifiable collectivity. Overall, the effect is always to victimize the society at large.

4.1.2 Direct and Indirect Victims

Direct victims are those who have suffered the direct effects of violence. They have been killed, or physically and psychologically abused, detained, discriminated against and so on. *Indirect victims* are those who are linked to direct victims in such a way that they too suffer because of that link.

According to the Declaration of the UN Commission on Human Rights (see box 4.1), indirect victims are the family members of a direct victim. Relatives often experience extreme hardship and pain because of the suffering of a family member or by being punished because of their connection to that person - through serious socio-economic deprivation, bereavement, the loss of a breadwinner, missed educational opportunities, family breakdown, police intimidation or humiliation. The Declaration also speaks of the people who suffer as a result of intervening to assist a victim or to prevent further violations.

Some observers work with an even wider definition of indirect victim that includes neighbours, friends and bystanders of direct victims - all who may have been traumatized because of what they witnessed. Others even query the usefulness of the distinction between direct and indirect victims in reality: one finding of the South African Truth and Reconciliation Commission (TRC) was that it is difficult to distinguish meaningfully between the physical harm and psychological grief experienced by the direct victim and the pain of those to whom this person is or was precious. Including a wider constituency of victims in this way is very significant. It extends the scope of victimhood, and consequently increases the number of people rightly claiming recognition and compensation for their suffering.

4.1.3 First-Generation and Second-Generation Victims

Most attention goes to what can be called first-generation victims - those who have been victimized during their lifetime. But studies have demonstrated that their children and sometimes even their grandchildren have to bear the consequences of what happened and may feel and behave like victims, displaying deep hurt and bitterness. Trauma can be handed down. The second generation, particularly, tends to absorb and retain pain and grief, consciously or unconsciously. They carry traces of the experience into adulthood, and this is a problematic heritage that can threaten the future of a society.

4.1.4 Gender

Brutal conflict causes immense suffering to all people, but it also has a different impact on men and women, because victimization is partly gender specific.

Men are more likely than women to be involved in fighting and to be killed or wounded - although there are cases where the participation of women in combat is considerable. Women have joined the ranks of several Latin American guerrilla forces, of the Irish Republican Army (IRA) and of the Liberation Tigers of Tamil Eelam (LTTE), among others. During the Ethiopian civil war of the 1980s, approximately one-third of the rebel Ethiopian People's Liberation Front (EPLF) fighters were women. Women combatants can be doubly victimized - not only by their enemies but also by their male comrades - and in the latter case the victimization takes the form of physical and psychological abuse.

Women suffer the brunt of various forms of sexual assault during times of violence or oppression. Mass rape of women belonging to an enemy group has been practised as a means of assaulting the role and identity of the men in the group as providers and protectors of the family and the group. In other cases, young girls have been forced to marry men either as a strategy of creating alliances or to satisfy the needs of men isolated from the family sphere during war. Women have also been exposed to increasing risk of rape, abuse and stigmatization by members of their own community as a result of their new and more public roles and responsibilities during conflict. And, in response to growing poverty, many more women have taken to prostitution for a living with a high risk of abuse and of becoming infected with HIV/AIDS. A long-term consequence of several of these acts of abuse is children who not only lack a father but who are also illegitimate and a continuous reminder of the violation.

One of the long-term consequences of men's engagement in war as combatants is their difficulty in redefining a post-conflict social role and a male identity. This may result in divorce, alcoholism, violence and criminality, with additional effects for the family and women.

Sexual assault is not the only form of conflict-related victimization that is gendered. Differences in rights and entitlements have proved to be of great importance in determining how conflicts impact on men's and women's livelihoods. For instance, women are not always registered as individual citizens, nor are they always registered (and recognized) as owners of land, houses, assets and utensils. In a situation of conflict and social upheaval, women may have difficulty protecting their resources and find it almost impossible to make claims for compensation and other kinds of assistance. This adds to their economic and social vulnerability.

Victimization is partly gender specific.

Not only do women suffer differently to men, but their response to victimization is often different too. In most cases, women hesitate to testify to sexual abuse as it would be considered shameful and, typically, result in stigmatization and perhaps even severe punishment, although men too, find it difficult to admit to repeated cases of rape, partly because it inverts prevailing notions of gender roles.

With regard to economic victimization, women's weakness is often their lack of knowledge about and experience in dealing with authorities. Their strength, however, is the existence of local self-help groups created in order to help women overcome hardships and create supportive relationships. It can be said that women have succeeded better than men in identifying a commonality and uniting as victims across national, ethnic, class, religious and other boundaries. This is a reminder of the important point that no victim is only a victim, but also an actor with many identities, roles and resources.

Finally, victimization may not cease with the establishment of a peace agreement. Cases from Cambodia and Sierra Leone demonstrate that sexual abuse unfortunately often continues with the appearance of peacekeepers and humanitarian workers. Experience in Rwanda and South Africa illustrates the difficulties - and double victimization - that women may face when they try to make the state recognize and compensate the injustice and sufferings they have undergone during conflict. In some cases, limited representation on political bodies prevents them from giving voice to their grievances; in others it is a woman's affiliation with a particular ethnic or social group or her husband's position and role in the struggle that determines her entitlements.

4.1.5 Children as Victims

Children are the most defenceless victims in civil war and other forms of violence and oppression. Two groups are particularly vulnerable - refugee children and child soldiers.

More than half of the world's refugee population is made up of children. They are often separated from their family, suffer socio-economic deprivation, usually have no access to schooling and, more importantly, are seriously traumatized by what they have experienced. Child soldiers have frequently been intimidated or abducted, brutalized and coerced to commit atrocities. A special case is the fate of the Latin American children of murdered members of the opposition, who as orphans were then forced into a kind of adoption by the families of soldiers or police officers. Another group of child victims are the many girls who are either forced into marriage at a young age or removed from their families and homes and sold as prostitutes. And, finally, there are the many invisible and indirect victims - the children who are prevented from receiving an education and employed as child labour-ers, or who are abused at home by parents and relatives - a symptom that is found in many societies but is reinforced in times of conflict and distress.

In general, widespread and sustained violent conflict can produce a whole generation of variously victimized young people. These young victims of political, ethnic or religious aggression carry the effects of their traumatic experiences throughout their lives. The risk that this unhealed hurt and resentment can become the basis for new violence highlights the need to develop special protection, healing and rehabilitation programmes specifically for children and young people, such as assistance in family tracing (which the Red Cross and Red Crescent Societies provide for orphans and refugee children) and schooling opportunities. Truth commissions sometimes hold thematic hearings specifically on the suffering of children. The UN Convention on the Rights of the Child can assist in setting the basis for action to address the particular problems of these young victims.

> *Young victims of political, ethnic or religious aggression carry the effects of their traumatic experiences throughout their lives. This unhealed hurt and resentment can become the basis for new violence.*

Box 4.1: Official Definitions of "Victim"

1. According to the United Nations Declaration of Basic Principles of Justice for Victims of Crime and Abuse of Power, General Assembly Resolution 40/34, 29 November 1985: "victim" means, in the case of abuse of power, "persons who, individually or collectively, have suffered harm, including physical or mental injury, emotional suffering, economic loss or substantial impairment of their fundamental rights, through acts or omissions that do not yet constitute violations of national criminal laws but of internationally recognized norms relating to human rights".

2. In the United Nations Commission on Human Rights, "The right to restitution, compensation and rehabilitation for victims of gross violations of human rights and fundamental freedoms: final report of the Special Rapporteur, Mr M. Bassiouni, submitted in accordance with Commission Resolution 1999/33", UN document E/CN.4/2000/62, "A person is a 'victim'

where, as a result of acts or omissions that constitute a violation of international human rights or humanitarian law norms, that person, individually or collectively, suffered harm, including physical or mental injury, emotional suffering, economic loss, or impairment of that person's fundamental legal rights. A 'victim' may also be a dependant or a member of the immediate family or household of the direct victim as well as a person who, in intervening to assist a victim or prevent the occurrence of further violations, has suffered physical, mental or economic harm"
(*Declaration on the Right to Restitution for Victims of Gross Human Rights Violations, 1999*).

3. In the International Criminal Court, "For the purposes of the Statute and the Rules of Procedure and Evidence", finalized draft text, adopted by the Preparatory Commission at its 23rd meeting, 30 June 2000, document PCNICC/2000/

1/add.1): "(a) 'Victims' means natural persons who have suffered harm as a result of the commission of any crime within the jurisdiction of the Court; (b) Victims may include organizations or institutions that have sustained direct harm to any of their property which is dedicated to religion, education, art or science or charitable purposes, and to their historic monuments, hospitals and other places and objects for humanitarian purposes".

4. In the report of the Truth and Reconciliation Commission of South Africa, the Reparation and Rehabilitation Committee defines relatives and dependants of a victim as follows: "a) parents (or those who acted/act in place of a parent); b) spouse (according to customary, common, religious or indigenous law); c) children (either in or out of wedlock or adopted); d) someone the victim has/had a customary or legal duty to support".

4.2 The Identification of Victims

Socially, becoming a victim is a process that involves a number of mechanisms. The simple fact of having been physically, psychologically or economically harmed is a necessary but not sufficient element. Other factors play important roles. Social norms and customs, developed in politics, law and culture, partly shape the selection of those who will be allocated victim status.

No post-conflict state can involve every single victim in healing activities, truth-telling, trials and reparation measures. Material resources and manpower are too scarce. Of necessity, usually only a fraction of those whose fundamental rights have been violated will be accepted as "real" victims, but even so they may fulfil a positive role of representing symbolically the wider constituency of victims in the formal reconciliation process.

4.2.1 The Definition of a Victim

Society's influence in this process of defining who exactly qualifies as a victim comes from three sources:
- socio-political factors;
- legal definitions of victims; and
- cultural influences on definitions.

Equally important is the perception of the person who has been victimized. Is he or she aware of this victimization? Does he or she aspire to the status of victim or is there a conscious refusal of this label?

Socio-Political Factors

Official agencies define victims. Initiatives in the area of healing, truth-telling, justice and reparation obviously contribute to the definition of who will be included in the category of victims.

This is most clearly visible in the activities of truth commissions. No doubt, such bodies stimulate the recognition of victims. This has clearly been the case with the TRC in South Africa. Hundreds of statement-takers talked to victims; many witnesses were heard during public sessions; its official report publicly acknowledged the distress of tens of thousands of men and women. Yet still its mandate excluded many others whose pain fell outside the terms of reference, and this was also true of all the other truth commissions of the 1980s and 1990s. Such exclusion comes about as the result of political, time and economic restraints.

The political definition of which crimes are to be identified and registered as relevant has major consequences, precisely because any such definition necessarily also excludes some crimes as irrelevant. But, irrespective of the definition, all such crimes are relevant to the victims. One possible effect is gender bias in a commission's mandate: definitions of gross human rights violations have often masked or sidelined the types of abuse more frequently suffered by women. (A major step in correcting such prejudice is the recognition of sexual violence, in the statutes of the International Criminal Tribunal for Yugoslavia (ICTY) and of the International Criminal Court (ICC), as a crime against humanity and a war crime.)

Time, too, is a significant factor. Truth commissions or commissions of enquiry usually examine events during a specifically defined period of history. Violations that occurred before or after this period will therefore not be addressed, despite the real suffering and victimization they have caused. Economic constraints can also have huge effects on restricting either the definition of victimhood or the capacity to fulfil the resulting mandate.

Reparation programmes have similar effects. These include individuals and communities in the definition of victimhood. But they, too, have to make painful decisions.

In post-conflict states, where economic infrastructure has often been destroyed, resources are scarce.

So the reality tends to be that only a section of all the injured parties, perhaps just direct victims, or just those with the most serious physical injuries, will qualify for compensation. Others will be excluded. For example, refugees are a category of victims that can easily be forgotten. Their voices in the debate around defining victimhood are weak; they have often lived outside the country, perhaps for a generation or more. Reparation to them, for example, through restitution of property, is consequently a difficult, contentious and expensive enterprise. Women may be another group who because of their socio-political status or the nature of their victimization risk being excluding from reparation programmes. In many cases their suffering is considered a private issue which should mainly be dealt with at the private level.

The role of NGOs, both local and international, also contributes to the identification and definition of victims.

Their role in these processes often starts before the demise of an inhuman regime or the end of a violent conflict. Civil society groups monitor human rights abuses, gather information on victims and provide assistance to them. In Argentina during the 1970s and early 1980s, NGOs collected information on "the disappeared" while the generals were still in power. In 1983 they gave copies of their files to the state-initiated National Commission on the Disappearance of Persons. In Guatemala, the Human Rights Office of the Archbishop gathered information on victims well in advance of the activities of the official truth commission. Most of the information these NGOs collected was of critical importance in the post-conflict situation.

NGOs are also active in the area of healing, rehabilitation and reintegration of victims. All these activities have effects both on how victims come to perceive their own status and on official definitions and policies. While international and local NGOs may help to give silenced and invisible victims a voice, the engagement of NGOs is not always neutral. Sometimes they select victims on a sectarian basis and exploit humanitarian assistance to create or strengthen partisan relationships. Another problem inherent in humanitarian assistance work by NGOs and other agencies is a tendency to overstress the victimhood of individuals and groups, overlooking the fact that they have multiple other identities, experiences, resources, capacities, interests and aspirations, which are equally important in defining and positioning them as individuals and citizens.

Legal Definitions

It took the international community many years to reach an agreed definition of victim.

The UN Declaration of Justice for Victims of Crime and Abuse of Power of 1985 (see box 4.1) was a first step. This general description served as the basis for the UN Commission on Human Rights' Declaration on the Right to Restitution for Victims of Gross Human Rights Violations of 1999. The statutes of the ad hoc international tribunals in The Hague and Arusha, and of the ICC, also contain formal definitions (see box 4.1 for the last of these).

The criminal legislation of a post-conflict state, combined with international humanitarian and human rights law and the state's customary, indigenous and religious law, constitutes a second element in the identification and recognition of victims. The broader the scope of such legislation, the higher the number of victims who can be included in the legal category of "injured parties".

In transitional societies, it is usually the task of parliament to oversee the process of adapting existing criminal legislation to develop a suitable prosecutorial system to try the perpetrators of violent acts. Political and time constraints usually result in limits being set on the scope of the new system. Further problems often occur later at the operational level, when a department of justice tries to put the procedural machinery into gear. These are exemplified in Ethiopia's transitional justice system.

The courts there can deal with only a fraction of the crimes committed by the Marxist–Leninist Mengistu regime, and are forced to prioritize crimes and prosecute only the most serious, such as genocidal acts. Other major crimes - arbitrary arrests, seizure and theft of property, forced migration of farmers, the use of famine as a weapon of war and so on - remain outside their reach. The consequence is that the suffering of millions of victims will not be acknowledged or taken into account. In addition, as is often the case in such situations, the process focuses only on the actions of the previous regime, while the human rights violations of the armed opposition movements remain outside consideration.

> *Views on rights are to some degree culturally rooted.*

Finally, prosecutors and adjudicating judges in national and international tribunals are also key actors in the definition process: it is they who decide, in a very formal way, who is a perpetrator and who is his or her victim.

Cultural Influences

The debate on the universality of human rights has demonstrated that views on these rights are to some degree culturally rooted, as are opinions as to what constitute gross violations of these norms and, consequently, as to how the notion of "victim" should be constructed. Culture is also significant in delineating the extent of the circles of indirect victims. At a very general level, it is fair to say that societies in Africa and Asia work with broader definitions of the scope of the immediate family and of community ties than do many in Europe (see box 4.1 for an example from South Africa).

Personal Perception

Political programmes and legal texts are not the only foundations for defining a victim in the context of state crimes and civil war. The inclusion of people in (or their exclusion from) the broad category of "victim" also depends on the personal perception of the individuals involved and on the prevalent visions within a society or a culture of what is a crime and, thus, of what is acknowledged as producing physical, mental and economic harm.

Individuals differ in the way they perceive what was inflicted on them. Some deliberately refuse to be labelled as victims. They see themselves as soldiers, heroes, freedom fighters or martyrs. Others prefer the label of "survivor" because, in the words of Rama Mani, a scholar who has worked in several African countries, "The term victim defines individuals in terms of their past; makes them appear ill and in need of treatment; impotent and in need of help".

Awareness of victimization is another important factor. To perceive oneself as a victim requires naming the pain one suffered, blaming the offender and claiming some type of restitution. Obvious though this may sound, people regularly fail to do this. There are many understandable reasons. They may lack access to the public debate. They may lack the social skills necessary to make their voices heard. The effects of their trauma may have removed their belief that anything can be done to help. They may remain passive because of feelings of guilt at having survived or at not having helped others. Women's experiences of harm differ from those of men. When making a statement, for example, to a truth commission, women sometimes tend to speak about the agonies of their children or their husbands rather than their own anguish. Often, talking publicly about sexual abuse would only bring them more shame and social exclusion.

Victims have the right to remain silent. But, as noted earlier, in some ways those victims who do speak out and engage in the reconciliation process can act as the symbolic representatives of those who remain silent.

4.2.2 Re-victimization

There are ways in which a person who is already the victim of political, ethnic or religious violence can receive additional hurt after the direct cause of victimization has disappeared.

Sources of re-victimization tend to appear in one or more of the following ways:

- denial of the status of victim;
- unfulfilled expectations in dealing with official agencies;
- unwanted effects of victim-centred initiatives; and
- social stigmatization and exclusion.

The first mechanism was partly discussed in section 4.2.1: socio-political, cultural and legal definitions of victimhood result in the exclusion of individuals and communities. Inevitably, despite the best attempts, some victims will be denied acknowledgement. Sometimes denying the status of victim is vicious in nature. It may rest on a conscious attempt to make the suffering appear banal (for example, the harm done to European Gypsies during World War II was publicly denounced as negligible). It may result from stigmatization (for example, in the late 1940s and early 1950s Jewish Holocaust victims were almost blamed for a perceived passivity to their fate - "going like sheep to the slaughter"). Or it may be the effect of denying victims' suffering by dismissing them en masse as terrorists, murderers, criminals and so on.

Victims become engaged in a broad range of relations with a variety of government and non-governmental agents - police, judges, civil servants, medical doctors, journalists and professionals from victim support associations. In these engagements, victims expect an expression of understanding, sympathy and comfort. But in fact the actions and reactions of these people can sometimes merely cause extra grief. The treatment received may be unprofessional, inadequate or humiliating. The information given may be incorrect or insufficient. The formal process may be too impersonal and cold. Such negative experiences leave the victims even more mentally scarred. They increase emotional stress and feelings of incomprehension, hopelessness and isolation. Sometimes the structures of the system establish hierarchies of suffering, causing great offence and renewed hurt to those whose pain is labelled as minor.

A different but equally hurtful effect happens when victims' agony is used and/or abused for political means. Sometimes a new regime may be tempted to exploit the misery of its victims as a sort of emotional blackmail in order to gain more assistance from the international community. Conscious or unconscious, such manipulation of victims, by politically "hijacking" the victim issue, can bring short-term rewards, but its internal effect in the society - alienating the victims - is seriously counterproductive to sustainable reconciliation.

Ironically, re-victimization can even arise in institutions that are developed to serve the interests of victims. Truth commissions, for example, may reopen the wounds of testifying victims because of the confrontation with their aggressors or because of negative exposure by the victimizer. The procedures of retributive justice can have a similar effect. They are perpetrator-oriented and thus tend to exclude the voices of the victims from the whole process, or directly hurt them through a vicious cross-examination procedure that simply serves to make the victim relive the trauma in public.

> *Re-victimization can even arise in institutions that are developed to serve the interests of victims.*

Regardless of whether a violation has been officially recognized or not, victims will also be at risk of longer-term re-victimization as a result of social stigmatization and exclusion. The human will to forgive is considerable, but there are many cases where individuals, especially women, continue to be punished for having become a victim. Widows may not be allowed to remarry; women who have been raped, forced to sell their sexual services or who have simply taken a job outside their home are treated as prostitutes; their children are ostracized. Such denials of social recognition and reintegration may have serious ramifications for women's economic position and ability to contribute to efforts to counter structural marginalization.

4.2.3 "Self-Victimization"

It happens that perpetrators of violence themselves lay claim to victimhood. They blame the ideological indoctrination they were subjected to or refer to earlier periods in history when it was their group or community who was victimized. They may even blame "the system" for what they did. The effect is to render their actions excusable, and to shift the responsibility to some more anonymous "system", "ideology" or "regime".

> *Victim empowerment is a prerequisite of any reconciliation policy.*

Observing the conflict in Northern Ireland, Marie Smyth writes: "The status of victim renders the victim deserving of sympathy, support, outside help. Victims, by definition, are vulnerable, and any violence on their part can be construed as the consequences of their victimization. The acquisition of the status of victim becomes an institutionalized way of escaping guilt, shame, or responsibility".

The argument of victimization through indoctrination is, to a certain degree, acceptable in the case of bystanders and onlookers, who are faced with the charge of being morally, if indirectly, guilty (see chapter 5). But it can encourage them to avoid any responsibility for the construction of a just political and economic future for all members of society. Where offenders call on the "we are all victims" argument, the effect may be to seriously obstruct reconciliation programmes. Such blurring of guilt can become an obstacle on the path to coexistence, trust and empathy from the point of view of many victims.

4.3 Victim Mobilization

Passive victimhood - the state in which people avoid addressing their pain and trauma through silence, disengagement and resignation - is an enemy to reconciliation. It blocks the return of the very integrity and self-confidence of the victim. It also tempts the victimizers to define and organize reconciliation as a painless forgiving and forgetting. Victim empowerment, the way to escape from this submissive position, is a prerequisite of any reconciliation policy.

4.3.1 Victim Empowerment

Almost all reconciliation programmes, particularly in the area of healing and truth-telling (see chapters 6 and 8), aim to empower the victims of brutal conflict. They mobilize resources that restore the dignity, the reputation and the life chances of victims.

Victim associations are key actors in this area. They operate in most post-conflict societies and range from small groups, like the Mothers of the Plaza de Mayo in Chile, to large-scale organizations of survivors, like IBUKA in Rwanda. They cover a whole array of activities in the area of empowerment. They act as pressure groups, inform public opinion, offer legal aid.

Victim identification is one of their most important goals. IBUKA (kinyarwanda for "remember") has published a list of 59,050 genocide victims, all from the prefecture of Kibuye situated in the west of the country, on the border of Lake Kivu. This record contains personal data (name, sex, age and so on), and information on the circumstances of the killing (place, weapon used etc.). In Argentina,

Chile and Guatemala, where atrocities have for a long time been denied, the collection of such basic data by victim associations can work to break the conspiracy of silence.

Victim self-help organizations have another, equally crucial role to play. The healing effect of "suffering together" has been described by group therapists. While trauma can silently continue to kill victims from within, talking about it in the company of fellow-sufferers may give them a sense of relief and can start a cathartic process. The exchange of information, the learning process of listening to other people's problems and questions, the gradual discovering of the power of alliances - all these facilitate the development of social and politico-legal skills. Members of such groups will slowly but surely enable each other to master the techniques of naming the pain they suffered, blaming those who are responsible and claiming recognition and reparation. To resent wrong done is conducive to regaining self-esteem, a crucial step towards rebuilding trust in oneself and in others. An additional effect is to counteract the attitudes and types of behaviour that develop in silent isolation.

Self-help groups, like the associations of widows in Rwanda, create for their members a supportive social fabric. Victims who, through their involvement in such networks, make the transition from passive disengagement to active engagement may even grow into the role of moral beacons and play a significant leadership role in reconciliation projects.

One recent development - the rise of what has been called a victim culture - may make it easier for victims to achieve the much-needed empowerment. Public opinion, in part stimulated by and partly followed by policy makers and NGOs, has altered in two ways.

First, there has been a shift from the cult of the hero or victor to the cult of the victim. Suffering instead of heroism now attracts public and political consideration. This cultural reversal is evidenced in what has been called the "rediscovery of historical victims", such as the forced labourers of the Third Reich, the sex slaves (known as "comfort women") of the Japanese Army in World War II, the Japanese-Americans who were detained in concentration camps after the Pearl Harbour attack, Native Americans in the USA, Aborigines in Australia, and the millions of men and women abused and killed during the merciless period of European colonialism and slavery. This has led to the demand that political descendants apologize for past acts, and to claims for restitution and reparation, all in the name of reconciliation.

A second shift has diverted attention, in the reaction to crime, away from an exclusive focus on the offender and turned the emphasis towards the victim. In a general way, this trend is detectable in the proliferation of victim support programmes and in the growth of victimology as a scholarly discipline. More specifically in the context of dealing with a violent past, transitional societies now seem to prefer restorative justice and truth-telling above outright retribution, partly because penal action is perpetrator-oriented and largely excludes or ignores victims, while the alternative instruments focus much more on the victim and the effects of the crime.

Victim empowerment is not a blessing in all circumstances. It can become an obstacle to peaceful coexistence and mutual trust. Victim associations may organize opposition to measures that are aimed at reconciling former conflicting parties, such as conditional amnesties or reintegration of offenders. They can become trapped in the past, searching continually for recognition of their suffering but with no strategy for the future. Rwanda's IBUKA, for example, has been criticized for its opposition to the release of prisoners who were detained without any indictment and for its initial refusal to accept the reconciliation-oriented gacaca tribunals (see the case study following chapter 7). Victim associations in Northern Ireland have opposed conciliatory measures, such as the inclusion of convicted prisoners in the government's Victim Liaison Unit. Activities and groups that serve to strengthen victim identities and communities can sometimes lock people into the past, or encourage partisan groupings among sufferers. At worst, this can even lead to the use of past suffering as a justification for new retaliatory violence.

4.3.2 Victim Competition

It is tempting to see all those who have suffered from violent conflict as natural allies, even as members of one harmonious family. History, however, teaches us that victims frequently compete fiercely with each other for recognition, for material resources such as compensation and positive discrimination in the areas of housing and education, and for symbolic goods such as monuments, medals, memorial days and other types of commemoration.

Most common is competition between victims of the same atrocities. There are historical studies of the bitter post-World War II struggles between the various victims of the German invasion in Belgium, France and the Netherlands. Resistance fighters, forced labourers, persecuted patriots, anti-fascists, communists and surviving Jews all tried to represent their own suffering as greater than that of others and to make their experiences dominant in the national war memory. The pattern is repeated again and again in many contexts today. In Burundi, for example, it is usual for Tutsi leaders to boycott the inauguration of any memorial to Hutu victims, and vice versa.

A second kind of competition develops between victims of different aggressions. American historian Peter Novick speaks cynically of "the fight for the gold medal in the Olympics of genocides". Some Jews in particular have emphasized the uniqueness of the Holocaust, even denying other victim groups (e.g., the Armenians in early twentieth-century Turkey) the right to call their suffering "genocide". This reaction is easy to understand. Not only is it the product of massive trauma, but its aim is to monopolize the symbolic capital that such a unique fate brings and to convert it into political and economic opportunities that might begin to compensate for the massive injustice.

4.4 Victims and Offenders: Interchangeable Roles

There are post-conflict circumstances in which it is almost impossible to draw a clear line between victims and perpetrators.

Authoritarian regimes, particularly if they stay in power for many years, have the effect of blurring the distinction between being victimized and being an accessory: large sections of the population become casualties of the totalitarian use of continuous indoctrination and ideology, but they may also collaborate in state crimes. In the case of a civil war, almost all rival groups have committed flagrant violations of human rights. The cycle of violence in such countries as Burundi, Colombia, Northern Ireland, Rwanda and Sri Lanka continually turns victims into aggressors and vice versa.

Most extremely, people are sometimes brutally forced into aggression: Guatemalan peasants were coerced by the army to eliminate "informers" passing information on to the guerrilla movements.

> The alternation of roles between victims and offenders is an important consideration in preparing and implementing reconciliation programmes.

This alternation of roles is an important consideration in preparing and implementing reconciliation programmes. It is clear that no coexistence or mutual trust will develop if the rotating nature of violence is not recognized and admitted. Many will refuse to accept accountability: "Peoples who believe themselves to be victims of aggression have an understandable incapacity to believe that they also committed atrocities. Myths of innocence and victimhood are a powerful obstacle in the way of confronting unwelcome facts", writes Michael Ignatieff. Mutual aggression also creates a post-conflict situation in which retributive justice is almost impossible to achieve. Penal systems are not devised to deal with such intricacies.

Child soldiers who have participated in extreme cruelty (as in Liberia and Sierra Leone) are a particular case of the strange mix of being perpetrator and victim. They deserve special attention. NGOs, such as the Coalition to Stop the Use of Child Soldiers, are rightly fighting for demobilization and reintegration measures in the Congo, Eritrea, Ethiopia, Sierra Leone, the Philippines and Paraguay (see chapter 5, section 2 on their reintegration).

The ambiguities that follow from these situations have prompted some observers to question the usefulness of the distinction between victim and offender. They prefer the transcending notion of survivor, encompassing all those who need to be reconciled after conflict. This argument provokes fierce opposition from those who claim that it will hurt certain victims and will be a source of re-victimization. It could also give perpetrators a neat alibi for self-victimization. However, the bridging notion of survivor may be useful in situations where a climate has developed that might enable victims and offenders to develop some cooperative activities towards reconciliation.

4.5 Concluding Remarks

The recognition of victims is a crucial issue in the search for reconciliation. The following list of principles to be considered may help domestic and international agencies deal adequately with this matter:

• Be aware of the many consequences of selecting a particular political and legal definition of a "victim".

• Respect the victims' very personal perception of what has happened to them. In some cases this means approaching them not as victims but as survivors. At the same time policy makers have to accept that perceptions are flexible and change with time. Trauma is a slow-working virus.

• Recognize that a victim's recovery proceeds through several different stages.

• Provide for collective measures in the areas of health care, education and housing that assist whole communities and thus include the many who fall outside reparation programmes.

• Listen to the needs of victims who stay as refugees in neighbouring countries.

References and Further Reading
Main Sources

South African Truth and Reconciliation Commission. *Report, Vol. IV*. Cape Town: Juta & Co., Ltd, 1998.

Rombouts, Heidy and Stef Vandeginste. "Reparation for Victims of Gross and Systematic Human Rights Violations: The Notion of Victim." *Third World Legal Studies, 2001–2002* (forthcoming).

Other References

Boyden, Jo and Sara Gibbs. *Children of War: Responses to Psycho-Social Distress in Cambodia*. Geneva: United Nations Research Institute for Social Development (UNRISD), 1997.

Gibbs, Sara. "Postwar Social Reconstruction in Mozambique: Reframing Children's Experiences of Trauma and Healing." In *Rebuilding Societies after Civil War: Critical Roles for International Assistance*, edited by Krishna Kumar. Boulder, Colo.: Lynne Rienner, 1997:227–238.

Ignatieff, Michael. "Articles of Faith." *Index on Censorship* 5(1996):110–122

Lorentzen, Lois Ann and Jennifer Turpin. *The Women and War Reader.* New York: New York University Press, 1998.

Mani, Rama. *Beyond Retribution: Seeking Justice in the Shadows of War.* Cambridge and Malden, Mass: Polity Press and Blackwell, 2002.

Minow, Martha. *Between Vengeance and Forgiveness: Facing History after Genocide and Mass Violence.* Boston: Beacon Press, 1998.

Novick, Peter. *The Holocaust in American Life.* Boston: Hougton Mifflin, 1999.

Smyth, Marie. "Putting the Past in its Place: Issues of Victimhood and Reconciliation in Northern Ireland's Peace Process." In *Burying the Past: Making Peace and Doing Justice after Civil Conflict*, edited by Nigel Biggar. Washington, DC: Georgetown University Press, 2001:107–130.

Tushen, Meredith and C. Twagiramariya. *What Women Do in Wartime: Gender and Conflict in Africa.* London: Zed Books, 1998.

CHAPTER 5

Offenders

LUC HUYSE

Violent conflict produces a wide variety of offenders - men and women, state and non-state actors, local and foreign individuals and organizations, generals and foot soldiers. Ideally, the processes aimed at reconciliation should touch them all. In practice, many of them will remain outside the reach of healing, truth-telling, justice and reparation initiatives. Perpetrators may be unknown, on the run or simply unwilling to engage in reconciliation activities. Whatever the situation, it is essential to understand and recognize their role and motives (section 5.1). It is also in the interests of a post-conflict society that perpetrators be reintegrated in their community (section 5.2).

5.1 Understanding Offenders

Understanding the "why" and "how" of offenders' actions is not by any means the same as excusing them. But it is a precondition for any reconciliation policy. It is necessary to understand the diversity of their guilt, the gravity of their offence and their motives.

> Understanding the "why" and "how" of offenders' actions is a precondition for any reconciliation policy.

5.1.1 Varieties of Offender

Offenders can be classified according to the nature of guilt. Is it criminal, political or moral? Is it individual or collective? The range of sources and forms of guilt demands that a reconciliation policy reflect a diversity of approach.

"Primary" and "Indirect" Offenders

The presence of criminal guilt is the distinctive factor for what are called primary offenders. They are the ones who, on the basis of national or international law, can be brought before a criminal court. This is the category that receives most attention from political actors, international institutions, public opinion and NGOs working in the field of human rights, the media and the academic community.

In the case of indirect offenders, guilt is of a political and/or moral nature. Their offence is caused (a) by the direct or indirect advantages they enjoyed as a result of the offences of others, (b) by inaction when witnessing violations of human rights, or (c) by unintentional harmful action.

Each regime that is based on gross inequalities, each civil war, has its many silent beneficiaries. They do not kill, torture, abduct or abuse physically. But they profit whenever scarce resources are allocated - jobs and income, health care and education, housing and personal security, status and political power. In many cases the benefits they receive continue from the past over the present into the future. The report of the South African Truth and Reconciliation Commission (TRC) rightly says:

> Silent, indirect beneficiaries do not kill, torture, abduct or abuse. But they profit from the past.

"Reconciliation requires a commitment, especially by those who have benefited and continue to benefit from past discrimination, to the transformation of unjust inequalities and dehumanizing poverty". Focusing on beneficiaries also sheds more light on the victimhood of the majority, whereas an emphasis solely on the primary offenders inevitably limits the scope to individual victims whose suffering is most visible. The accountability of indirect beneficiaries must also be addressed in reconciliation processes.

Domestic beneficiaries are those among the population who benefit most from the unjust situation. Their accountability, too, must be addressed in a reconciliation process. Otherwise, certain key aims, such as distributive or social justice, will remain a distant goal. (It was in this context that the South African TRC proposed the introduction of a wealth tax to enable those who benefited from apartheid policies to contribute towards the alleviation of poverty. Up to now the scheme has not been put in place.)

Bystanders and onlookers are another type of indirect offender. Complicity here is due to inaction when confronted with victims of violent conflict. They know what happens, or choose not to know, and remain silent. Their guilt is moral. Sometimes bystanders belong to the international community. The inaction of the UN in general, and of Belgium, France and the United States in particular, at the start of the genocide in Rwanda was a forceful demonstration of such guilt. Another example was the passive attitude of the Dutch UN battalion in Srebrenica, Bosnia, while thousands of Muslim men were abducted and killed by Bosnian Serb forces.

Unintentionally harmful action is a further sort of indirect offence. This is a problem that continually haunts UN institutions such as the United Nations Development Programme (UNDP) and the United Nations Commission for Human Rights (UNHCR), and large NGOs like Médecins Sans Frontières (MSF). They have sometimes been involved in actions that involuntarily led to the persistence of a civil war or of human rights violations. For example, the genocide in Rwanda produced massive Hutu refugee camps in East Congo. MSF played a prominent role in the camps in responding to a major food and health crisis that broke out, while extremist Hutu elements in the camps exploited the crisis for the purposes of mobilization and indoctrination. It has been argued that a section of MSF, by maintaining aid provision for a year in the camps, in fact fuelled the war between Hutu and Tutsi by indirectly facilitating the reorganization and regrouping of Hutu combatants.

Individual and Collective Offenders

Criminal courts deal with individual guilt. Truth commissions, on the other hand, can look at cases of collective guilt (see chapter 8). Their findings confirm that churches, professional groups such as the judiciary and the medical profession, business and the media have contributed to human injustice. In many countries they act at least as beneficiaries and bystanders. Business leaders refrain from criticizing state violations of human rights because they need government contracts. In South Africa, the mining industry supported the migrant labour system that damaged black family life. Faith communities chose to look the other way when confronted with the effects of state-sponsored terrorism. The line between being silent or active supporters of apartheid often became extremely thin. Churches provided theological arguments in support of apartheid. Members of the medical profession advised police on torture techniques that left no marks.

> Churches, the judiciary, the medical profession, business and the media have contributed to human injustice.

Gender

The perpetrators of genocide and mass atrocities are chiefly men. Understanding of the biological, psychological, cultural and political foundations of male violence in the area of human rights is extremely limited, and knowledge about the role of women in this domain is even more lacking. Basic statistical information is scarce and, where it exists, merely anecdotal. For example, the report of the

South African TRC has a section on women as perpetrators, but the only information is that one per cent of amnesty applications of those where the applicant's sex was known came from women.

In effect, the inclusion of a gender perspective and information about the roles of women in situations of armed conflict is both recent and restricted, and there has been a tendency to depict women as natural peace-lovers who altruistically take care of others. But, even when there is a difference between the social behaviour of men and that of women in conflict situations, it is important to recognize the roles that women may play as offenders as well. It has already been mentioned that women have been active members in a number of liberation movements and armed forces. In Sri Lanka, for instance, there are women in both the national army and the Tamil liberation movement, the Liberation Tigers of Tamil Eelam (LTTE). In the LTTE women are said to be involved in the torture of enemy soldiers, and they play an important role as suicide bombers and in recruiting for and justifying the war among civilian Tamils through seminars and public meetings. Women also play a significant role in justifying war through the upbringing of children, particularly sons. We know from Sri Lanka, Palestine and other places that mothers actively encourage their sons to take up arms and fight the enemy. Also, women, like men, may take advantage of a militarized situation to involve armed factions in resolving local and domestic disputes.

5.1.2 Hierarchies of Cruelty, Hierarchies of Offenders

The term "perpetrator" is not applicable in all cases of victimization. Actions that produce considerable harm may be unintentional or the result of plain errors. In civil war, for example, collateral damage - killing or wounding civilians, destroying homes and communal infrastructure - is sometimes

---

Box 5.1: Categories of Offence

International Crimes*
(crimes posing a threat to international security and the safety of humankind; these cannot be modified by any treaty or domestic law):

• *Crimes against humanity* as defined in the Statute of the International Criminal Court (ICC) of 1998 (article 7) are crimes committed as part of a widespread or systematic attack directed against any civilian population: murder, extermination, enslavement, deportation, severe deprivation of physical liberty in violation of fundamental rules of international law, torture, rape, sex slavery, forced prostitution, forced pregnancy and sterilization, and all other forms of severe sexual violence, persecution, enforced disappearance of persons, apartheid or other inhuman acts of a similar nature.

• *Genocide* (ICC Statute, article 6) is acts committed with the intent to destroy, in whole or in part, a national, ethnic, racial or religious group as such, by killing members of the group, causing serious bodily or mental harm, deliberately inflicting on the group conditions of life calculated to bring about its physical destruction in whole or in part, imposing measures intended to prevent birth within the group or forcibly transferring children of the group to another.

• *War crimes* (ICC Statute, article 8) are severe violations, committed during an international or domestic armed conflict, of the Geneva Conventions of 12 August 1949 and of other international humanitarian laws, in particular if these acts are directed against people not actively participating in combat (e.g., civilians or prisoners).

Gross Violations of Human Rights*
(severe violations of human rights (e.g., torture, disappearances committed by state or non-state agencies).
This category entails (isolated) acts that are not necessarily part of a widespread or systematic attack, hence the difference with crimes against humanity.

Associated Violations**
These are not gross violations of human rights but cause all the same victimization (e.g., violating a corpse after death, sexual harassment including threats of rape, deprivation of essentials such as medical attention, ruin of business, intimidation by dismissal from work).

* Based on Gunnar Theissen.
** Based on vol. V, chapter 1 of the report of the Truth and Reconciliation Commission of South Africa.

unavoidable. No humanitarian or moral laws may have been violated. The strict notion of a perpetrator must be reserved for those whose acts fall into the categories of international crimes, gross violations of human rights and associated violations. Box 5.1 offers a short definition of these categories, portraying the faces of cruelty. It also helps to answer the questions whom to prosecute and/or whom to involve as perpetrators in programmes of healing, truth-seeking and reparation.

Information on offenders must be located, processed and utilized. One of the first steps is to classify offenders according to the gravity of the crimes they committed or are suspected of having committed. This often proves to be difficult: the majority of the population has participated in human rights violations; records have been destroyed; the new regime lacks the logistical capacities.

Two quite different approaches to offender classification can be found in Rwanda and Ethiopia.

In Rwanda, the Organic Law of 12 October 2000 creating the special gacaca tribunals (see the case study following chapter 7) provides for the classification of (suspected) perpetrators into four categories. Category 1 includes the planners, organizers and leaders of the genocide, persons acting in their official capacity, famous and excessively cruel killers and those who committed torture and sexual crimes. Persons suspected of physical assault resulting in the death of the victim belong to category 2. Category 3 is made up of criminals who committed serious but not deadly physical assaults and violence. Finally, persons who committed offences against property (theft, destruction, looting etc.) fall into category 4. However, the obstacles and handicaps in information management are immense and the implementation of this classification has proved to be extremely difficult.

In Ethiopia, the Special Prosecutor's Office had a double advantage: the former regime had kept meticulous records and the US-based Carter Center contributed to the establishment of an information management system. The Special Prosecutor's Office divided the suspects of genocide and other human rights violations into three groups. Category I consists of the policy and decision makers. These are the people being tried in the so-called Dergue trials. (The Dergue was the government in the previous regime.) Category II consists of the field commanders. They passed on the orders from the Dergue to the lower echelons. In the third category are the individual perpetrators of crimes. Right from the start, the Special Prosecutor has given priority to bringing category I offenders to court. This means that the most complicated cases are dealt with first, causing considerable delays to the proceedings. In the meantime, some 9,000 suspects of the two other categories have been on remand since May 1991. The philosophy behind the Special Prosecutor's strategy is that it will yield an understanding of the chains of command.

5.1.3 The Motives of Offenders

Understanding offenders requires the examination of a multitude of potential sources of violent deeds - biological, psychological, cultural and political. Asking offenders what their motives were is important, but it opens only one window on this immensely complicated matter. Many of the causes of vicious behaviour are consciously or unconsciously repressed.

The Context as a Source of Motives

Psychological sources of acts of atrocity (e.g., pure revenge or sadism) are an important dimension to explaining and understanding violent behaviour. However, in the context of reconciliation processes, factors of a social, cultural and political nature are even more significant, because they are more tangible targets for change-oriented policies than the psychology of real and potential offenders.

Offenders may have acted or thought that they were acting under orders or under threat. Or, given the context (e.g., an authoritarian regime), their actions may not have been unlawful when they were committed. A major discussion in France, during and just after World War II, focused precisely on the legality of the Vichy regime, which had collaborated with the German occupiers, and on the actions of those who, believing Vichy to be the legal and legitimate government of France during the war, obeyed its laws and committed ugly crimes. Some of the physical and psychological violence carried out by the communist regimes of Central and Eastern Europe was sanctioned by the legal codes then in force. Claus Offe, a German sociologist, gives the example of a communist offender who might argue that he was "unaware of the now alleged criminal nature of the acts of which he is accused; given the fact that he has been brought up in a regime that pardons and in fact mandates acts (now deemed criminal) for the sake of higher political purposes, he had no reason to doubt the rightfulness of what he had been doing".

Perpetrators may themselves be "victims" of hate speech, as in Rwanda, where Radio Mille Collines incited the Hutu population to exterminate the "cockroaches" (i.e., the Tutsi). The use of such dehumanizing language is a well-known technique that can turn ordinary citizens into violators of human rights. As Alex Boraine says: "The moment one designates a person as sub-human, one can act against them as an object with very little feeling. After all, if they are not quite human, then they don't feel as we do, they don't hurt as we do, and in a sense they don't bleed as we do". In yet other ways, language creates confusion about the sources of, and the accountability for, violent behaviour. Authoritarian regimes tend to use ambiguous words and codes when they discuss security matters with the military, the police and secret services - "take out", "neutralize", "methods after detention" and "informal policing". Adriaan Vlok, Minister of Law and Order in the last South African apartheid government, said in his testimony to the TRC: "We at the top took certain decisions and we used terminology without actually really thinking about it and that worked its way through to the people on the ground and they misinterpreted it".

> Perpetrators may themselves be "victims".

Finally, the existence of a culture of impunity also adds to the ambiguity of some forms of violence. The Zimbabwe Human Rights NGO Forum published a report on alleged perpetrators and their crimes during the 2000 parliamentary elections. They saw the culture of impunity in their country as one of the explanations for the violent behaviour of some of the followers of the governing Zimbabwe African National Union-Patriotic Front (ZANU-PF) party.

Amnesties have proven to be a dangerous practice in Zimbabwe and have set an unfortunate precedent. A general amnesty was imposed both after the Liberation War and after the Matebeleland massacres in the 1980s. As a result, Zimbabwe's disinclination towards seeking accountability in both these eras has been instructive to the populace in general: crimes will not be prosecuted, criminals are free and are even encouraged to terrorize again, and victims will be denied justice.

Latin American countries such as Colombia have a similar legacy of impunity, giving perpetrators the impression that their acts are politically, socially and morally accepted. (See chapter 7 on the question of amnesty and impunity.)

Political Motives

Violence in the area of human rights is a multidimensional phenomenon. The political motives which often lie behind it are similarly varied.

A frequent excuse is "We were at war". This can be a genuine explanation in situations of civil war between ethnic or religious groups. But it appears just as often in the context of colonial and anti-colonial operations. The Cold War, too, was an extremely effective context for similar self-justification. Ideology and a true "belief in the cause" can operate in the same way. Another, almost inexhaustible, source of rationalization appears when a society is caught in a cycle of violence. Revenge then becomes the fuel that continually causes breaches of human rights: new violence is justified, or even demanded, as retaliation or punishment for previous violence.

Non-state actors (paramilitary groups, rebels, and so on) who use violence will often explain their acts as justifiable "politically-motivated violence", unavoidable in response to state violence. Their fight for freedom or against repression, for example, is purely motivated by political and/or moral aims, and is only dismissed as criminal in the eyes of an unjust regime. Setting aside for the moment the question of the morality of violence in general, undoubtedly this is a genuine explanation of why many "ordinary" people around the world feel compelled to engage in "extraordinary" acts (i.e., violence) and see themselves as freedom fighters and reluctant heroes.

> *Distinguishing political from other motives for atrocities is a crucial mission in truth-telling and prosecution.*

Political motives can sometimes be used merely to camouflage criminal purposes. Examples can be found in the recent history of countries like the former Yugoslavia, Liberia, Sierra Leone and Somalia. The violence employed by official agencies (such as military and paramilitary units, police and so on) and by rebel movements is meant purely to protect their control over drug traffic, illegal migration routes or smuggling operations.

Distinguishing political from other motives for atrocities is a crucial mission in truth-telling and prosecution. Victims will never accept amnesty, for example, as the outcome of a testimony in a truth commission if there is no clear and unambiguous certainty that a human rights crime had a political foundation. And transitional justice trials frequently use the notion of a "political offence" as a way to identify attenuating circumstances. (See chapter 7.)

5.2 Offenders and Reconciliation

What can facilitate the reconciliation of offenders with their victims, with their society and with their own destiny? Much depends on the context in which the victimization of fellow citizens was committed and on the motives of the perpetrators. In some cases background, motives and perspectives raise serious obstacles to reconciliation; but experience suggests that under certain circumstances the reintegration of offenders is a principal step towards reconciliation.

5.2.1 Obstacles
Denial of Guilt

The findings of truth commissions demonstrate that rejection of guilt and responsibility is based on a variety of discourses. "We are heroes, not perpetrators" is the interpretation repeatedly given when violence is committed against a background of civil war or of colonial and anti-colonial wars. In addition, where impunity is a dominant theme in the political and legal culture (as was the case in many Latin American countries), offenders feel that they were entitled to do what they did. Others refuse to be called offenders, employing the well-known argument that they were "only obeying orders". They experience and acknowledge no guilt.

Michael Ignatieff, writing on the tragic events in the former Yugoslavia, identifies yet other forms of denial, such as complex strategies of relativization: "One accepts the facts but argues that the enemy was equally culpable or that the accusing party is also to blame or that such 'excesses' are regrettable necessities in time of war. To relativize is to have it both ways: to admit the facts while denying full responsibility for them".

The "Magnitude Gap"

Roy Baumeister, a German philosopher, has compared the per-spectives of victims and perpetrators on the importance of the violence that took place, on the intensity of emotions, on the duration of the effects of the events, and on the moral evalua-tion and interpretation of what happened. He argues that the differences are such that a "magnitude gap" exists between the two perspectives. Offenders generally tend to undervalue the

> A "magnitude gap" exists between the perspectives of victims and perpetrators on the importance of the violence that took place.

significance and consequences of their acts, while victims understandably feel the full weight of their suffering. This "disconnect" is a major obstacle on the route to reconciliation. (See box 5.2 for a concrete application of this analysis.)

Box 5.2: The "Magnitude Gap" in South Africa

This magnitude gap has a number of features:

1. The importance of the act is usually far greater for the victim. Horror of the experience is usually seen in the victim's terms; for the perpetrator it is often "a very small thing".

2. Perpetrators tend to have less emotion about their acts than do victims.

3. The experience of violence typically fades faster for perpetrators than for victims. For victims, the suffering may continue long after the event.

4. Moral evaluations of the events may differ: actions may appear less wrong, less evil, to the per-petrator than to the victim. While victims tend to rate events in stark categories of right and wrong, perpetrators may see large grey areas.

5. Discrepancies exist between victims and perpetrators regarding the question of motives and intentions, the crucial question of why? Victims' accounts show two versions, one which emphasizes sheer incomprehensibility - the

perpetrator had no reason at all - and one which presents the perpetrator's action as deliberately malicious, as sadistic, as an end in itself. By contrast, the vast majority of perpetrators, even if they admit wrongfulness, provide comprehensible reasons for their actions.

Source: South African Truth and Reconciliation Commission. *Report,* *Vol. V:*271–272

Apologies without Accountability

Some observers, reflecting on reconciliatory steps taken by offenders, have emphasized the impor-tance of apologies. Others ask if saying "Sorry" is enough. They argue that apologies without admit-ting responsibility to the victims will not lead to genuine reconciliation. This question has been debated fiercely in South Africa after former President de Klerk's appearance before the TRC. He apologized in the following terms: "Apartheid was wrong. I apologize in my capacity as leader of the National Party to the millions of South Africans who suffered the wretched disruption of forced removals in respect of their homes, businesses and land. Who over the years suffered the shame of being arrested for pass law offences. Who over the decades and indeed centuries suffered the indignities and humiliation of racial discrimination". But he also told the TRC that he did not feel responsible because, "I have not been involved in anything which can…constitute any form of cred-ible charge that I have been guilty of any crime".

While apologies can indeed add significantly to the reconciliation process, at the same time many victims can find incomplete apologies insulting, thus actually creating a further obstacle to reconciliation.

5.2.2 Reintegration of Perpetrators

It is ultimately in the interests of the society as a whole that perpetrators be reintegrated into their community. Their continued exclusion from the community threatens the overall integration and reconciliation of the society.

Perpetrators' continued exclusion from the community threatens the overall integration and reconciliation of the society.

Why Reintegrate?

The reasons for setting up reintegration programmes vary according to the context of the transition. Several practical considerations may lead state authorities to advocate the reintegration of perpetrators:

• Quite soon after the end of a violent conflict prisons often have to cope with overpopulation, exerting untenable pressure on public resources.

• Lengthy punishment of one particular category of offenders, namely administrative and managerial staff, risks being very counterproductive as it could endanger the badly needed political and economic reconstruction of the country.

• External threats may speed up the urge to reincorporate former perpetrators in view of a much-needed national reconciliation. This is what happened in France and the Netherlands a few years after World War II ended. Both countries became involved in a colonial war, France in Indochina and the Netherlands in Indonesia, and sought domestic unity through the reconciliation of the Resistance and those who had been punished for their collaboration with the Germans.

• Other motives are of a politico-moral order. The prolonged physical and social exclusion of certain sections of the population may drive the perpetrators into social and political isolation, giving birth to a class of outcasts who will take revenge on society. It can also result in the creation of subcultures and networks which, in the long run, will become hostile to democracy.

• Easy access to weapons in many societies emerging from conflict contributes to creating a highly explosive situation.

All these considerations may obstruct the processes leading to reconciliation.

Sooner or later most offenders will return to their community of origin. This homecoming could become a source of re-traumatization of the surviving victims if no explicit measures with respect to adequate reintegration are taken.

Sooner or later most offenders will return to their community of origin. This homecoming could become a source of re-traumatization of the surviving victims if no explicit measures with respect to adequate reintegration are taken.

How to Reintegrate?

There is a host of strategies available to national policy makers.

• Removing legal and administrative obstacles. Such measures include release on parole, reduction or remission of financial sanctions, restitution of office and of civil rights, and rehabilitation.

• Actively promoting reintegration by way of re-socialization is a further, but quite difficult, task. Moral persuasion is rarely enough: instilling democracy and human rights values requires intricate education programmes and is a long-term enterprise.

• Reintegrating offenders at the level of the local community. This is generally carried out by NGOs, religious institutions and other civil society groups. Local authorities may involve offenders in community-based projects, asking them to offer their skills and time in rebuilding schools, hospitals and roads. That is precisely the reconciliation-oriented sanction that the Rwandan gacaca tribunals at the level of the cell will be able to impose (see the case study following chapter 7).

In countries such as Cambodia, Indonesia, South Africa and Mozambique, reintegration initiatives are often based on traditional rituals which express the acceptance of offenders back into the community. In Canada, Aboriginal ceremonies, called healing circles and including contacts with elders, have been integrated into official prisoner release preparation programmes. The philosophy behind such schemes is that modern criminal justice systems have disempowered local communities with respect to reintegrating offenders by giving all the power to professionals such as social workers, psychologists and psychiatrists. These cleansing rituals place the crime back in the context in which it happened. This approach is part of the broader perspective of restorative justice (see chapter 7).

Reconciliation between offenders and victims will profit if both national and local policy makers can retrieve, reassemble or combine elements of traditional mechanisms of healing, reintegration and rehabilitation.

A Top-Down or Bottom-Up Approach?

Balancing the needs of the political system against the desires of individuals and local communities, state authorities often give full priority to a top-down approach, developing policies such as amnesty or collective pardon. These may be perceived in the population as imposed solutions and, thus, be resented. Local initiatives, on the other hand, are frequently too few in number and too small in scope to constitute an adequate form of policy. The reintegration of members of the army or of armed rebellion movements, for example, needs to take place preferably in the context of a national demobilization policy. What is wanted is a suitable mix of programmes and projects, both top–down and bottom–up.

That is exactly what is planned in East Timor. The Commission for Reception, Truth and Reconciliation, created in late 2001, will try to achieve the objective of "reception" or reintegration by using East Timorese traditional justice mechanisms and by facilitating "community reconciliation agreements" between the local community and the perpetrators of less serious crimes such as looting, burning and minor assault.

Such a blend is particularly needed where child soldiers form an important part of the ex-combatant population. Approximately 300,000 children, some as young as 10 years, are currently serving as soldiers in more than 40 armed conflicts. They have often been kidnapped. (One of the most brutal examples is the abduction of some 10,000 children by the Lord's Resistance Army in Northern Uganda.) According to Human Rights Watch, child soldiers in post-conflict societies are schooled only in war and tend to be drawn into crime or to become easy prey for future military recruitment. Breaking this cycle of violence entails specific demobilization and reintegration projects, based on creating opportunities for education, training and employment.

5.3 Concluding Remarks

Ideally, reconciliatory steps by offenders include fully exposing the facts, looking the victims in the eye, listening to them, repairing (part of) the harm done, acknowledging sorrow, guilt or shame, and ultimately feeling empathy with them. However, in many cases a variety of obstacles will block the way to such moves. Offenders may be unwilling to engage in reconciliation projects because they underestimate the consequences of their acts. Or ideology and a culture of impunity may incite them to reject guilt and responsibility or, even worse, look for revenge.

Overcoming such obstacles should be the ambition of any reconciliation policy. Positive developments include accepting the diversity of guilt in violent conflict and distinguishing political from other motives in atrocities. Reintegration of offenders into their local communities once a reasonable degree of coexistence has been reached is another possibility. There is no guarantee that reintegration programmes will convince offenders to reconcile with their victims, or vice versa. But such programmes certainly create opportunities for perpetrators to break out of their isolation and, in the case of community-based initiatives, to realize the harmful impact their behaviour has had on the victims and thus to consider how they might respond.

References and Further Reading
Main Sources

South African Truth and Reconciliation Commission. *Report, Vol. V.* Cape Town: Juta & Co., Ltd, 1998.

Theissen, Gunnar. "*Supporting Justice, Co-Existence and Reconciliation after Armed Conflict: Strategies for Dealing with the Past*". In *Berghof Handbook for Conflict Transformation*. Berlin: Berghof Research Center for Constructive Conflict Management, 2001,

http://userpage.fu-berlin.de/~theissen/biblio/index.html.

Other References

Baumeister, Roy. *Evil: Inside Human Cruelty and Violence.* New York: Freeman, 1996.

Boraine, Alex. *A Country Unmasked: Inside South Africa's Truth and Reconciliation Commission.* Oxford: University Press, 2000.

Gibbs, Sara. "Postwar Social Reconstruction in Mozambique: Reframing Children's Experiences of Trauma and Healing." In *Rebuilding Societies after Civil War: Critical Roles for International Assistance*, edited by Krishna Kumar. Boulder, Colo.: Lynne Rienner Publishers, 1997:227–238

Human Rights Watch, http://www.hrw.org/campaigns/crp/index.htm.

Ignatieff, Michael. "Articles of Faith." *Index on Censorship* 5(1996):110–122

Lorentzen, Lois Ann and Jennifer Turpin. *The Women and War Reader.* New York: New York University Press, 1998.

Offe, Claus. "Coming to Terms with Past Injustices." *Archives Européennes de Sociologie* 33(1992):195.

Tushen, Meredith and C. Twagiramariya. *What Women Do in Wartime: Gender and Conflict in Africa.* London: Zed Books, 1998.

Zimbabwe Human Rights NGO Forum report, http://www.hrforumzim.com

CHAPTER 6

Healing

BRANDON HAMBER

There is no magic solution to the problem of dealing with the impact of extensive violence. Truth commissions, criminal trials, or even extensive counselling and support, will not miraculously deal with the legacies of violence in a society. Healing is inevitably a lengthy and culturally-bound process. There is often no clear starting point and there will be few markers along the way - indeed, it is rare for the psychological impact of the past ever to be completely dealt with. This does not, of course, mean that programmes in pursuit of healing are a waste of time - quite the contrary. Assistance with healing can be invaluable for individuals and their communities. But the inherent limitations of attempts to deal with the legacies of extreme violence and the long-term nature of any such project must be accepted.

> *Healing is inevitably a lengthy and culturally-bound process.*

6.1 What is Healing?

The World Health Organization (WHO) defines health as not merely the absence of disease and infirmity but a positive state of physical, emotional and social well-being. Psychological health is understood by the WHO as encapsulating, among other factors, subjective well-being, perceived self-efficacy, autonomy, competence, inter-generational dependence, and self-actualization of one's intellectual and emotional potential. Psychological, emotional, physical and social health are not only interlinked but interdependent.

> *It is not only important to help people deal with the impact of the conflict on them, but it is also essential to deal with the causes of the distress.*

This chapter is primarily concerned with healing after what is often referred to as a "traumatic situation", an event or series of events of extreme violence that occur within a social context - most typically, war. Building on his experience working as a psychologist after the period of dictatorship in Chile, practitioner David Becker uses the term "extreme traumatization" to describe a situation where the psychological make-up of individuals and communities is continuously overridden, resulting in the destruction of individuals' senses of belonging to society and their being unable to perform the normal activities required for society to function.

Box 6.1: The Definition of Healing

For the purposes of this Handbook, healing is defined as any strategy, process or activity that improves the psychological health of individuals following extensive violent conflict. Strategies, processes or activities aimed at rehabilitating and reconstructing local and national communities more broadly are also integrally linked to this process. As such, healing is not only about assisting individuals to address their psychological health needs in an isolated way, but is dependent upon and integrally linked to repairing and rebuilding communities and the social context. This implies restoring a normalized everyday life that can recreate and confirm people's sense of being and belonging.

It is important constantly to bear in mind that trauma is not simply a collection of symptoms, as it is often portrayed - in fact symptoms may not follow all traumatic situations. In its essence, trauma is the destruction of individual and/or collective structures of a society. In this sense, it is not only important to help people deal with the impact of the conflict on them - to help them through, for example, a grieving process in a constructive way. It is also essential to deal with the causes of the distress and the symptoms. What needs to be "healed" is therefore the multitude of individual, political, social and cultural responses to a traumatic situation and its aftermath.

6.2 Violence and its Impacts

Violence in most conflict situations generally includes a structural element, for instance, systematic deprivation, racism or the denial of human rights.

The devastating impact of structural forms of violence on psychological well-being cannot be ignored. The psychological consequences of deprivation - one form of structural breakdown that can occur during conflict - are well documented. They include the effects of poor nutrition on the mental and physical development of children, as well as anxiety, depression and stress-related conditions caused by poor living and occupational conditions. Repression of culture and expression, ethnic intolerance and discrimination - also common in conflict situations - can severely undermine and even destroy social and cultural norms and feelings of identity, belonging and trust in institutions. Such micro-effects of violence can continue to ripple through communities for decades thereafter.

Acts of extreme violence are not always isolated and can extend over a period of time in such a way that an individual is victimized more than once. Or individuals may be exposed to multiple traumas simultaneously. For example, a person may be traumatically injured while at the same time witnessing another person being killed or severely injured. An individual may be subjected to torture during prolonged incarceration while knowing that his or her family is suffering economic hardship and systematic intimidation.

The South African Truth and Reconciliation Commission (TRC) provides a useful example of the complexities of dealing with extensive political violence. Various psychological symptoms and signs have been observed in some of those who have testified. On the whole, most individuals present a mixture of issues related to social, psychological and medical problems. In most cases, individual past traumas (e.g., torture or abuse by the police) have been overshadowed by present psychological, personal and social problems. Furthermore, the ability to draw direct causative links between the initial traumatic incident and the present difficulties experienced by some survivors has generally been complicated by the protracted period of time that has passed since the violations took place. In some cases, survivors and families have testified about violations that took place in the 1960s.

Different violent and political incidents can have distinctive cultural meanings and thus specific impacts. It is not only the traumatic event that requires attention: most particularly, the way in which the individual (or community) interprets the event is vitally important when considering a strategy for healing. Psychologist Michael Wessels, reflecting on his experience of working in Angola, argues that in Sub-Saharan Africa it is spirituality and community that are at the centre of life. For example, an Angolan boy whose parents were killed after the family was forced to flee may not need in the first instance to talk through his experience in a safe and supportive environment: rather the major stressor for the boy may be the spiritual discord and resultant communal problems following from his inability to conduct the proper burial ritual for his parents. Similarly, in Zimbabwe, survivors of the Matabeleland massacre (see the case study following chapter 2) consider the corruption of community values more offensive and disturbing than any other aspect of the conflict. It is primarily this loss that is still being mourned years after the massacres

Different violent and political incidents can have distinctive cultural meanings and thus specific impacts.

of the 1980s.

There is always a significant subjective component in an individual's response to a traumatic situation. This can be seen most clearly in disasters where, although a broad cross-section of the population is exposed in an objective sense to the same traumatic experience, individual psychological reactions are markedly different. The individual's reaction depends as much on his or her pre-traumatic personality structure, personal resources, coping strategies, understandings of the cause of the event, resilience and extended community support structure as on the actual traumatic incident.

Other factors such as gender and age are also significant. A traumatic incident has different impacts on children, young adults and older persons. In any healing process it may be necessary to specifically target vulnerable groups. According to the United Nations High Commission for Refugees (UNHCR), vulnerable groups include children, adolescents, victims of torture and sexual torture, those who have been repeatedly traumatized, the elderly, psychiatric patients, ex-detainees, prisoners of war and relatives of missing persons. A percentage of individuals (some estimates are as high as 30 per cent) will develop a severe emotional response to a traumatic situation (e.g., psychosis or suicidal tendencies).

The proximity in time of the traumatic incident should also be taken into consideration. Immediately following an incident victims often appear cut off, dislocated and unable to participate in a healing process. At a later stage they may be more ready to begin to move towards resolution or integrate the event into a broader web of personal and community meaning.

There is no linear progression to the healing process and no typical or universal response to violence. What we do know, however, is that individual and social impacts of extreme forms of violence and social disruption caused by conflict can have an effect for decades thereafter. Any strategy aimed at addressing the impact of political conflict and extreme violence needs to be long-term in its outlook. Some specific responses to direct political violence include self-blame, vivid re-experiencing of the event, fear, nightmares, feelings of helplessness, hypervigilance, depression, relationship difficulties, feelings of social disconnectedness, anxiety and even substance abuse-related difficulties. In Western practice, the term "post-traumatic stress disorder" (PTSD) is often used to describe this collection of symptoms. However, the relevance of using this medical language is questionable. Again, it is important to stress that the objective of a healing programme is not merely to address the symptoms of trauma or make a diagnosis. PTSD should not be used as the principal vehicle for explaining the impact of the traumatic situation on the individual or society. Rather the symptoms (or reactions) must be viewed from a position of understanding the origins of violence and its meaning to those involved, as well as the social and cultural context.

> *There is no linear progression to the healing process and no typical or universal response to violence.*

The case of the Angolan boy mentioned above is useful to consider in this regard. Focusing on his signs of distress (sleep disturbance and hypervigilance) could divert attention from strategies at the communal and spiritual level where they are most needed. Even in a Western context, focusing solely on the distress of an individual and their symptoms can divert attention from the important role of social interventions such as justice, truth and reparation. These issues are discussed in more depth below.

6.3 Reconciliation and Healing

Healing should be sought at the individual level but dependent upon and interrelated with the social context.

Much of this Handbook is about the use of broader social strategies aimed at restoring the social context and society. It explores a number of strategies and approaches aimed at helping victims to acknowledge pain and providing space for victims or survivors of political atrocities to speak out if they so wish, or to participate in processes of justice or mediation. Such processes are necessary starting points and preconditions for creating a social context that is conducive to healing. Strategies for healing (explored in section 6.5) are also part of this process.

Just as healing is dependent on the collective and political context, so too can individual and community healing strategies bolster national attempts to re-establish society.

When considering healing, particularly at the individual level, it is important to acknowledge that its trajectory is naturally haphazard and it is a slow process. While, on the one hand, political processes and strategies aimed at reconciliation are important in establishing the context for individual healing and coming to terms with violence, each individual's healing path is personal and unique. It can often be at odds with political, social and international political demands on people to leave the past behind.

> *Often politicians and political processes are ready to move on before those who are the direct survivors of political violence.*

In this sense, some survivors can experience national processes of reconciliation, especially in the absence of full truth and justice, as "false reconciliation". This is because the national process of "moving forward and making amends" does not coincide with the process of the individual's coming to terms with the situation, or because reconciliation has not ensured sufficient social justice to complement the individual healing process. This situation is intensified when survivors feel that the social space in which they can vent their anger is closed down, or when their disenchantment with peace processes (e.g., over amnesties or prisoner releases) results in them being branded as "anti-reconciliation". The result is that often the politicians and the political processes are ready to move on before those who are the direct survivors of political violence.

6.4 Approaches to Healing

There is no single healing process. What is called for is a blend of facilitating transformation of the social world that causes distress, while attending to individuals' needs. To this end, it is useful to highlight some approaches that can be used to address the suffering of those affected by violent conflict. However, before doing this, it is important to acknowledge a set of broad principles that should guide all strategies aimed at healing. These are:
• understand the context;
• use local resources; and
• link healing with wider reconstruction efforts.

6.4.1 Understanding the Context

Any strategy developed to deal with the needs of victims after conflict must acknowledge the social and cultural context and address the individual as a whole. Often - especially from a Western perspective - this is understood to mean that any intervention (e.g., counselling) should be tailored or reworked to be culturally relevant. This is, in fact, a wrong approach. Context is not a minor variable whose influence on a programme needs to be considered and accommodated; rather it is the major variable which should be the starting point when developing the healing strategy in the first place.

6.4.2 Using Local Resources

It would be mistaken to see conflict and violence as always resulting in the complete breakdown of social, community and psychological functioning. Psychiatrist Derek Summerfield writes that the "human responses to war are not analogous to physical trauma: people do not passively register the impact of external forces (unlike, say, a leg hit by a bullet) but engage with them in an active and problem-solving way".

Some communities and individuals can become extremely good at coping with adversity. Localized coping mechanisms and models of social and emotional resilience should be identified, supported and built upon where possible. At the same time, one needs to guard against overvaluing or glorifying existing mechanisms. It is often the case that traditional mechanisms are destroyed in the violence. To take the view that only local supports should be used, especially in a context where these may be almost non-existent, could also mean denying people services and relevant supports. It is also possible that some coping mechanisms, such as silence, may in fact be counterproductive in the long run.

> *Localized coping mechanisms and models of social and emotional resilience should be identified, supported and built upon where possible.*

6.4.3 Linking Healing with Broader Reconstruction Programmes

Truth, acknowledgement and justice cannot be separated out from the healing process. Psychosocial interventions which operate in a vacuum are less effective than, and cannot in themselves replace the need for, truth, acknowledgement and justice. Bringing perpetrators to justice is an important, legitimate and sometimes essential component of a victim's recovery and psychological healing. Amnesties are generally unacceptable to victims.

Today, some members of survivor self-help groups in South Africa will speak of a sense of closure, but for most the past is still very much alive. Some of this is merely a reflection of the long-term nature of healing. However, it is also largely due to the fact that, despite various healing initiatives, the truth about many cases has still not been revealed, while amnesty has been granted to perpetrators and reparations have been slow to be delivered. The cry that there can be no reconciliation without truth is still common for many victims. This is not an uncommon occurrence in societies following extensive conflict: groups started over two decades ago in Chile, Argentina and Brazil can be heard to say the same thing.

The result of this is that psychosocial programmes (see section 6.5.1) often need to delve into the political world. It may be necessary for those working with individual victims (e.g., with counselling and complementary therapies) to be aware of broader processes and even be involved in activities such as working for the discovery of the truth of past events or supporting processes such as commissions of enquiry or prosecutions. This activist perspective can pose problems for some traditional psychotherapy models which demand objectivity.

> *Healing initiatives need to be part of socio-economic and cultural reconstruction in the post-conflict phase.*

One of the main interventions needed in terms of genuine healing is to re-establish as far as possible a socio-political context conducive to helping those victimized to begin to reclaim their sense of identity and dignity. A favourable context is necessary if local and traditional forms of support (and resilience) are to be identified and built upon. This means that healing initiatives need to be part of socio-economic and cultural reconstruction in the post-conflict phase.

6.5 Healing Programmes and Strategies

A wide range of healing strategies has been used in different contexts, and they can be useful sources of inspiration and guidance when building a healing programme. However, two points to bear in mind are that: (a) all strategies should ideally grow out of the local context; and (b) most contexts demand that multiple strategies be undertaken simultaneously.

Some healing-oriented programmes typically seen in post-conflict situations are:

- psychosocial programmes;
- individual counselling and support interventions;
- training of local communities with psychosocial support skills;
- self-help support groups; and
- symbolic forms of healing.

6.5.1 Psychosocial Programmes

Intervention is generally described as psychosocial when it is built on the assumption that there is a strong and important relationship between the individual's psychological status and the social context. Psychosocial programmes address the psychological and general health needs of post-conflict populations by promoting and rebuilding the social and cultural context.

The methods used in such programmes can vary, often including creative expression through arts and story-telling; the development and promotion of self-help groups; assisting with the completion of grieving and reburial rituals; an emphasis on re-training, education and re-skilling; the reintegration and reunion of individuals dislocated from communities and families; counselling and group support; information dissemination and connecting people to resources; and at times simply focusing on creating a safe environment where those affected by conflict can meet, network, share experiences and focus on establishing new routines. While in many cases it may be sound to locate such programmes within a community or at least within an ethnic group, experience from Sri Lanka shows that the bringing together of women from all ethnic groups - and different sides to the conflict - often helped women to face and give voice to their grievances, and turned the healing process into a more proactive fight against the armed conflict that had victimized so many.

Inger Agger highlights several levels at which psychosocial programmes were used in the former Yugoslavia. These included community development interventions, such as establishing schooling and day care for refugee children; network-strengthening interventions, such as organizing knitting groups; language courses or other types of occupational and educational activities; and mutual support-building interventions such as facilitating women's self-help groups and youth groups. These were complemented by counselling and psychotherapy interventions at the individual, group and family levels.

Obviously, not all levels of intervention may be appropriate in all contexts, but addressing traumatic situations in this multifaceted way is generally found to be most effective.

Imported Methods and the Local Agenda

There has been much criticism of the way in which some psychosocial programmes have been set up and foisted onto post-conflict societies, particularly in the former Yugoslavia and more recently in Sierra Leone. Criticisms touch on the way international NGOs have shaped the local agenda with the use of foreign methods of explaining the impact of conflict, specifically using terms like "trauma" or "post-traumatic stress disorder" and disregarding local "ethno-psychologies" and the existing notions of self which influence people's suffering. Some international efforts have also increased local competition, giving rise to hierarchies of "victimhood" (see chapter 4) and resulting in a lack of coordination and duplication between the international organizations themselves.

To prevent this, guidelines for running psychosocial programmes have been published. It is worth reviewing the draft guidelines published by the Netherlands Institute for Care and Welfare, and the WHO's 2000 Declaration of Cooperation: Mental Health of Refugees, Displaced and Other Populations Affected by Conflict and Post-Conflict Situations.

6.5.2 Individual Counselling and Other Interventions

Individual interventions characterized by culturally-specific counselling, or as part of a psychosocial programme, can be useful. This can include a range of individualized forms of psychotherapy, group work, family therapy, counselling or support from the community. These forms of support need not only be professional services or psychotherapy. The case study at the end of this chapter is a very good example of a voluntary, community-based initiative from Northern Ireland. In another example from Northern Ireland, there is befriending: trained befrienders visit those who have lost relatives and develop a supportive relationship with them. Making space for individuals and groups to share experiences, if they so wish, can be beneficial in itself. This may entail a simple process of survivors gathering and sharing (with or without a trained professional) in a familiar space, such as a community centre, religious building or other traditional meeting place.

Over the past decade there has been a growing trend to develop trauma-specific counselling, often generically referred to as "trauma counselling". If done appropriately and in the relevant context, this can be helpful.

This is not to say that individual interventions are more relevant or useful than other methods. Different individual methods have been useful in different contexts. In addition, individual interventions should not be equated with giving public testimony, as has been evidenced in some truth commissions (see chapter 8). Giving testimony at a truth commission can be useful in breaking down some of the previous social barriers and silences - and for some individuals may even be the end-point of a personal healing process - but, generally, individual, social and group interventions will be needed to address adequately the impact of extensive violent conflict.

6.5.3 Training Local Communities in Psychosocial Support Skills

It has become popular to involve (international) psychological health care professionals in the training of local people to help with trauma counselling. In some contexts this has been wholly inappropriate, and those trained have been left in difficult circumstances with little back-up support. The language of traumatology has also been imported and local methods of dealing with suffering overridden. As guidelines produced recently by the International Society for Traumatic Stress Studies noted: "The arrival of international agencies and their personnel has the potential of creating irreversible cultural change . . . offering training without properly understanding the ongoing political process [and this] risks accusations of uninvited intrusion".

That said, training programmes for local people that are built on a genuine appreciation of the interplay between different methods and ideas, local and borrowed, can be valuable. These programmes seldom use the word "trauma" and certainly do not advocate "trauma counselling" as the panacea. The Christian Children's Fund (CCF) Angola project provides an interesting and useful example. The goal of the project was to improve the ability of adults working with children to recognize psychological trauma in children and help them come to terms with their experiences. The CCF set up training for adults who were selected through ongoing dialogue with local communities and traditional leaders. The training courses were built on a bedrock of understanding developed through seminars and discussions at the local level, focusing on local customs and healing methods in the regions. They concentrated on a range of issues, including children's psychosocial needs and development; the impact of war and violence on children; rites associated with death and bereavement; Western and traditional methods of assisting war-affected children; and non-violent conflict resolution. Seminars also focused on different interpretations of problems, such as sleep disturbance or severe isolation and withdrawal. Through discussion, participants analyzed how best to help children using a mixture of traditional, ritual, expressive and Western methods. This resulted in trainees going into communities equipped with skills to encourage culturally-appropriate group activities among the children they saw, such as play, singing, story-telling, drama and dancing.

These methods served as vehicles for the construction of social meaning as children learned the songs, myths and symbols of their community and ethnic group. The trainees also worked as agents of change, encouraging communities to address the needs of children sensitively. Trainees were even drawn into community rebuilding projects, which were identified as being central to the healing process. Over the course of the project, discourses evolved well beyond trauma. Over an extensive period of time, new communities of practice were built.

This experience is shared by many community-based or small-scale NGO interventions in this field. Experience suggests, however, that it is difficult to mobilize the required human and financial resources for such an ambitious programme all at once. It is also advisable to allow for a gradual expansion of activities in order to enable the participants themselves to play a decisive role in defining activities and implementing them.

6.5.4 Self-Help Support Groups

Self-help groups offer emotional or practical help to their members. Members generally share a common problem and pursue their goals through mutual aid. The groups are normally member-led.

Self-help groups are common in many societies, typically forming around those who have a common illness, addiction and/or disability. It has also become fairly commonplace for such groups to develop in conflict situations. They are generally made up of survivors of political violence and the families of those killed or "disappeared". They can be instrumental in healing and reconciliation. Born out of conflict situations, they are often referred to as "victim" or "survivor" groups. Perhaps the best known is the Mothers of the Plaza de Mayo in Argentina. Similar initiatives, however, have been seen across the world in societies as diverse as Sri Lanka, Rwanda, Chile, Northern Ireland and South Africa (see box 6.2).

> *Self-help groups can be instrumental in healing and reconciliation.*

Self-help victim support groups generally serve as:
• a forum for joining together and recognizing that others have had similar experiences and have common problems;
• a place for friendship, companionship and emotional support;
• a forum where first-hand experiences of support outside the group through other agencies can be shared and broader coping techniques exchanged;
• a safe place to recount events and break the cultures of silence that are common in conflict situations;
• a possible vehicle for social change and for lobbying and advocacy to get authorities to address their and other victims' needs;
• a means of raising awareness about exclusion and the "forgotten victims" of a conflict;
• a forum for networking about how to access resources, health care, support services, housing, employ-

ment and welfare benefits; and

• a focal point for information exchange and personal education about the predicament in which survivors find themselves.

The aims of victim or survivor self-help groups can be diverse, and the degree to which each sees its objectives as political, supportive or both may vary. While many offer direct support and services to their members (e.g., counselling and befriending), most have broader goals of continuing the fight for recognition, acknowledgement and justice in the post-conflict phase.

The Khulumani (Speak-out) Victim Support Group was formed in anticipation of the South African TRC to assist survivors to gain access to the TRC. It was founded on the premise that encouraging people to "speak out" about the atrocities of the past was psychologically beneficial and would advance their goal of being recognized as victims of apartheid violence. The group had a strong focus on advocacy activity with the intention of keeping the TRC and the reconciliation process victim-centred. At the height of the TRC process there were 35 Khulumani groups operating as a powerful voice for victims in the TRC process.

As the group developed, its work became broader than simply focusing on "speaking out" and influencing the TRC process. In some areas, local people were trained in basic counselling and small-income generation skills (e.g., sewing and gardening to grow food); some projects now even help victims of ordinary crime and not only "political" victims. This pattern, whereby the work of the group broadens as the environment changes, is also typical of similar groups in other parts of the world.

In 1997 the Khulumani Group developed a play entitled *The Story I am about to Tell*. Three members of Khulumani acted along with three professional actors, and the play was taken to communities as a way of educating people about the past. Such activities are linked directly to a healing agenda, where social justice is an integral part of the process. "Speaking out" was not simply about making the individual feel better, but was aimed at changing society.

6.5.5 Symbolic Forms of Healing

The healing value of symbolic acts, objects and rituals lies in the way they can help concretize a traumatic incident, serving as a focal point in the grieving process. Such symbols are most effective if they are personalized and culturally relevant. They can also have a wider community- or society-level benefit, as markers to remind society of the lessons of the past which need to be carried into the future.

• Memories of the past can be housed in symbols such as monuments, museums and plaques, and peace parks or sites of dignified burial can be useful places where the bereaved can remember their loved ones. The ideals, rights and aspirations of those who suffered can also be advanced by acknowledging their contribution to the birth of a new society through official statements, or naming official places, streets or buildings after them.

• Apologies, if genuine, can also have a significant impact.

• Reparation and compensation awards can manifest the state's acknowledgement of wrongdoing, restore survivors' dignity and raise public consciousness about the general population's moral responsibility to participate in healing the wounds of the past. Psychologically speaking, so-called symbolic acts of reparation (such as reburials) and material acts of reparation (e.g., payments) serve the same end. Both these forms of reparation, like monuments and other forms of symbolic remembrance, can play an important role in healing.

• Specific rituals and ceremonies can also have powerful symbolic and healing value. The forensic exhumations in Matabeleland, Zimbabwe, of people murdered in the political violence of the 1980s provide a useful example. According to AMANI, a Zimbabwean NGO, the exhumations were undertaken "with the primary intention of facilitating community healing processes". In Ndebele belief systems, the spirits of the dead play an essential role in the lives of every family, guiding and nurturing them. If a spirit is not honoured with a funeral and the *umbuyiso* ritual completed, it can become restless and angry, bringing bad luck to the family and the community. Clearly, the symbolic value of the burial and the subsequent rituals were vital to any sense of healing.

This example reinforces the importance of processes such as investigations, prosecutions and commissions of inquiry in post-conflict societies which can uncover the facts about what happened to individuals during the violence, including, for example, the locations of graves. However, it also highlights another important point: the process of healing occurs not through the delivery of an object - a pension, a monument or an exhumation - but through the process that takes place around this, such as the reburial ritual.

That said, symbolic forms of healing, like other strategies for healing, cannot be separated out completely from the broader context. Symbolic acts can place the survivors in a difficult position. Acknowledgement, apology, recognition and even substantial material assistance can never bring back the dead or be guaranteed to alleviate all the psychological pain suffered by a survivor. The essence of the problem of making amends for past violations is that the amount of distress, hurt, injustice and anger the survivor is personally struggling to come to terms with is immeasurable.

> If symbolic acts are not linked with the delivery of truth, justice and social change, they run the danger of being seen as a strategy to "buy off" the survivors.

Also, in accepting the reparation or apology, the survivor may feel as if his or her actions are finally putting their loved one to rest - a step he or she may understandably feel ambivalent about taking. Furthermore, if symbolic acts are not linked with the delivery of truth, justice and social change, they run the danger of being seen by the survivors as a government strategy to close the chapter of the past prematurely, leave its secrets hidden and "buy off" the survivors. It is in these cases that survivors or families of victims talk of reparations as a form of "blood money". If full truth and justice are not achieved, anger and other emotional responses from victims (e.g., refusing to accept reparations or protesting about what is granted) can be legitimately anticipated.

6.6 Concluding Remarks

Strategies for healing are integrally linked to the broader social context and interface with, and are part of, any broader process aimed at reconciliation. At the same time, healing is not one-dimensional or easily attained, and it is as much about what already exists within communities and cultures as about learning from other approaches or considering (if appropriate) the methods outlined in this chapter.

The journey from "victim" to the status of "survivor" is long and complex. In South Africa some members of the Khulumani Group (see box 6.2) say they will only use the word "survivor" when they feel that they have been properly acknowledged. In the CCF programme in Angola the term "war-affected children" has been used to explain the position of those affected, rather than words foreign to the context such as "victim" or "survivor". The language used to explain the impact of extreme violence belongs to those directly affected. In this respect, it is the meaning of the experience that is most important. Appropriate and culturally relevant healing strategies can provide the context in which alternative meanings to the experience of extreme trauma can be found.

If a broader concept of healing is used, in which the individual is not treated as separate from the social context, then the shift from "victim" to "survivor" is as much a question of social justice as a question about any personal process the individual undertakes. Summerfield argues that: "History has shown that social reform is the best medicine; for victims of war and atrocity this means public recognition and justice. Health and illness have social and political roots: post-traumatic reactions are not just a private problem, with the onus on the individual to recover, but an indictment on the socio-political forces that produced them."

> Social justice is a foundation stone of lasting healing.

Social justice is a foundation stone of lasting healing. Reconciliation processes can, in some instances, deliver social justice, and this will invariably aid the healing process. Either way, though - and much to the distress of people who want those directly affected by political conflict to "move on" as soon as possible - it is certain that genuine healing is protracted and requires sustained personal, community and political attempts to integrate the suffering of the past into the present.

References and Further Reading

Agger, I. "Psychosocial Assistance During Ethnopolitical Warfare in the Former Yugoslavia." In *Ethnopolitical Warfare: Causes, Consequences, and Possible Solutions*, edited by D. Chirot and M. E. P. Selgiman. Washington, DC: American Psychological Association, 2001:305–318.

Becker, D. "*Dealing with the Consequences of Organized Violence*". In *Berghof Handbook for Conflict Transformation*. Berlin: Berghof Research Center for Constructive Conflict Management, 2001.

Bracken, P. J. and C. Petty (editors). *Rethinking the Trauma of War*. London: Free Association Books, 1998.

Chirot, D. and M. E. P. Selgiman (editors). *Ethnopolitical Warfare: Causes, Consequences, and Possible Solutions*. Washington, DC: American Psychological Association, 2001.

Hamber, B. "Does the Truth Heal? A Psychological Perspective on the Political Strategies for Dealing with the Legacy of Political Violence." In *Burying the Past : Making Peace and Doing Justice after Civil Conflict*, edited by N. Biggar. Washington, DC: Georgetown University Press, 2001.

International Society for Traumatic Stress Studies, Taskforce on International Trauma Training. "Draft Guidelines for International Trauma Training",

Version 11.00, 2000, http://www.istss.org/guidelines.htm

Loughry, M. and A. Ager (editors). *The Refugee Experience: Psychosocial Training Module*. Oxford: Refugee Studies Centre, 1999, http://earlybird.qeh.ox.ac.uk/rfgexp/rsp_tre/copy.htm

Netherlands Institute for Care and Welfare. "Draft Guidelines for Programmes: Psychosocial and Mental Health Care Assistance in (Post) Disaster and Conflict Areas.' Utrecht: Netherlands Institute for Care and Welfare, 2002, http://websrv1.nizw.nl/nizwic/_Werkdocs/Publications/guidelines.htm

Summerfield, D. "War and Mental Health: a Brief Overview." *British Medical Journal* 321 (2000):232–235.

"The Nature of Conflict and Implications for Appropriate Psychosocial Responses." In *The Refugee Experience: Psychosocial Training Module*, edited by M. Loughry and A. Ager. Oxford: Refugee Studies Centre, 2001, http://earlybird.qeh.ox.ac.uk/rfgexp/rsp_tre/copy.htm

Wessels, M. and Monterio, C. "Healing Wounds of War in Angola." In *Addressing Childhood Adversity*, edited by D. Donald, A. Dawes and J. Louw. Cape Town: David Philip, 2000.

World Health Organization. "Declaration of Cooperation: Mental Health of Refugees, Displaced and Other Populations Affected by Conflict and Post-Conflict Situations, endorsed at the International Consultation on Mental Health of Refugees and Displaced Populations in Conflict and Post-Conflict Situations", 23–25 October 2000, Geneva, http://www.xs4all.nl/~mtrapman/xgasten/nizw/WHODeclaration.html

Victim–Combatant Dialogue in Northern Ireland

IAN WHITE

Background
The Conflict in Northern Ireland

The armed conflict that erupted in Northern Ireland in the late 1960s was only the latest manifestation of a centuries-old antagonism between Ireland and England. A partial resolution of this age-old quarrel had been attempted in 1921, when Britain conceded a degree of independence to what became the Irish Republic, but allowed the six counties of north-east Ireland to opt to remain within the United Kingdom. In the 17th century those counties saw the concentrated settlement of hundreds of thousands of English and Scottish incomers - all Protestants, in contrast to the predominantly Catholic Irish population of the time. The north-east was established as a province of the UK under the title Northern Ireland, with its own parliament, administration and police force (the Royal Ulster Constabulary, RUC). That parliament, with a fixed 2:1 Protestant: Catholic majority and a heavily armed, overwhelmingly Protestant police force to enforce its rule, settled into a 50-year pattern of anti-Catholic discrimination, using a combination of fear and heavy-handedness to maintain control.

Catholic discontent in Northern Ireland manifested itself in political organization around the cause of Irish nationalism - the wish to reunite the north-east with the Irish Republic - and in a sporadically violent campaign led by the Irish Republican Army (IRA). Control, however, remained with the Protestants, organized politically around Unionism - the wish to maintain the union with Britain - and backed up on occasion by British military strength. It is important to note that, although the two communities in Northern Ireland are still identifiable as Protestant and Catholic, because of the 17th century heritage, the conflict can only properly be understood as one over land, politics and power. While sectarian attitudes certainly remain, and have been fuelled by the conflict, few people in Ireland are arguing about the right way to worship a Christian God. The religious labels act as badges of identity for the two culturally distinct communities, not as indications of the core of the conflict.

Five decades of British attempts to ignore the simmering situation in Northern Ireland finally ended when Catholics took to the streets in the mid-1960s, inspired by the US civil rights campaign, to demand equal treatment. Robust repression of the protesters by the RUC resulted in the reinvigoration of an almost moribund IRA and intervention by the UK, which sent in the army. Eventually, in 1971, Britain suspended the Northern Ireland Parliament and implemented direct rule from Westminster. That set the pattern for the next 25 years, as the paramilitary IRA fought an increasingly sophisticated guerrilla war against the British Army and the RUC and as retaliatory Unionist paramilitaries were formed (calling themselves Loyalists). The war was mostly fought in Northern Ireland, but the IRA also launched sustained bombing campaigns against military and economic targets in Britain, and the Loyalists occasionally attacked across the border in the Republic. More than 3,000 people died during the period.

The war never completely destroyed Northern Ireland's infrastructure or completely prevented some semblance of continued normality, but by the 1990s a whole generation was reaching adulthood having lived its lifetime in a context of violence and bitterness.

A combination of many factors finally brought relief: war-weariness among the combatants as well as the wider population; a military stalemate with neither side capable of outright victory; a shift in British–Irish governmental relations from antagonism to partnership; a change of interest and emphasis in Irish affairs in the US administration; the economic influence of the EU, especially in developing the economy of the Irish Republic; a direct challenging by non-violent Nationalist politicians of the violent tactics of the IRA and the Republican movement; and so on. There were sporadic secret talks between the British Government and the IRA regarding a ceasefire and eventually, after many hiccups, an IRA ceasefire was declared in 1994. The Loyalist paramilitaries followed suit. After 18 months of political frustration, the IRA returned to violence, until a change of government in London persuaded it to reinstate the ceasefire in 1997. Following from that, inclusive peace talks under the chairmanship of former US Senator George Mitchell eventually produced the Good Friday Agreement in April 1998. The implementation of the agreement continues to be difficult, with many issues unresolved, but Northern Ireland has not yet slipped back into the pre-Agreement years of violence and pessimism.

The Glencree Centre for Reconciliation

The Glencree Centre was established in 1974 in the Irish Republic as an NGO response to the situation in Northern Ireland. Its focus is on peacemaking primarily, but not exclusively, within and between communities in Ireland and Britain. The Centre attempts, through its evolving programme of activities, to respond to the changing political environment within which it works. It is currently involved in dialogue facilitation, mediation, negotiation, peacemaking and peace education in various forms.

In the post-Agreement context of 1998, the Glencree Centre devised its dialogue programme, Let's Involve the Victims' Experience (LIVE). The following description of the programme is provided by the Director of the Glencree Centre.

The LIVE Programme

Many reconciliation activities, particularly those which engage victims who have experienced trauma as a direct result of violent conflict, tend to be associated with psychological and even spiritual dynamics. However, it is essential to fully understand the political implications of such work and the political context within which it takes place. This understanding of the political as well as the more human elements of reconciliation - and even the degree to which such work can be politically manipulated - is an essential prerequisite for engagement in the work.

Victims in Three Geographical Regions

In the post-Agreement context of 1998, the Glencree Centre identified a need to start to consolidate the fragile peace process. The paramilitary ceasefires had softened the attitudes of society generally, making some reconciliation initiatives possible for the first time. From its limited previous experience of working with victims/survivors, the Glencree Centre realized that there were many unacknowledged individuals and groups of victims/survivors located in the three regions.

The great majority of victims/survivors were in Northern Ireland. Their experience of suffering was wide-ranging, some having been bereaved or maimed by Loyalist or Republican paramilitaries, while others had suffered loss as a result of actions carried out by the RUC or the British Army. Although such suffering clearly has a deeply personal impact, any attack on an individual is also perceived as an attack on the individual's entire community. It was also essential when designing LIVE to recognize the very diverse political and cultural backgrounds from which Northern Irish participants would be coming. Some of the victims were relatives of combatants, both paramilitary and state, while others were relatives of civilians who had been caught in the crossfire. Even civilians have their own political values which, in the Northern Irish context, are likely to align them to some degree with one of the two main conflicting communities.

In Britain most of the casualties of the three decades of violence were army personnel, leaving a large number of grieving families. In the vast majority of cases their suffering had been caused by the actions of Republican paramilitary groups. There had also been civilian casualties.

In the Republic of Ireland the direct casualties from the conflict were much fewer, but included the victims/survivors of actions of mainly Republican paramilitaries and state security forces. The only formally organized group of victims in the Republic of Ireland was united by a shared tragedy in that they were all bereaved on the same day in 1974 by a series of Loyalist paramilitary bombings in two cities in the Republic. This particular group is involved in legal action concerning possible British security services complicity in the bombings, and so chose not to engage with the LIVE programme in case its involvement might prove detrimental to the legal proceedings.

Objectives of the LIVE Programme

The initiative focused on the issue of relationship-building between some of the most vulnerable members of the communities which have caused lasting hurt to each other and, as a result, have developed very negative perceptions of each other. The LIVE programme was established to create opportunities for relationship-building within and between the victims/survivors from the three geographical regions outlined above. The basic belief which inspired this was that, regardless of political affiliations or the affiliations of the deceased family member, the loss of a loved one in the conflict or an injury caused by it is a common denominator which should to some degree transcend sectarian or political differences.

The primary objective of the LIVE programme was therefore to build relationships between victim/survivor communities in the three jurisdictions which represent the main opponents engaged in the conflict. The secondary objective was to facilitate dialogue between former combatants in the conflict and those victims/survivors who felt "ready" for such engagement.

Participation

In Northern Ireland, violent deaths have been well recorded by both state bodies and NGOs. Additionally, many victim/survivor groups have developed over the years. Some provide support and psychological services. Others adopt a more political or campaigning approach to the need for truth and recognition, and are often perceived as aligned to one or other community. In Britain and the Irish Republic, in contrast, much less attention has been given to victims of the conflict, and there is a serious absence of accurate records. This fact, which demonstrates to some degree a lack of acknowledgement of the suffering of victims/survivors, was an obvious obstacle to the delivery of the programme.

An important channel for recruiting participants to the LIVE programme was advertisements placed in national daily newspapers. In recruiting participants it was important to define the term "victim" in such a way as to include all who have suffered as a result of the protracted social conflict. To define it more narrowly would almost certainly have excluded some participants from some sections of the three targeted jurisdictions.

It was the participants themselves who designated themselves as victims. A small percentage of the total number had been physically injured as a result of the conflict, but the vast majority had suffered bereavement. In total, about 20 victims each from both Britain and the Republic of Ireland, and 60 in total from both Protestant and Catholic communities in Northern Ireland, participated in the programme. Participants were approximately 70 per cent women and 30 per cent men, about 80 per cent being over 40 years old.

Structure

The experimental programme was based upon 10 three-day workshops held over a period of 12 months, where victims/survivors told their stories of suffering and heard each other's. There were three main components in each workshop:

• structured opportunities for discussion and the telling of participants' stories;
• inputs from professionals and therapists on issues directly related to managing post-traumatic stress; and
• social activities aimed at allowing participants the chance to build relationships and share experiences in a less formal environment.

Stage 1: Single-Identity Workshops

The first three workshops were single-identity events, that is, each involved victims/survivors from one region only. This allowed participants to begin to trust the Glencree Centre, an organization with which most had had no previous contact. The fact that participants came from the same jurisdiction gave them a sense of safety and familiarity, which helped in building a group commitment to the LIVE programme. These workshops also allowed Glencree personnel to hear and make provision for some of the expectations and fears of the participants. The objectives of the programme were explained to participants. The possibility of moving on into a dialogue process between victims and perpetrators was also outlined as an option for those participants who felt they might be "ready" for such a step. These workshops were poorly attended, with an average of 15 participants in each, but those who attended came away feeling very positive about the experience.

Stage 2: Bilateral and Multilateral Workshops

The Glencree Centre then hosted seven workshops for victims/survivors, either bilateral (involving two regions) or multilateral (involving all three regions), with members drawn from the participants of the initial single-identity workshops. Because of their very positive experience of stage 1, these participants encouraged more victims/survivors to participate at the second stage. Consequently, numbers rarely fell below 30 per workshop at this point.

By the time of the third multilateral workshop, participants had built sufficient trust in each other and in the Glencree Centre for some now to ask for the opportunity to hold a dialogue with representatives from the organizations which had caused their suffering. These dialogue sessions were organized as part of the formal sessions within the workshop programme and involved former combatants from Republican paramilitary organizations. Given that they involved both a personal and a political dynamic, it was thought best that they should be facilitated by Glencree staff with both political and psychological expertise and sensitivity.

Victim–Combatant Dialogue

As part of the bilateral stage of the LIVE programme, a number of dialogue sessions took place between former paramilitary combatants and victims/survivors. Each session lasted roughly four hours. The following account focuses on one such dialogue, which took place between a former IRA member, who has since become an elected politician, and 28 victims/survivors, most of whom had suffered as a result of IRA violence.

Trust had been built with and between the different groups of victims in the earlier stages of the process. In order to engage a former IRA combatant, a series of preparatory meetings were held to reassure him about the aims of the work and the procedures involved. A previous relationship between him and the Glencree Centre helped allay any fears, some of which were political: he was interested to know who would hear of this dialogue, whether it could be used by his political opponents to undermine him, or indeed whether his own community might view his participation as betrayal.

The dialogue session started with the facilitator explaining the process and then inviting participants to introduce themselves briefly, to allow the former IRA combatant to realize the diversity of experience within the group. Then the victims/survivors were invited to ask questions of the former combatant or make observations and comments. No restrictions were placed on the dialogue. One of the victims/survivors started by praising the former combatant for his bravery in coming to meet them. This was a most fortunate and positive way to start the workshop, as it helped to create an appropriate environment for constructive dialogue by allowing the former combatant to be less defensive. The facilitator then praised the participants for their bravery in inviting the dialogue. The former combatant was accompanied by his wife, who offered him support throughout in the form of physical contact and other gestures.

Although neither the victims/survivors nor the former combatant had had experience of this type of dialogue before, there was a rapid engagement. It was as if, on both sides, they had been hanging on to unanswered questions and unresolved uncertainties, in some cases for many years, waiting for the right opportunity. The composition of the group of victims/survivors was established by the Glencree Centre to create a balance of experience. This proved to be more helpful to the process than anticipated. Some of the participants had been bereaved not by the actions of the IRA but by the actions of the British Army. They became a kind of bridge between the former combatant, with whom they shared some political perceptions or aspirations, and the other victims/survivors who had suffered IRA violence, with whom they had now established a strong relationship through the previous multilateral workshops.

The questions came in the form of the detailed stories of the suffering caused, mainly but not exclusively by IRA activity. The retelling of the stories brought much grief with it, from both the story-teller and other members of the group. The former combatant listened attentively and carefully. All the stories were followed by questions, ranging from the general, such as, "Why do you think violence will achieve your desired outcome?" to the more specific, such as, "Why him?" or "Where did you take him after the abduction?"

In response, the former combatant was able to answer some of the general questions with his explanation of the historical causes of the conflict, which he knew had to be conveyed with sensitivity and his natural conviction. His answer to the more general questions appeared to be welcomed in particular by the victims from Britain, who had little or no understanding of the causes of the conflict. It appeared that they were gaining an understanding for the first time of the IRA perspective that this conflict was a war against the British. While the former combatant offered a sincere apology for the casualties of his actions, he could not apologize for the war itself which was, he believed, a just war.

The more specific questions were more difficult for the former combatant to answer, as he simply did not have full information on all the actions ever carried out by the IRA. However, he was able to offer some insights into the way the IRA might have been thinking at the time of particular actions, and he undertook in one case to try to find out more information.

The former combatant was then invited by the facilitator to tell his own story, and was asked to focus on his total life experience in order that victims/survivors might understand more clearly his motivation for engaging in the conflict. He explained the injustice he had experienced as a young man, which provided his motivation to engage in the conflict. He also explained his two decades in prison and the consequences of that for his family and community.

The engagement for the most part was respectful and, while it was filled with emotion, outbursts of anger were few. The word "forgiveness" was not mentioned in the workshop by either the victims/ survivors or the former combatant. There was, however, a clear sense of a growth of understanding by both parties of each other's sacrifice.

Two of the victims/survivors left the room at different stages as they did not feel comfortable with the dialogue. Therapists accompanied them to offer support. When the session was over, some participants felt the need to continue their discussions in a more private and even less formal one-to-one context. These discussions mainly comprised expressions of reciprocal gratitude between combatant and victim in relation to the value of the dialogue and the bravery of each person who engaged in it.

Following this dialogue session, there was a reflection session for the participating victims/survivors, which allowed the encounter to be fully processed. In addition to verifying the well-being of the individuals involved, it also allowed many of the learning outcomes which follow to be identified. The experience of the group was overwhelmingly positive and, in addition to the essential conversations which took place within the session, participants were generally keen to continue this interaction further. We know that discussions on a one-to-one basis between the former combatant and the victims have continued outside the remit of the LIVE programme.

This encounter created the conditions through which a subsequent dialogue took place between one of the victims/survivors of the conflict and the former IRA combatant who had killed her father.

Learning Outcomes

1.   This programme was designed for victims/survivors of the conflict, and at the time it was designed did not include former combatants. Preparation and support mechanisms for victims/ survivors were put in place within the programme, but little support was provided to look after the psychological needs of the former combatant. This is now being addressed through a planned parallel programme for former combatants.

2.   An integral part of the LIVE programme is an ongoing telephone support service. Great demands were made on this, following the victim–combatant session.

3.   Participation in such dialogue must be completely voluntary. In addition, care must be taken not to imply in any way that any victims/survivors who do not engage in dialogue are either weak or resistant to reconciliation. Everyone involved must realize that, while the opportunities for dialogue exist, no one is a bad person if he or she does not feel ready to participate. In reality, victims/survivors encouraged each other to participate.

4.   The conclusion that this dialogue was a success is based on participants' views and comments,

which suggest that, for most, their pain is at least a little easier to manage after the encounter.

5.   Inter-group dialogue is to be preferred, rather than one-to-one dialogue. It is less threatening for all and also allows a diversity of life-experience to be shared, rather than just that of a victim/survivor and a combatant.

6.   The staff involved in the delivery of the LIVE programme come from the same communities as both the victims/survivors and combatants. It is important therefore to remember that, despite their best efforts, staff are directly affected by this type of reconciliation dialogue. They therefore have a capacity to impact on the process both positively and negatively. It is for this reason that the Glencree Centre often reminds itself that it does reconciliation work *with* and not *to* people.

7.   No one has a monopoly on guilt or innocence.

Follow-Up and Future Activities

Since the events described here, the Glencree Centre has received EU funding for workshop activities to build relationships between the various different groups of combatants engaged in the conflict. The combatant groupings involved are:
• republican paramilitaries - the IRA and the Irish National Liberation Army (INLA);
• loyalist paramilitaries - the Ulster Defence Association (UDA) and Ulster Volunteer Force (UVF);
• the former RUC (Northern Ireland police force) (now the Northern Ireland Police Service);
• the British Army;
• the Irish Defence Forces (state army of the Irish Republic); and
• the Northern Irish Prison Service.

Activities have begun, with the Glencree Centre doing some intensive work with a small core group who will in turn recruit other combatants from their groupings. When relationships have been established between these combatant groupings, it is the intention to introduce those of them who feel it is appropriate to groupings of victims/survivors from the LIVE programme.

Much is already being learned from the development of these two parallel programmes, one with victims/survivors, the other with combatants.

First, the fact that many combatants have also been bereaved or injured renders strict delineations between the two groupings impossible. It is now even more important than before that the Glencree Centre allow people non-judgementally to make their own definitions of themselves as survivor/ victim and/or combatant.

Second, the combatant participants, although divided into several categories above, can also be considered as belonging to one or other of just two categories - governmental and paramilitary. It is vital to take these categories into consideration, as there are different cultures, different structures and different personal motivations for each which can impact on the way in which they view participation in the programme. While members of government security forces have come forward to participate as individuals, the authorities seem to have problems with this kind of reconciliation activity. For example, governments can be held responsible for violating the European Convention on Human Rights but paramilitaries cannot. This makes the authorities very wary of the possibility of litigation by victims who could use the information gained in the dialogue to pursue a case through the legal system.

Third, great differences exist in the motivation for involvement in the conflict between government and paramilitary combatants. A paramilitary often becomes involved in violence because of an emotional reaction to real or perceived injustice. A soldier or police officer, in contrast, often treats the work as a profession, and many have little say in the selection of the particular field of conflict in which they find themselves. It is, therefore, a fair assumption that, if the Irish peace process fails, a high percentage of paramilitaries will return to armed struggle, whereas former government combatants, if still serving, will be directed to the next arena of conflict.

Concluding Remarks

In general, the process of reconciliation can be very painful as well as rewarding. As one former combatant remarked after a dialogue session with a group of victims/survivors: "Prison was easy compared to that encounter". There are many reasons, both genuine and otherwise, for not participating in such initiatives. One argument often put forward is that reconciliation dialogue is only appropriate and effective in a post-conflict environment. There is certainly no doubt that reconciliation work helps significantly to consolidate a settlement already reached. But this kind of work can also be very effective at an earlier stage by helping to heal relationships, which in turn creates a more auspicious atmosphere in which to reach a settlement. Indeed, NGOs in Northern Ireland have been developing a range of reconciliation activities aimed at relationship-building and dialogue since the early 1970s. The personal risks to participants working in a pre-settlement context, however, will usually be considerably higher, and might create an added barrier to full, inclusive participation.

Most conflicts around the globe are civil conflicts in which state and non-state combatants engage. This particular model of reconciliation dialogue could be applied to many of those situations, and will produce positive outcomes, provided that the approach is:

- inclusive of all opinions and constituencies to the conflict;
- non-judgemental;
- voluntary; and
- supportive of all at the psychological level.

The Glencree Centre is now examining how best to take the healing and relationship-building that has been witnessed through the victim/survivor-combatant dialogue programme at the personal level and produce an impact at the broader community level. In partial response to this challenge, some of the interactions were recorded for broadcast in 2002, and an annual convention has been established where the public can hear the stories of victims and combatants generated from the programme.

CHAPTER 7

Justice

LUC HUYSE

Reconciliation and justice are almost twin notions. Many people argue that the search for peaceful coexistence, trust, empathy and democratic power sharing demands that "justice be done" - that in one way or another the crimes of the past are acknowledged and punished. But justice has many faces:

- It can be retributive and based on prosecution.
- It can be restorative and based on mediation.
- Truth commissions produce historical justice.
- Reparation policies aim for compensatory justice.

The tendency in thinking about justice, especially in the West, is to focus on the retributive dimension. Central to this view is the idea that perpetrators should not go unpunished - that they should pay a price. This chapter reviews the potential role of criminal justice in reconciliation processes.

Practitioners in the field argue that "there is no peace and no reconciliation without punitive justice". Sceptics have raised four general objections to the use of trials and criminal prosecutions in dealing with a violent past:
- Political circumstances may mean that retributive justice is simply not possible as a post-conflict strategy.
- Retributive justice tends to ignore or sideline the real feelings and needs of victims.
- Material obstacles can seriously hinder the delivery of adequate justice.
- Trials have the potential to thwart reconciliation processes.

Justice has many faces.

In cases where trials may not be possible or may be counterproductive to reconciliation, alternatives are amnesty, mechanisms of restorative justice, truth-telling and reparation. Amnesty and restorative justice are discussed in sections 7.2 and 7.3. Truth commissions and reparations are the subjects of chapter 8 and chapter 9.

7.1 Retributive Justice: the Promise, the Practice and the Risks

This section of the chapter poses four questions:
- Why is it that criminal prosecution in post-conflict societies can be conducive to reconciliation?
- How is retributive justice to be organized in a transitional context?
- Under what circumstances can trials and other forms of punishment obstruct reconciliation processes?
- What are the available alternatives?

7.1.1 The Potential Role of Retributive Justice in the Reconciliation Process

For reconciliation to stand any chance in the immediate aftermath of a civil war or a regime transition, it is crucial to limit the danger of renewed violence and terror. If the fire re-ignites, coexistence (the first step in reconciliation) will be further away than before. Reconciliation also involves the gradual building of self-confidence and mutual trust, and implanting a culture of human rights and democracy. Some say retributive justice is the obvious instrument to realize both these conditions.

Supporters of retributive justice have identified the following list of its possible benefits, which may help policy makers in assessing its potential contribution to reconciliation:

Avoiding unbridled private revenge. If there is no criminal prosecution at all, victims may be tempted to take justice into their own hands: the risks then are vigilante justice, summary executions, spirals of revenge and so on. In addition, such "self-help justice" can trigger social and political disturbance. Refraining from prosecuting may also encourage conspiracy theories according to which the leaders of the new regime are suspected of collusion with one side in the former conflict.

Protecting against the return to power of perpetrators. In the first months after a violent conflict has ended, the survival of a newly-established regime depends on swift and firm judicial action against those who are responsible for the gravest violations of human rights. This is seen as a necessary protection against sabotage "from within" and as a way of achieving some minimal physical security.

Fulfilling an obligation to the victims. Advocates of punitive justice argue that retaliation is exactly what most victims want. It serves to heal their wounds and to restore their self-confidence because it publicly acknowledges who was right and who was wrong and, hence, clears the victims of any criminal labels that were placed on them by the authorities of the past or, indeed, by rebel groups or the new authorities. Only trials, the argument runs, lead to a full recognition of the worth and dignity of those victimized by past abuses. A post-conflict society thus has a moral obligation to prosecute and punish the perpetrators.

Individualizing guilt. Criminal courts establish individual accountability. This is crucial in the eradication of the dangerous perception that a whole community (e.g., "the Serbs", "the Muslims", "the Hutu", "the Tutsi") is responsible for violence and atrocities. This idea of collective guilt is often the source of negative stereotypes, which may provoke more violence in turn.

Strengthening legitimacy and the democratization process. Prosecutions, it is said, also advance long-term democratic consolidation. Retributive justice, as a sort of ritual sacrifice and purification process, paves the way for an ethical and political renaissance. It also consolidates the values of democracy, instils public confidence in the capacity of the new regime to implement these values, and encourages the population to believe in them. Failure to prosecute, on the other hand, may generate in the public feelings of cynicism and distrust towards the political system and its values. This is precisely what happened in many newly-democratized Latin American countries.

Breaking the cycle of impunity. Prosecutions are seen as the most potent deterrence against future abuses of human rights and the most effective insurance against sustained violence and atrocities. They can successfully put an end to the vicious circle of impunity that is at the origin of human rights abuse and injustice in

---

Box 7.1: How Retributive Justice Can Help Reconciliation

- avoiding unbridled revenge;
- protecting against return to power of perpetrators;
- fulfilling an obligation to the victims;
- individualizing guilt;
- strengthening legitimacy and process of democratization; and
- breaking the cycle of impunity.

---

many parts of the world. This argument has been heard in several countries that have emerged from painful conflicts. It is also behind the establishment of the international criminal tribunals for the former Yugoslavia and Rwanda at The Hague and Arusha, respectively, and the creation of the permanent International Criminal Court (ICC).

7.1.2 Forms of Retributive Justice
Criminal Prosecution in Operation

Tribunals are the primary instruments for policing a violent past. They operate at a national and an international level.

National Tribunals

Domestic prosecution of the perpetrators of crimes against humanity, genocide and other gross violations of human rights has been extremely rare, largely because these crimes were not recognized in domestic legislation in the past. In Greece in 1974, after the fall of the generals, national tribunals tried some of the top military. In Argentina in 1985, a few junta leaders and army officers were brought before the courts, but because of heavy pressure from the army proceedings stopped after two years. A more recent example is the prosecution of the suspected Rwandan *génocidaires* in national tribunals in Kigali.

Another current case worth discussing in more detail is Ethiopia, where the authorities of the Marxist–Leninist regime have been brought before domestic criminal courts. Immediately after the capture of Addis Ababa in May 1991 by the troops of the Ethiopian People's Revolutionary Democratic Front (PRDF) and the Tigrean People's Liberation Front (TPLF), thousands of members of the defeated Mengistu regime were arrested. The new government asked a special presidential committee to set out a retributive justice policy. A central role was allocated to a Special Prosecutor's Office, created in August 1992. The first charges, against 73 members of the former government, were submitted to the Central High Court in October 1994. Their trial started two months later and was still going on in mid-2002. More than 1,500 witnesses have appeared at the hearings of the court. In the meantime, the Special Prosecutor drew up charges against a further 5,200 suspects, of whom nearly 3,000 will be judged by default as they cannot be traced. These proceedings, mainly in regional courts, began in late 1997 and have not been completed at the time of writing. A total of 14,209 victims of genocide and torture have been identified.

The heart of the applicable penal law is Article 281 of the Ethiopian Penal Code on genocide, which says that any person is punishable who "with intent to destroy, in whole or in part, a national, ethnic, racial, religious or political group, organizes, orders or engages in, be it in time of war or in time of peace: killings, bodily harm or serious injury to the physical or mental health of members of the group in any way whatsoever". In order to avoid the risk of Article 281 being considered as inapplicable by the courts, the Special Prosecutor has also included in the indictment "homicide in the first degree" (Article 522 of the Penal Code). For other charges (disappearances, enforced migration of entire population groups) international customary law has been invoked.

> A consensus has emerged on the duty to prosecute those responsible for gross human rights violations, if necessary by courts that operate outside the country where the crimes were committed.

International Tribunals as Supplementary to National Justice

For centuries criminal justice was based on a purely territorial logic: a state's tribunals could only try crimes that were committed within the borders of that state. The only exception to this rule of national judicial sovereignty was the prosecution of piracy. This has changed dramatically since the 1950s. A consensus has emerged on the duty to prosecute those responsible for gross human rights violations, if necessary by courts that operate outside the country where the crimes were committed.

The legal foundations of such a duty are found in an array of UN conventions and in the principle of universal jurisdiction (see subsection below on universal jurisdiction).

At the practical level, international jurisprudence takes the following forms:
• ad hoc tribunals;
• the International Criminal Court (ICC); and
• national trials based on universal jurisdiction.

International ad hoc tribunals. The UN Security Council, confronted with the atrocities on the territory of the former Yugoslavia and in Rwanda, has established two international criminal tribunals.

The International Criminal Tribunal for the Former Yugoslavia (ICTY) was created in 1993 by UN Security Council Resolution 827. It was mandated to prosecute individuals allegedly responsible for violations of international humanitarian law during armed conflict in the territory of the former Yugoslavia. It is based in The Hague, Netherlands.

The International Criminal Tribunal for Rwanda (ICTR) was established in 1994 by UN Security Council Resolution 955. Like the ICTY, the tribunal for Rwanda was tasked with prosecuting individuals responsible for genocide and crimes against humanity committed in Rwanda between 1 January and 31 December 1994. The ICTR also has jurisdiction for prosecuting Rwandan citizens who committed such violations in neighbouring states. Its proceedings are held in Arusha, Tanzania.

Both tribunals have the same three-section structure. The three arms are the Judges' Chambers, the Office of the Prosecutor and the Registry. The judges are divided into two trial courts of three judges each and a five-judge appeals chamber. The judges are responsible for issuing indictments and hearing and deciding cases. The UN General Assembly elects the judges serving on the tribunals. The Office of the Prosecutor has the responsibility for investigating alleged crimes, framing indictments and prosecuting cases. He or she is appointed by the UN Security Council and is assisted by a Deputy Prosecutor and other staff. The Registry is the administrative division of the tribunal and performs a wide array of functions, including recommending protective measures for witnesses, providing counselling for victims and handling the appointment of defence counsel.

Although the ICTY and the ICTR are separate entities, they share some of the same personnel, such as the five appellate judges and the Chief Prosecutor.

> The ICC will have jurisdiction over the most serious crimes of concern to the international community, such as genocide, crimes against humanity and war crimes.

International ad hoc tribunals give a country the chance to take strong, concrete steps towards building a society based on the rule of law through a process that is seen to be fair and law-based. The criticism of the post-World War II Nuremberg trials - that they imposed norms on the accused and victors' justice on the accused retroactively - no longer applies. In the intervening years, the notion of individual responsibility for war and related crimes has become internationally accepted. Additionally, as with Rwanda and Yugoslavia, an international tribunal under the UN need not be controlled by the "victors", and therefore cannot be accused of seeking revenge.

A new departure in international jurisprudence is the creation of hybrid national–international criminal courts. In the case of Sierra Leone, the UN Security Council has set up, at the government's request, a tribunal that is a mixture of international and Sierra Leonean law and judges. The UN Secretary General appoints the foreign judges. The (planned) international court for Cambodia that was to prosecute Khmer Rouge leaders would have consisted of three Cambodian and two foreign judges. However, many problems arose at the implementation phase of this special court, and in

February 2002 the UN decided to abandon all plans. It was no longer sure that the Cambodian political elite wanted to respect the independence and impartiality of the proposed tribunal (see the case study following chapter 3).

Box 7.2: Questions and Answers about the ICC

What is the ICC? The International Criminal Court is a permanent international tribunal which will try individuals responsible for the most serious international crimes. One hundred and sixty countries attended a UN-sponsored conference in Rome in 1998 to draft a treaty establishing the ICC. After five weeks of intense negotiations, 120 countries voted to adopt the treaty. Only seven countries voted against it (including China, Iraq, Libya and the United States) and 21 abstained. For the court to be set up, 60 countries needed to ratify the treaty. The court was established on 1 July 2002 and is based in The Hague, the Netherlands. By 5 August 2002, 77 countries had ratified the Rome Statute.

What crimes will the ICC prosecute? The ICC will prosecute individuals accused of genocide, war crimes and crimes against humanity, all defined in the treaty setting up the court. It will help to ensure that these serious crimes, which have long been recognized by the international community, no longer go unpunished because of the unwillingness or inability of individual countries to prosecute them.

Who can be brought to trial before the ICC? The ICC will have jurisdiction over crimes committed by the nationals of governments which ratify the treaty or in the territories of governments which ratify it. It can try any individual responsible for such crimes, regardless of his or her civilian or military status or official position.

What are the rights of those accused of a crime by the ICC? The ICC treaty contains a detailed list of the rights that any accused person shall enjoy, including the presumption of innocence, the right to counsel, the right to present evidence, the right to remain silent and the right to have charges proved beyond all reasonable doubt.

How will national courts and the ICC work together? The treaty gives the ICC jurisdiction that is complementary to national jurisdictions. This "principle of complementarity" gives states the primary responsibility and duty to prosecute the most serious international crimes, while allowing the ICC to step in only as a last resort if the states fail to implement their duty - that is, only if investigations and, if appropriate, prosecutions are not carried out in good faith. Bona fide efforts to discover the truth and to hold accountable those responsible for any acts of genocide, crimes against humanity, or war crimes will bar the ICC from proceeding.

How is the ICC different from the International Court of Justice and other existing international tribunals? The International Court of Justice (ICJ or World Court) is a civil tribunal that hears disputes between countries. The ICC is a criminal tribunal that will prosecute individuals. The two ad hoc war crimes tribunals for the former Yugoslavia and Rwanda are similar to the ICC but have limited geographical scope, while the ICC will be global in its reach. The ICC, as a permanent court, will also avoid the delay and start-up costs of creating country-specific tribunals from scratch each time the need arises.

What good can the ICC do? The ICC will help to end the impunity often enjoyed by those responsible for the most serious international human rights crimes. It will provide incentives and guidance for countries that want to prosecute such criminals in their own courts and offer permanent back-up in cases where countries are unwilling or unable to try these cases themselves because of violence, intimidation, or a lack of resources or political will. As noted, the ICC is not intended to replace national courts. Domestic judicial systems remain the first line of accountability in prosecuting these crimes. The ICC will ensure that those who commit the most serious human rights crimes are punished even if national courts are unable or unwilling to do so. Indeed, the possibility of an ICC proceeding may encourage national prosecutions in states that would otherwise avoid bringing war criminals to trial.

How can politically motivated cases be avoided? Many safeguards exist in the ICC treaty to prevent frivolous or politically motivated cases from being brought. For example, all indictments will require confirmation by a Pre-Trial Chamber of judges, which will examine the evidence supporting the indictment before issuing it. The accused and any concerned countries will have an opportunity to challenge the indictment during confirmation hearings before the Pre-Trial Chamber. In addition, any investigation initiated by the Prosecutor will first have to be approved by the Pre-Trial Chamber. Prosecutors and judges will all undergo rigorous scrutiny before they are elected and appointed. *Source:* Reproduced with permission from the Human Rights Watch web site, http://www.hrw.org/campaigns/icc/.

The *International Criminal Court*. The establishment of a permanent international criminal court (the ICC) under the Rome Statute of July 1998 is another illustration of the emerging international consensus on the issue of transitional justice. It will effectively supplant the temporary mechanisms used since World War II to prosecute crimes against humanity, such as the Nuremberg and Tokyo war crimes tribunals and the ad hoc UN tribunals for Rwanda and former Yugoslavia. The ICC will have jurisdiction over the most serious crimes of concern to the international community, such as genocide, crimes against humanity and war crimes. Box 7.2 presents the key issues of the ICC.

Trials based on universal jurisdiction. The perpetrators of genocide, torture and other crimes against humanity are generally brought to justice by either domestic or international tribunals. There is, however, a growing tendency to accept the so-called "rule of universal jurisdiction". This principle entails that the prosecution of genocide and related crimes is achievable by and in every state, no matter where the crimes were committed and regardless of the nationality of the victim or the offender.

Various countries have incorporated the rule of universal jurisdiction into their national criminal legislation. This development led to the Spanish indictment of former Chilean President Pinochet, to complaints in Belgium against Israeli Prime Minister Ariel Sharon, and to the conviction by a Swiss tribunal of a Rwandan official who was involved in the 1994 genocide. According to some observers, further diffusion of the principle will be a major step in the direction of "global justice".

Administrative Justice: Disciplinary Measures Outside the Criminal Court System

Disqualification (or "lustration") of agents of the secret police, of military personnel, judges and other functionaries is an alternative way to address the question of punishing those who are responsible for aggression and repression. Such non-judicial disciplinary measures are usually meted out by administrative agencies. They come in various forms:
• political disqualification, for example, loss of suffrage;
• barring high-ranking officials from public service in the police, the army and the state administration; and
• softer types of penalty for senior officials, such as forced early retirement or transfer to less strategic posts.

> Outright punishment of those responsible may not be appropriate in every context.

Political and professional disqualification was the preferred transitional justice measure in the Central European states after 1989, often as a way to side-step criminal prosecution. It involves intricate vetting and screening operations which, as has been demonstrated in post-communist Europe, tend to become highly politicized. Leaders of political parties, for example, in Poland, have manipulated screening legislation to pin suspicion on rivals and eventually to expel them temporarily or permanently from public office.

7.1.3 The Limits to and Risks of Retributive Justice

Outright punishment of those responsible for violence and human rights violations may not be appropriate in every context.
• In some cases, political leaders consider retributive justice too risky as a strategy for dealing with the past because of the many dangers it provokes for a successor regime.
• Just as prosecutions have the potential to facilitate reconciliation, they can also produce inadequate results that could actually harm reconciliation.

Political Risks

The end of a civil war or of a period of violent repression creates an intricate agenda - rebuilding the political machinery and the civil service, guaranteeing a minimum of physical security, healing the victims, repairing the damage inflicted to them and so on. Dealing with the perpetrators, eventually by means of criminal prosecution, is only one of many challenges. More often than not it will be impossible to tackle all tasks simultaneously. Choices have to be made. The place of justice in general, and of trials in particular, on the post-conflict agenda depends on the particular conjunction of political, cultural and historic forces. There may be legitimate arguments that other problems and needs are more important and/or more urgent than seeking justice through trials.

In addition, prosecutions are ambivalent in certain transitional contexts. They can have highly destabilizing effects on a peace settlement or a fragile shift to democracy. In fact, precisely to avoid such an outcome, Latin American policy makers throughout the 1980s deliberately opted against trials. Refusal to prosecute appears to be based on the argument that harsh punishment may have one or more of the following negative results:

Destabilizing a fragile peace settlement. Former military leaders may respond to the threat of prosecution by trying to reverse the course of events with a coup or a rebellion. The risk of a destabilizing backlash especially haunted the young democracies of Latin America in the 1980s and 1990s. Immediately after he came to power, President Sanguinetti of Uruguay, for example, rejected a punitive justice operation with the following argument: "What is more just - to consolidate the peace of a country where human rights are guaranteed today or to seek retroactive justice that could compromise that peace?". The general attitude has been that there is a sleeping lion in the background, which trials will inevitably provoke, thus risking a return to military dictatorship.

Provoking hostile subcultures and networks. A prolonged physical and social expulsion of certain sections of the population, based on criminal court decisions, may obstruct democratic consolidation by driving the convicted perpetrators into social and political isolation. This in turn could result in the creation of destabilizing subcultures and networks which in the long run will become hostile to democracy.

> **Box 7.3: Retributive Justice: Priority Questions and Political Risks**
>
> - Other points on the agenda are more important and/or more urgent.
> - It risks destabilizing a fragile peace.
> - It can provoke subcultures and networks, hostile to democracy.
> - It may have crippling effects on governance.

Causing crippling effects on governance. The viability of a post-conflict state depends also on its efficacy. A far-reaching purge of administrative and managerial staff can have crippling effects on governance and endanger the vital political and economic development of the country. Prudent considerations of the problematic consequences of large-scale dismissals from the civil service and from high-level posts in industry have been heard regularly in post-communist Central and Eastern Europe.

Other Shortcomings and Risks

Even where the establishment and operation of prosecutions is appropriate to the context, a number of reasons may still be found not to prioritize retributive justice in a reconciliation policy. Constraining factors tend to appear in one or more of the following ways:
- The general deficiencies of retributive justice are accentuated.
- Material obstacles may prevent the adequate operation of the criminal justice system of a post-conflict society.
- Post-transition trials may directly impede other routes to reconciliation.

General shortcomings

- Prosecutions are perpetrator-oriented.
- Trials may lead to re-victimization.
- Criminal courts restrict the flow of information.

Material obstacles in times of transition

- Evidence may have been destroyed.
- The criminal justice system may be in shock or crippled.

Shortcomings and risks in a transitional context

- Post-transition trials may be emergency justice.
- Post-transition trials may violate rule-of-law norms.
- Trials identify individual guilt, not patterns in atrocities.
- The penal system is not adapted to handle large-scale atrocities.
- Trials may work against the culture of a post-conflict society.

General Shortcomings of Retributive Justice

Any criminal justice operation, even under normal conditions, has certain drawbacks. Among the most important are the following:

Prosecutions are perpetrator-oriented. Prosecution as a form of repairing past injustices concerns itself almost exclusively with the perpetrators. It is badly equipped to give the victims the attention they need in order to be healed from the injustices they suffered.

Trials may lead to re-victimization. Criminal proceedings usually involve cross-examination, turning a courtroom into a hostile environment for victims. This may result in humiliation and renewed trauma. Re-victimization may also happen if trials do not meet victims' expectations because of lack of proof, inadequate judicial decision making or legal loopholes that assist the defence.

> Prosecution concerns itself almost exclusively with the perpetrators and is badly equipped to give victims the attention they need.

Criminal courts restrict the flow of information. The logic of criminal law is to generate "yes or no" decisions. The outcome of a trial must be "guilty" or "not guilty". To arrive at such clear verdicts, criminal courts restrict the amount of information that is processed. However, during violent conflict the behaviour of perpetrators often falls into a "grey area" in which various forms of guilt and innocence are mixed. (See chapter 5 for a discussion of this question.) Courtrooms are not usually capable of the subtlety needed to deal with such complexities.

Material Obstacles in Times of Transition

Societies emerging from painful conflict are usually impoverished and thus short of the material and human resources to support a formal criminal justice operation. Among the most important problems are the following:

Evidence may have been destroyed. In collecting proof, tribunals are particularly dependent on the cooperation of security agencies, such as the army and the police, which may still reflect in their composition and culture the spirit of the old order. Their personnel often include the very individuals who are responsible for some of the most heinous crimes. This may result in the obstruction of the tribunal's work, for example, by destroying or concealing evidence. Consequently lack of proof can lead to acquittals of well-known perpetrators. Such justice, perceived as arbitrary, will seriously damage victims' trust in the whole system.

The criminal justice system may be in shock or crippled. The judiciary may have been one of the sources of injustice and/or the infrastructure may be badly damaged. The history of transitional justice in post-1991 Ethiopia or in post-genocide Rwanda, for example, demonstrates that the absence of legal technical expertise in trying violations of human rights is a serious handicap. One negative outcome is serious delay in the trials. In Ethiopia, almost all arrested suspects have now been on remand since the summer of 1991 and will undoubtedly continue to be so for years to come. Some will eventually be acquitted for lack of evidence after an extremely lengthy captivity. The same situation exists in Rwanda. By the end of 2000, six years after the genocide and with some 130,000 arrested suspects, the Rwandan tribunals had only pronounced 5,200 verdicts. In 2001 no more than 1,200 new cases were dealt with. (Of these 6,400 individuals judged, approximately 25 per cent were acquitted.) The saying "Justice delayed is justice denied" is certainly very applicable here. And nothing is more damaging than ineffective justice.

Shortcomings and Risks in a Context of Transition

Criminal prosecutions may also directly block or even reverse a reconciliation process. In transitional contexts, ranging from Spain in the 1970s to Cambodia in the 1980s to Mozambique in the 1990s, civil and political leaders have sometimes consciously opted not to try to bring perpetrators to court, precisely out of fear that prosecutions would endanger reconciliation initiatives. The following reasons have been given:

Post-transition trials may be "emergency justice". The sooner trials start after the end of a conflict, the bigger is the danger of "emergency justice" being dispensed. The political and social climate is not yet well suited to a scrupulous sorting of all the levels of responsibility for the abuses of the past, and the criminal justice system is therefore incapable of dispensing fair and effective rulings. Consequently rash and hurried trials can actually add to injustice and inequality, especially if those who are tried first receive the most severe punishment, even if they are not the worst offenders. The resulting resentment will become an obstacle to reconciliation initiatives.

Post-transition trials may violate rule-of-law norms. Retributive justice after violent conflict involves a number of decisions that may trespass on rule-of-law norms and human rights. A key question is how to punish persons for activities that were approved, legalized and encouraged by those in power during a civil war or a cruel authoritarian regime. Political leaders may feel the need to issue retroactive penal legislation, thus breaking the rule that no conduct can be held punishable unless it is covered by a law that existed before the offence was committed. Or they may, with good intentions, renew the statute of limitation once it has run out because major perpetrators would otherwise escape punishment. In addition, in this volatile context, judicial impartiality may fall victim to political pressure, time constraints, shortage of trained judges and lawyers and, in the case of ad hoc courts, the appointment of non-career judges who are more amenable to pressure from politicians, the media and public opinion. The risk of partisan verdicts, or so-called "victors' justice", is very real. Tribunals may even turn into opportunities for settling old personal and political vendettas. The effect will almost certainly be that new victims are created and that new hatred and bitterness arise. Criminal prosecution must be discarded as a priority option if procedural standards cannot be maintained.

The penal system is not adapted to handle large-scale atrocities. Criminal justice systems are not well resourced to deal with the most extreme of crimes, such as gross human rights violations, particularly if these offences come in large numbers. There is a real risk that only a small percentage of perpetrators will be prosecuted and punished so that the process will appear merely arbitrary. Criminal courts are, moreover, not adapted to the complexities that arise when all sides have committed atrocities, as is usually the case in civil war.

Trials identify individual guilt, not patterns in atrocities. Criminal courts are, generally speaking, not able to get at the broader patterns of the multiple causes and (state) practices that contributed - and might still contribute in the future - to violence and terror. Moreover, trials only recognize criminal guilt, not political or moral responsibility.

Trials may conflict with the culture of a post-conflict society. Desmond Tutu, Chair of the South African Truth and Reconciliation Commission (TRC), argues that retributive justice is not character-istic of traditional African jurisprudence. It is too impersonal and has too little consideration for victims. The African view of justice is aimed at "the healing of breaches, the redressing of imbalances, the restoration of broken relationships. This kind of justice seeks to rehabilitate both the victim and the perpetrator, who should be given the opportunity to be reintegrated into the community he or she has injured by his or her offence". Retributive justice, in contrast, may make reintegration much harder. Writing on the legacy of the 1967–1970 civil war in Biafra, when three million people died, Ifi Amadiume explains that, for Africans: "The evil is in the social system, in the guise of inequality and oppression. According to this African logic, guilt is collective; Africans turn to their own social mediators, healers and reclassifiers, such as diviners and prophets. It is a modern arrogance to assume that courts are instruments of healing". Similar arguments have been developed with respect to the Asian vision of dealing with victims and perpetrators, exemplified by the hesitation of the Cambodian people about instituting a retributive reaction to the crimes of the Khmer Rouge.

> Trials only recognize criminal guilt, not political or moral responsibility.

The Need for a Multiple Cost–Benefit Analysis

The cry "No peace, no reconciliation without retribution" is a key argument in ongoing debates on how to deal with a violent past. As a public argument, it cannot be discarded without creating heavy opposition and re-victimization. It is clear from the preceding discussion that political, material and legal constraints may make retributive justice almost impracticable. However, this call for cau-tion should not lead automatically to the abandonment of criminal prosecution as a dimension of transitional justice. Some problems can be resolved. Political leaders and civil society, both local and international, may develop measures that neutralize the paralysing effects of the limitations and risks. Past experiences suggest that the best practice is to balance all costs and benefits of a given policy against each other, above all taking into account the particular conjunction of political, cultural and historical forces in a transitional society.

Moral Requirements and Political Constraints

It is critically important that those who, in good faith, advocate the use of criminal justice understand the obstacles and risks in advance. But the political costs of criminal prosecutions should not be exaggerated. This is a difficult and delicate calculation, balancing short-term gains against long-term costs. But post-conflict policy makers can also make use of the international community at such a juncture. Outside actors can put pressure on dissidents who threaten stability. The ICC now offers permanent back-up in cases where countries are unable to try these criminals themselves because of violence, intimidation or a lack of political will and, finally, foreign criminal justice systems too can, on the basis of universal jurisdiction, bring offenders to their courts.

The crucial challenge is to strike a balance between the demands of retributive justice and political prudence or, in other words, to reconcile moral imperatives and political constraints. It entails a difficult and, on occasion, tortuous cost–benefit analysis.

Overcoming Practical Limitations

Retributive justice, especially in the context of a post-conflict society, is at best plagued by certain shortcomings and, at worst, may endanger reconciliation and democratization processes.

One of the major risks relates to the problem of maintaining procedural standards. Countering the danger of rule-of-law violations requires drastic interventions in the criminal justice system - restoring the judicial infrastructure, reforming the police force, recruiting and training judges and defence lawyers, and developing a human rights culture in the prison system. In other words, keeping prosecution as an option in transitional justice is only justified if there is a simultaneous reorganization of the justice system. This is no easy enterprise. It may imply the mobilization of the international community, as is currently demonstrated in Burundi and Rwanda, where Avocats Sans Frontières (an international NGO) offers training to judges and lawyers.

> Retributive justice, at worst, may endanger reconciliation and democratization processes.

Many of the other limitations discussed above necessitate even more radical interventions, several of which will be presented later in this and the following chapters.

International Jurisprudence as a Complementary Instrument

International tribunals, or national trials based on universal jurisdiction, are less vulnerable to intimidation, material obstacles, violation of procedural standards, lack of trained personnel and "victors' justice". This makes them seem a perfect complement, or even an alternative, to local trials. But the actual experience of the ad hoc tribunals in The Hague and Arusha suggests that they are constrained by several factors: [*]

Lack of an enforcement mechanism. Tribunals have the power to issue arrest warrants for perpetrators but do not have the police authority to apprehend those who have been indicted. Lack of enforcement may severely hinder the effectiveness of tribunals, thereby eroding public confidence in their usefulness.

Tribunals cannot stop a conflict in progress. Although tribunals may begin their work before hostilities completely cease (as in the case of the former Yugoslavia), they cannot themselves stop a conflict that is in progress. This problem can be alleviated to the extent that tribunals are established before a war arises, as will be the case now that the ICC has been set up. Questions have been raised, however, about the potential for interference by the ICC in delicate local or regional peacemaking: for example, ICC prosecutions might work against local amnesty measures, producing a serious clash of interests.

The scope of prosecutions depends on whether the conflict is internal or international. Under the Geneva Conventions, if a conflict is internal, a perpetrator can only be prosecuted for genocide or crimes against humanity but not for grave breaches of the Geneva Conventions on humanitarian law or other war crimes. The ICC, however, will not be hindered by this limitation.

The danger of imposing retributive justice as the universal response to human rights crimes. In the course of their vigorous lobbying for an effective ICC and for the extension of universal jurisdiction, international institutions (such as the UN) and NGOs (such as Human Rights Watch and Amnesty International) have tended to put a one-sided emphasis on retributive justice. This has been happening simultaneously with, and in contradiction to, the growing support - particularly but not solely in developing countries - for more informal and mediation-oriented mechanisms of restorative justice (see section 7.3).

Ad hoc tribunals tend to be costly, time-consuming and too distanced from the population. The innovation of tribunals that are a mixture of international and national elements (as in the case of the special

---

[*] *Parts of the following are based on Michael Lund, "Reckoning for Past Wrongs: Truth Commissions and War Crimes Tribunals". In* **Democracy and Deep-Rooted Conflict: Options for Negotiators,** *edited by Peter Harris and Ben Reilly. Stockholm: International IDEA, 1998:291.*

courts in Sierra Leone and Cambodia), together with the establishment of the ICC, may eliminate some of these problems. Mixed tribunals are less expensive and closer to the population, can develop a stronger deterrent effect, and have easier access to evidence.

7.1.4 The Alternatives

It is perfectly conceivable that policy makers and civil society, after weighing the pros and cons, will conclude in a particular situation that retributive justice is too dangerous a path or that the obstacles are insurmountable. Various alternative routes are then available. One is amnesty, an approach whose political appeal is often irresistible. Section 7.2 examines this policy option at length. Other options are (a) the use of restorative justice, possibly based on traditional mechanisms of conflict resolution; and (b) the establishment of a truth commission and/or reparation programmes - the two latter being forms of justice without formal punishment. Restorative justice is the subject of section 7.3. Truth-telling and reparation are discussed in chapters 8 and 9.

These alternatives all raise a preliminary but crucial question: how do they relate to the duty under international law to prosecute genocide, war crimes and gross violations of human rights? The spirited debate over this question is still unresolved. Some participants in the debate accept no exceptions to this international obligation. Others argue that a post-conflict society may refrain from the duty to prosecute if certain strict conditions are met. Among the most important conditions are:
• Blanket amnesty must be completely out of the question.
• Irrefutable proof must be given that national courts are unable to prosecute.
• The population in general, and victims in particular, must have a voice in the decision not to prosecute.
• The state authorities must accept the commitment to acknowledge as much as possible of the truth about the past.
• Firm promises must be given with respect to reparation for victims.
• Those who profit from a pardon must express regret.

7.2 Amnesty: a Questionable Alternative

Reconciliation processes are ineffective as long as the vicious circle of impunity is not broken. The nasty reality is that in most post-conflict societies gross atrocities go unpunished, unacknowledged and without redress.

Impunity has many sources. In some countries silence is the main cause. It can be officially induced or simply a case of public amnesia. In Zimbabwe, for example, the army committed gross human rights violations in Matabeleland between 1983 and 1985. This remained unacknowledged until 1997, when two NGOs published a report titled *Breaking the Silence* (see the case study following chapter 2).

> Reconciliation processes are ineffective as long as the vicious circle of impunity is not broken.

In other societies impunity is the product of a deliberate attempt by the authorities to camouflage certain painful episodes by imposing a selective reading of the past. Post-World War II France is a compelling illustration of this. After the war, the French Government presented a picture of a society that had been united in resistance to the German occupiers and ignored the collaboration of the domestic Vichy regime and its participation in the Holocaust. As a result, high-ranking officials of the Vichy regime went totally unpunished until new trials in the 1990s put an end to this anomaly.

Impunity also occurs when domestic criminal courts, and often military courts, fail to deal adequately with perpetrators.

Immunity is a variant of impunity. It is embedded in international customary practice which provides protection against prosecution for heads of state. In some cases, for instance Burundi in 2002–2003, peacemaking is facilitated by granting leaders of rebel movements provisional and limited immunity through domestic legislation.

However, the most frequent source of impunity is amnesty legislation, an officially declared and imposed forgiving and forgetting. The next two subsections discuss the various forms of amnesty and its close relationship with the notion of "political offence".

7.2.1 Amnesty in its Many Forms

Amnesty comes in a variety of forms. Which particular form it takes depends both on the way it is decided upon and on the range of perpetrators and crimes it indemnifies.

The Origin: a Unilateral or Negotiated Decision?

Some sort of self-amnesty accompanied the transitions to democracy in many Latin American countries in the 1980s. The outgoing elites unilaterally pardoned most of their political leaders and senior army officers. For example, in Argentina in 1983 democratic elections were held in October, but in September the military junta had passed the so-called Law on National Pacification, granting amnesty for all political and related crimes by its officials and military. In 1978, years before Chile's transition to democracy, the Pinochet government unilaterally pardoned all criminal acts committed during the state of siege (between September 1973 and March 1978). In Zimbabwe, after each election in the period 1980–2000 the Zimbabwe African Nationalist Union-Patriotic Front (ZANU-PF) government enacted amnesty laws pardoning violence against opposition parties and their members.

Pre-transitional negotiations between warring parties are a similar source of amnesty laws. This type of reciprocal amnesty became a dominant feature from the early 1990s. The end of the apartheid regime in South Africa was preceded by negotiations that facilitated amnesty for

---

Box 7.5: The Notion of "Political Offence" in South Africa

The law and practice of states show that there is now a considerable degree of consensus both as to the types of offence which may in principle be classified as "political" and as to the sort of factors which should be taken into account in deciding whether an offence is political or not.

The following factors will be considered when making a recommendation for the grant of pardon or indemnity as may be appropriate in individual cases:

• the motive of the offender, i.e., whether the offence was committed for a political motive (e.g., to further or oppose the aims of a political organization, institution or body) or for a personal motive;

• the context in which the offence was committed, and in particular whether it was committed in the course of or as part of a political uprising or disturbance, or in reaction thereto;

• the nature of the political objective (e.g., whether to force a change in the policy of or to overthrow or destroy the political opponent);

• the legal and factual nature of the offence, including its gravity;

• the object and/or objective of the offence (e.g., whether it was committed against the political opponent or his property, or directed primarily against private individuals or property; or was committed on the assumption that a particular cause, governmental or otherwise, was being served);

• the relationship between the offence and the political objective being pursued (e.g., the directness or proximity of the relationship, or the proportionality between the offence and the objective pursued); and

• the question whether the act was committed in the execution of an order or with the approval of the organization, institution or body concerned.

Source: South African Government Gazette, 7 November 1990.

both sides. The Madrid peace accords of December 1996 between the government of Guatemala and the rebel Guatemalan National Revolutionary Unit (Unidad Revolucionaria Nacional Guatemalteca, URNG) produced a similar result. The 2002 ceasefire agreement between the Angolan government army and the military commanders of the National Union for the Total Independence of Angola (União Nacional para a Independencia Total de Angola, UNITA) included the promise of amnesty for former UNITA rebels: a few days before the official signing of the agreement the Angolan Parliament passed an amnesty law. The Nicaraguan "general amnesty and national reconciliation law" of March 1990 was the result of negotiations between the Sandinista government and opposition parties.

The Scope: Total or Conditional?

Total amnesty is rare. In most legislation, pardon is reserved for crimes that are political in nature. Limiting conditions can be:
• amnesty after full exposure of the facts by the author of the crime, as in South Africa;
• amnesty reserved for certain perpetrators (for example, child soldiers);
• amnesty reserved for crimes committed during a specified period; or
• amnesty laws which specifically exclude crimes that fall under the country's international obligations (such as the UN conventions on genocide and torture and the Inter-American Convention on Human Rights). Examples are Peru's amnesty law of June 1995, Uruguay's "law of national pacification" of 1995, Suriname's amnesty act of August 1992, and the amnesty proclamations of 1994 in the Philippines.

However, there are cases where the definition of a political offence is so broad as to produce a de facto total amnesty. The 1993 "general amnesty law for the consolidation of peace" in El Salvador, for example, granted amnesty to all those who participated "in any way in the commission of political crimes or common crimes linked to political crimes or common crimes in which the number of persons involved is not less than twenty".

Evaluation

Amnesty legislation - the imposition of official forgiving and forgetting - is, then, a disputed instrument in the context of post-conflict societies. More often than not it obstructs the reconciliation process. It is a general rule that unilateral amnesties that are total in scope should be avoided. A different situation arises when amnesty is the price to be paid for negotiating a fragile peace. If the end of a violent conflict is otherwise not attainable, amnesty can be a last resort. But even then, according to most observers, strict conditions must be met. These include, among others, a public debate preceding the enactment of an amnesty law, as much truth-seeking and reparation as possible, and full respect for a state's international obligations under any human rights treaty.

> Amnesty legislation more often than not obstructs the reconciliation process.

7.2.2 The Notion of a "Political Offence"

Almost all amnesty legislation explicitly refers to crimes or offences that in one way or another are of a political nature. In many cases, particularly in the indemnity laws of the 1980s, the notion "political" remained extremely vague, allowing authorities to bend the scope of the legislation to their needs. Change has come with the transitions in Mozambique and South Africa. The parties at the negotiation table agreed on a set of guidelines on political offences drawn from extradition law. These criteria are a mix of elements (see box 7.5):

- the subjective dimension - the motive of the perpetrator;
- the objective dimension - the context, nature and intention of the act; and
- the proportionality question: does the objective of the act justify its severity?

7.3 Restorative Justice

The growing dissatisfaction with the purely punitive handling of common crimes has stimulated the search for mechanisms that could serve as complements, or even alternatives, to retribution. Inspiration has been found in indigenous mediation-based justice institutions in Africa, Australia, New Zealand and Canada. This led practitioners and scholars to develop a model of "restorative justice".

> *Restorative justice works with the full participation of the victim and of the relevant communities in discussing the facts, identifying the causes of misconduct and defining the sanctions.*

7.3.1 What is Restorative Justice?

Section 7.1.3 discussed the main shortcomings of retributive justice: it is perpetrator-oriented; the whole process may, consequently, frustrate the victim and even lead to re-victimization; and it emphasizes individual guilt and punishment, and thus overlooks the community dimension in conflict, in crime and in the reaction to it.

Restorative justice is thought to handle wrongdoing differently: it works with the full participation of the victim and of the relevant communities in discussing the facts, identifying the causes of misconduct and the defining sanctions. The ultimate aim is to restore relations as far as possible, both between victim and offender and within the broader community to which they belong. Box 7.6 gives a presentation of the underlying values of restorative justice.

One example of an application of restorative justice in the Western legal system is victim–offender reconciliation programmes. These were developed in North America in the early 1970s. Howard Zehr describes them as follows: "In its classic form, it is operated in cooperation with the courts, but often housed in separate non-profit organizations. Upon referral of a case by the court or proba-

---

Box 7.6 : Values of Restorative Justice

- Restorative justice is concerned far more about restoration of the victim and the victimized community than about the increasingly costly punishment of the offender.

- It elevates the importance of the victim in the criminal justice process through increased involvement, input and services.

- It requires that offenders be held directly accountable to the person or community they have victimized.

- It encourages the entire community to be involved in holding the offender accountable and promoting a healing response to the needs of victims and offenders.

- It places greater emphasis on getting offenders to accept responsibility for their behaviour and make amendments, whenever possible, than on the severity of punishment.

- It recognizes a community responsibility for the social conditions that contribute to offender behaviour.

Source: Umbreit, M. *The Handbook of Victim Offender Mediation: An Essential Guide to Practice and Research.* San Francisco, Calif.: Jossey-Bass, 2001:xxviii–xxix.

---

tion service, trained volunteers separately contact victim and offender to explore what happened and determine their willingness to proceed. If they agree, victim and offender are brought together in a meeting facilitated by the volunteer mediator who serves as a neutral third party. In this meeting, the facts of the offence are fully explored, feelings are expressed, and a written restitution contract is worked out." The programme has been used predominantly to handle fairly minor crimes, although initiatives in conflict contexts such as Northern Ireland have tried to extend the concept.

7.3.2 Traditional Forms of Restorative Justice

The Western search for a justice mechanism that can balance a purely punitive approach has generated renewed interest in traditional non-state systems of dealing with crime. Some of these have existed since antiquity in African and Asian societies. In countries like Australia, New Zealand, Canada and the United States, on the other hand, traditional justice systems belong to the aboriginal heritage and have only recently been revived.

It has been argued that traditional forms of justice might be of great value as instruments in the reconciliation processes in developing post-conflict countries. Punitive measures are often a risky and/or unattainable strategy in such societies. Mediation- and reconciliation-oriented procedures have fewer disadvantages. Existing institutions could, it is thought, be adapted to play a role in dealing with past atrocities. There is thus good reason to take a closer look at these mechanisms and their salient features, strengths and weaknesses.

Salient Features

- The problem is viewed as that of the whole community or group.
- The emphasis is on reconciliation and restoring social harmony.
- Traditional arbitrators are appointed from within the community on the basis of status or lineage.
- There is a high degree of public participation.
- Customary law is merely one factor considered in reaching a compromise.
- The rules of evidence and procedure are flexible.
- There is no professional legal representation.
- The process is voluntary and decisions are based on agreement.
- There is an emphasis on restorative penalties.
- The enforcement of decisions is secured through social pressure.
- Decisions are confirmed through rituals aimed at reintegration.
- Like cases need not be treated alike.

Strengths

- They are accessible to local and rural people in that their proceedings are carried out in the local language, within walking distance, with simple procedures which do not require the services of a lawyer, and without the delays associated with the formal system.
- In most cases, the type of justice they offer - based on reconciliation, compensation, restoration and rehabilitation - is more appropriate to people living in close-knit communities who must rely on continuous social and economic cooperation with their neighbours.
- They are highly participatory, giving the victim, the offender and the community as a whole a real voice in finding a lasting solution to the conflict.
- They help in educating all members of the community as to the rules to be followed, the circumstances which may lead to them being broken, and how ensuing conflict may be peacefully resolved.
- The fact that they employ non-custodial sentences effectively reduces prison overcrowding, may allow prison budget allocations to be diverted towards social development purposes, permits the offender to continue to contribute to the economy and to pay compensation to the victim, and prevents the economic and social dislocation of the family.

Weaknesses

- The compromise reached may reflect the unequal bargaining strengths of the parties. While checks and balances exist (particularly public participation), existing social attitudes may in fact reinforce inequalities on the basis of gender, age or other status.

• Traditional leaders may favour certain parties depending on their political allegiance, or power in terms of wealth, education or status.

• Another major flaw, not mentioned in the report, is that procedural safeguards are often insufficient.

(Reproduced with permission from a study published in 2000 by Penal Reform International.)

7.3.3 Restorative Justice in Post-Conflict Societies

Traditional forms of justice may complement and even replace more formal and punitive ways of dealing with past human rights violations. However, many doubts remain. These traditional mechanisms have some significant weak points, resulting in many instances in a denial of fair trial. This has recently been pointed out by the African Commission on Human and Peoples' Rights: "It is recognized that traditional courts are capable of playing a role in the achievement of peaceful societies and exercise authority over a significant proportion of the population of African countries. [However,] traditional courts are not exempt from the provisions of the African Charter relating to fair trial".

Traditional forms of justice are designed to deal with relatively small numbers of cases of minor wrongdoing - theft, conflicts between neighbours and so on. Do they have the capacity to restore years and sometimes decades of oppression? Can they bear the weight of the most serious crimes? This is the most important reservation. The problem in answering these questions is that there are as yet only a few and fairly recent experiences of restorative justice being implemented in post-conflict situations. Box 7.7 gives a brief description of two examples. The most ambitious operation so far is the remodelling of the *gacaca* tribunals in Rwanda with the aims of speeding up the prosecution of suspected perpetrators of the 1994 genocide, increasing the participation of the population, and introducing elements of mediation and reconciliation into the process. The importance of this enterprise and its potential relevance for other post-conflict societies are indisputable. This chapter therefore ends with a case study on the Rwandan experiment.

Box 7.7: Restorative Justice in Sudan and Bougainville

"We in the Sudan have a group of experts called *ajaweed*. These are elders, mostly tribal chiefs, who are experienced in mediation. They are usually called upon to mediate in conflicts between groups other than their own. The process of mediation begins with an open discussion in which everything is aired. The parties express their grievances against one another in lengthy and often embittered speeches, which makes one wonder whether an agreement is possible. After an exhaustive exchange, in which the mediators labour against all odds to explore a common ground, there comes a point when the leaders come together and agree on the principles for resolving the conflict and living together. Rituals of reconciliation are then performed and the conflict is formally declared resolved."
Francis Deng

"The civil war on Bougainville (concerning secession of this island from Papua New Guinea, and fighting between different local factions) has been a testing ground for a restorative justice approach to peacemaking. The PEACE Foundation Melanesia, funded by Caritas, The New Zealand Overseas Development Agency and the Princess Diana Fund, has given basic restorative justice training to 10,000 people on Bougainville, 500 as facilitators, including many traditional chiefs, and 50 to 70 as trainers. Out of this, the PEACE Foundation Melanesia expects to have some 800 active village-based mediators to deal with the conflicts that have arisen in the aftermath of civil war, from petty instances of ethnic abuse up to rape and political killings. The Bougainvillians are discovering their own ways of doing restorative justice consistent with their Melanesian principle of *wan bel* (literally 'one belly') or reconciliation."
J. Braithwaite

7.4 Concluding Remarks

There are real problems with retributive justice in the context of post-conflict societies - political and legal risks, material obstacles and many more shortcomings (see section 7.1). But amnesty, often proposed as an alternative, is a deeply questionable strategy. As a result, a restorative approach based on existing traditional jurisdictions seems fairly appealing. Together with truth-telling and reparation programmes, it offers an attractive middle way between punitive justice and a blanket pardon. However, a great deal of imagination and creativity will be needed if traditional forms of justice are to be reframed for use in the context of massive atrocities such as genocide or prolonged human rights violations. Every initiative will have to take an uncharted path. Furthermore, recent developments in the international environment (the UN, large NGOs and so on) almost exclusively favour retributive institutions (ad hoc tribunals, the ICC, universal jurisdiction). This one-sided approach discourages experiments to develop a restorative approach.

> Recent developments in the international environment almost exclusively favour retributive institutions.

Throughout this Handbook the emphasis is on the need for reconciliation policies which are a mix of culturally appropriate strategies and instruments. This general concern is also valid in the domain of justice. A combination of domestic trials (where possible), of international punitive reactions *and* of justice mechanisms outside the formal criminal system may well provide the richest possibilities.

References and Further Reading
Main Sources

Lund, Michael. "Reckoning for Past Wrongs: Truth Commissions and War Crimes Tribunals." In *Democracy and Deep-Rooted Conflict: Options for Negotiators*, edited by Peter Harris and Ben Reilly. Stockholm: International IDEA, 1998.

Mani, Rama. *Beyond Retribution: Seeking Justice in the Shadows of War*. Cambridge and Malden, Mass: Polity Press and Blackwell, 2002.

Penal Reform International. *Access to Justice in Sub-Saharan Africa: The Role of Traditional and Informal Justice Systems*. London: PRI, 2002.

Other References

Amadiume, Ifi. "The Politics of Memory: Biafra and Intellectual Responsibility." In *The Politics of Memory: Truth, Healing and Social Justice*, edited by Ifi Amadiume and Abdullahi An-Na'im. London: Zed Books, 2000:38–55.

Braithwaite, John. *Restorative Justice and Responsive Regulation*. Oxford: University Press, 2002.

Deng, Francis. "Conclusion: The Cause of Justice behind Civil Wars." In *The Politics of Memory: Truth, Healing and Social Justice*, edited by Ifi Amadiume and Abdullahi An-Na'im. London: Zed Books, 2000:184–2000.

Tutu, Desmond. *No Future without Forgiveness.* London: Rider, 1999.

Umbreit, Mark. *The Handbook of Victim Offender Mediation: An Essential Guide to Practice and Research.* San Francisco, Calif.: Jossey-Bass, 2001.

Zehr, Howard. "Restorative Justice." In *Peacebuilding: A Field Guide*, edited by Luc Reychler and Thania Paffenholz. London: Lynne Rienner, 2001:330–335.

The *Gacaca* Tribunals in Rwanda

PETER UVIN

Introduction

Between April and July 1994, more than 700,000 Tutsi were killed in the Rwandan genocide. In parallel massacres, tens of thousands Hutu were killed for being too moderate, too sympathetic to Tutsi, too wealthy or too politically inconvenient. After the genocide a new government came to power, dominated by Ugandan-born Tutsi returnees but with the participation of other political parties. It inherited a totally destroyed country, with a traumatized and impoverished population, a collapsed state and a destroyed infrastructure. Eight years later, much of the physical fabric of the state and the economy has been rebuilt - at times better than it was before. However, the giant tear in the fabric of Rwanda's society has not been repaired. Achieving justice and reconciliation remains the great challenge for Rwanda.

From the beginning, the new government argued that unless the "culture of impunity" was once and for all ended in Rwanda the vicious cycle of violence would never end. Although some donors were interested in the South African "truth and reconciliation" model, the government firmly rejected this: only when the guilty had been punished would it be possible for the victims and the innocent to create a joint future together. As a result, the Rwandan Government and the donor community invested heavily in the (re)construction of the justice system. More than 100 justice-related projects have been funded - training lawyers, judges, investigators and policemen; supporting reform of administrative and court procedures; funding the construction of courts, libraries and prisons; paying for vehicles and fuel; supplementing the salaries of judges; and supplying technical assistance to the Ministry of Justice and the Supreme Court.

All this has produced significant results. In 1996, the Rwandan National Assembly adopted a genocide law, creating four categories of crime and associated punishments, ranging from particularly cruel behaviour (category I) to simple property offences (category IV). Trials started by the end of the same year. By mid-2001, approximately 3,500 persons had been judged.

The quality of the trials has improved over the years as verdicts have become more nuanced, but serious problems remain. The quality of the justice delivered is deficient: there are too many instances of investigative bias, corruption of judges, intimidation of witnesses, weak defence counsel or absence of a defence counsel, and political pressure. A second major problem is quantitative: at the current pace, it would take more than a century to finish the trials of the 130,000 persons who are currently imprisoned, often in horrendous conditions. It is widely believed that the justice system simply cannot work much faster than it currently does (it could work faster but not, let us say, 50 times faster, which is what is really needed). More people accused of participation in the genocide die in Rwanda's prisons each year than are judged. This is socially, economically and politically very costly for the Rwandan Government and society.

From mid-1997, senior Rwandans began thinking about innovative ways of dealing with this challenge. Out of these discussions grew the idea of transforming a traditional Rwandan community-based conflict resolution mechanism called *gacaca* into a tool for judging those accused of participation in the genocide and the massacres. This system is labelled the "modernized *gacaca*" and constitutes an unprecedented legal–social experiment in its size and scope. In the summer of 1999, a draft law began to circulate. This was followed by a large number of meetings and discussions involving various segments of government and society, as well as the international donor community. The law underwent various modifications, which resolved some of the criticisms against it but not others, and was finally passed by the National Assembly in October 2000. Elections for approximately 255,000 *gacaca* judges took place in October 2001. Training for the judges followed in April and May 2002, with international support.

The System

Throughout the country *gacaca* tribunals have been created composed of persons of integrity elected by the inhabitants of cells, sectors, districts and provinces. Each prisoner (except those accused of category I crimes) will be brought before the tribunal in the community where he or she is alleged to have committed a crime. The entire community will be present and act as a "general assembly", discussing the alleged act or acts, providing testimony and counter-testimony, argument and counter-argument. The community will elect among those present 19 people to constitute the bench. These people must be of high moral standing, non-partisan and not related to those accused.

In the first phase, at the lowest level (the cell), *gacacas* will categorize all prisoners using the legal

The Structure of the **Gacaca** *Tribunals in Rwanda*			
Level	Number	Competence	Observations
Province	12	To judge appeals for category II crimes	The competence of *gacaca* tribunals to judge appeals for category II crimes, which carry a life sentence, has been controversial. Many believe such appeals should be heard before a formal tribunal
District	106	To judge category II crimes To judge appeals for category III crimes	Category II crimes were the major category in the traditional *gacaca* system, covering 80% of all cases
Sector	1,531	To judge category III crimes To judge appeals for category IV crimes	It is likely that there will be few category III crimes
Cell	9,189	To categorize the accused To list damages To judge category IV crimes	With respect to the categorization of crimes, a major innovation is the classification of rape as a category I crime, and therefore outside the scope of the *gacaca* tribunals The penalty for category IV crimes is restitution not imprisonment

categories established in the 1996 genocide law. In so doing they can use the case files drawn up against the prisoners insofar as that these dossiers exist. However, they are expected to draw primarily on testimony from the accused and the community assembly. In the second phase, *gacaca* tribunals at different levels will judge the accused, with each level having competence to judge appeals from the level below.

One of the innovative elements of the *gacaca* law is the confession procedure. Prisoners who confess and ask for forgiveness can receive dramatic reductions in penalties. Reductions are greatest for those who confess before the proceedings against them start, either while in prison or at the very beginning of the *gacaca* proceedings, when they are explicitly asked if they want to confess. Reductions are smaller for those who confess only during the *gacaca* procedure, while penalties are unchanged for those who do not confess at all but are found guilty. Additionally, up to half of the sentence of all convicted can be transmuted into community service (*travaux d'intérêt général*), the modalities of which are yet to be determined by further laws. To benefit from the community service provisions, the accused have to ask for forgiveness publicly.

Finally, the *gacaca* law greatly simplifies the reparation procedure for survivors of genocide. Part of the *gacaca* proceedings consists of a detailed listing of all the damages suffered by each survivor - destruction of property, physical harm or loss of relatives and providers. When the procedure is completed the claimants receive a statement of their losses and can use this to receive reparations from a public fund which will be set up for this purpose.

Merits and Limitations: the Debate

The aim of the *gacaca* system is twofold:
• to speed up the trials and empty the prisons; and
• to involve the community in establishing the truth and, through that, promoting reconciliation.

On paper, the system should be able to achieve these two aims much better than the formal justice system. With approximately 10,000 tribunals, it should be possible to judge all prisoners over a much shorter period of time. Given its decentralized nature, its relatively simple and recognizable procedures and the importance attached to local participation, the *gacaca* ought to be much better at involving the entire community, including victims. As a result it is potentially more victim-centred, and may thus have a more profound impact in terms of reconciliation. Finally, through the process of local discussion and fact-finding, *gacaca* proceedings may well develop a fuller picture of the nature of the violence that occurred and the responsibilities of different people.

The *gacaca* law contains a politically astutely designed set of incentives to encourage popular participation and acceptance. The confessions procedure, with its requirement for complete confession, including the names of all other people involved in the crime, is already setting in motion an avalanche of confessions, including the implication of other people, which is likely to lead to significant debates as people seek to explain themselves, implicate others, contextualize events and so on. Hence the *gacaca* procedure could produce more truth than the formal justice system has so far managed to do. In addition, the confessions procedure and the community service commutation option bring significant reductions in length of prison sentences, even for those found guilty. As a result, many people should be able to finally rejoin their families and get on with life. Finally, the streamlining of the reparation procedure provides a way to buy some (grudging) support from the genocide survivor organizations. However, the *gacaca* system suffers from significant limitations:
• It compromises on principles of justice as defined in internationally-agreed human rights and criminal law.
• It could set in motion social dynamics that are unexpected and possibly violent.

On the first point, there is no separation between prosecutor and judge, no legal counsel, no legally reasoned verdict, great encouragement of self-incrimination, and a potential for major divergences in the punishments awarded. In short, the modernized *gacaca* system seems to provide inadequate guarantees for impartiality, defence and equality before the law. Many foreign legal specialists and human rights observers have consequently been highly sceptical about the *gacaca* proposal. However, the alternatives they propose, such as guaranteeing the right to legal counsel, basically end up reinventing the same formal justice system which is clearly not adequate.

At the same time, a number of "real-world" arguments have been proposed which may be sufficient to defend the *gacaca* system even from within a human rights perspective.

The practice of formal justice, which has been maintained for years with massive international assistance, also violates human rights. The basic right to a speedy trial, reasonable detention times and decent conditions of detention is being violated under the current practice, and no one has any credible ideas about how to change this. In addition, approximately 60 per cent of those brought to justice so far have not had legal counsel, and for many who had it this counsel was of low quality - as were the prosecutors, investigators and judges. Hence, when discussing *gacaca*, we are not comparing a "clean" system that respects criminal and human rights law with one that violates it, but rather two practices that are both weak and incomplete. This may well be unavoidable: in the aftermath of mass violence, full, formal justice and complete adherence to human rights standards may be unattainable. For that reason, Ian Martin wrote about "the impossibility of justice" in Rwanda. All this is compounded by conditions of extreme poverty, continued profound social polarization, civil war and the absence of a strong historical tradition of independent justice.

It is possible to argue that the *gacaca* proposal actually respects the spirit of justice, if not the letter of criminal and human rights law. In other words, the practice of *gacaca* may well produce fair trials, but in an original, locally appropriate form. For example, while there is indeed no independent legal counsel, the play of argument and counter-argument and of witness and counter-witness by the community basically amounts to a fair defence, possibly producing better results than the formal justice system has until now been able to achieve. Similarly, if one accepts that people in the community by and large know the truth about who did and did not kill, and how, why, and with what degree of ruthlessness people killed others, *gacaca* is a superior tool to that which the formal justice system has produced.

The categories of persons most affected - the prisoners, the survivors and all Rwandan communities - seem to be largely in favour of the proposed *gacaca* system. Indeed, there is strong evidence that the prisoners themselves overwhelmingly favour *gacaca*. Admittedly, people who have spent many years imprisoned in horrendous conditions are likely to be willing to try anything that gives them a chance to get out of prison, and thus this argument cannot be given any decisive weight. Since the public discussions about the *gacaca* law began, confession rates have skyrocketed, and these confessions have taken the form of mini-*gacaca*s. Prisoners thus seem to be giving, by their own behaviour, a certain legitimacy to the idea of *gacaca* and, although their behaviour is certainly heavily constrained, this is of importance. In addition, research results suggest that the great majority of the population, both Hutu and Tutsi, prefer the *gacaca* process to the current system. While they do fear its potential excesses or abuses, they also judge that under current conditions the *gacaca* system is superior to the continuation of the current formal justice practice.

In short, there seem to be a number of real-world reasons that may render the human rights and criminal law violations embedded in the *gacaca* process less devastating than may appear, either because there are few real-world alternatives, or because the process can be argued to constitute a locally appropriate, and popularly legitimate, form of justice, with a higher potential for contributing to reconciliation. This does not mean that the human rights and criminal law violations inherent in the *gacaca* proposal become suddenly irrelevant; it does mean, however, that the *gacaca* proposal should not be dismissed outright as inappropriate or unjust.

On the second point, the potentially positive effects of *gacaca* in terms of community participation and victim-centredness could well be undone by local social dynamics. A number of such issues must be mentioned here - (a) interference by power-holders, (b) neglect of the gender dimension, (c) population movements, and (d) the broader political and social dynamics in Rwanda.

One factor that can reduce or destroy the potential of *gacaca* to produce a measure of truth, justice and reconciliation is interference by power-holders - whether the power they possess is that of the gun, of money or of the state. Even if most power-holders are successfully excluded from election to the *gacaca* benches, they will be present during the sessions as well as the periods in between. For whatever reasons - personal vengeance, political conflict, issues of land and property, family ties or simply ideology - they may seek to influence the proceedings. If they do so, the *gacaca* process will not yield justice or truth, and it will not contribute to reconciliation. Indeed, it may even do the opposite, rendering people even more distrustful, bitter and ready to embrace ideologies of hatred and contempt. The total absence of witness protection is worrying in this regard. Clearly, then, the capacity of the police to stop attempts at intimidation and manipulation will be a crucial variable.

There is an important gender issue: if no special efforts are made, women's participation in the *gacaca* process may well be minimal. The election of *gacaca* judges in October 2001 was a worrying sign in this regard. Relatively few women were elected, varying from one-third of all judges at cell level to only one-fifth at the provincial level. There is concern that women may also be neglected during discussions about restitution and compensation, contrary to the law. As a consequence of their precarious economic situation, widows are particularly vulnerable to family and social pressure. Given the prevalence of social taboos, the horrific sexual crimes suffered by many of these women are likely to go undiscussed. The absence of trauma counselling; the fact that a fixed representation of women on the *gacaca* benches was not accepted; and the generally weak position of women in Rwandan society are all cause for concern. On the other hand, women's groups, often made up of widows, have sprung up all across the territory, and they may well act as strong new voices.

Underlying a neo-traditional mechanism such as the modernized *gacaca* jurisdictions is a notion of community - the existence of rather close-knit groups of people sharing certain values and expectations (at a minimum the expectation that they will live together for a long time to come). This condition is not always met in present-day Rwanda. In many areas, a significant proportion of the population has arrived since the genocide, and thus the process of witnessing and confrontation may be incomplete. This situation is bound to be worst in urban areas. In general, the degree of distrust that still reigns may well make any notion of community a mirage.

Finally, the way in which the *gacaca* process unfolds will be profoundly affected by broader social and political trends, both nationally and locally. The extent to which people distrust or dislike the government (perhaps because they suffered heavily from the counter-offensives against rebel infiltration, or because they judge the central government to be increasingly unrepresentative and exclusive), the memories they carry about of the behaviour of government soldiers immediately after the genocide, and even general economic trends (e.g., the impact of localized famines) - all these factors are bound to influence people's willingness to engage in the risky process of *gacaca*. While these factors fall outside the design of the law, they may well be the key factors that determine its success or failure.

Concluding Remarks

If successful, the *gacaca* proceedings could produce great benefits. They may solve problems of the current slow judicial practice; they also have the potential to create significant benefits in terms of truth, reconciliation and even empowerment. For these reasons the international community, including many human rights organizations, has decided to cautiously support the process. These potential benefits follow from the central role played by local communities, as well as from the fact that the system involves many more people, particularly victims, and involves fewer time-consuming rules than the formal justice system. However, for precisely the same reasons, the *gacaca* system is also very vulnerable to unpredictable political, social, psychological and economic dynamics. The results are potentially dangerous.

At the time of writing (summer 2002), the pilot phase has begun, with tribunals taking place in at least one cell of each province. The full-scale phase is expected to start in late 2002. *Gacaca* is a worthy gamble, but a gamble nonetheless. It is simultaneously one of the best and one of the most dangerous opportunities for justice and reconciliation in Rwanda. But in a country like Rwanda there are no easy, cheap or clean solutions.

References and Further Reading

Centre de Gestion des Conflits. *Les Juridictions* gacaca *et les processus de réconciliation nationale*. Cahier no 3. Butare: Université nationale du Rwanda, 2001.

Martin, Ian. "Hard Choices After Genocide: Human Rights and Political Failures in Rwanda." In *Hard Choices: Moral Dilemmas in Humanitarian Intervention*, edited by Jonathan Moore. Lanham, Md., Rowman & Littlefield, 1998:157–176.

Sarkin, Jeremy. "Using *Gacaca* Community Courts in Rwanda to Prosecute Genocide Suspects: Are Issues of Expediency and Efficiency More Important Than Those of Due Process, Fairness and Reconciliation?" (draft paper, unpublished, 2001).

Vandeginste, Stef. "Les juridictions *Gacaca* et la poursuite des suspects du génocide et des crimes contre l'humanité au Rwanda." *Dialogue* 220 (2001)

See also articles in http://www.Diplomatiejudiciaire.com

CHAPTER 8

Truth-Telling

MARK FREEMAN AND PRISCILLA B. HAYNER

INTERNATIONAL CENTER FOR TRANSITIONAL JUSTICE*

8.1 Introduction

Confronting the past in a reconciliatory way requires the mobilization of a variety of techniques. Historical accounting via truth-telling is one of the most important steps in the reconciliation process. But how does seeking accuracy about the past help a society to move from a divided past to a shared future?

The term "reconciliation" is widely used but not often clearly defined or understood. A study by the Johannesburg Centre for the Study of Violence and Reconciliation of the impact of the South African Truth and Reconciliation Commission (TRC) on one community showed that residents of the area had very different ideas of what reconciliation meant. A common underlying theme involved building a relationship between groups or individuals, but the definitions of that relationship differed depending on culture, particular experience of human rights abuse, position in the political structure and personal circumstances. There does, however, appear to be generally uniform agreement among most experts that reconciliation is more a process than an achievable objective.

In the context of truth commission work, perhaps the most important distinction that must be made is that between individual reconciliation and national or political reconciliation. While a truth commission may be a useful mechanism in advancing the latter to the extent that it may help prevent basic points of fact from continuing to be a source of conflict or bitterness among political elites, reconciliation on an individual level is much more complex and probably more difficult to achieve by means of a truth commission. Forgiveness, healing and reconciliation are deeply personal processes, and each person's needs and reactions to peacemaking and truth-telling may be different.

Nevertheless, many continue to assert that it is necessary to know the truth in order to advance reconciliation. It is of course possible to point to evidence and to quote survivors to show that this is the case: sometimes it is, for some people or in some circumstances. Yet it is easy to imagine that the opposite may also be true, or that reconciliation may be more affected by factors other than knowing or acknowledging the truth about past wrongs. For example, true reconciliation might depend on a clear end to the threat of further violence; acknowledgement by the state or by perpetrators of the injuries suffered; a reparation programme for those injured; attention to structural inequalities and the basic material needs of victimized communities; the existence of natural linkages in society that bring formerly opposing parties together; or, most simply, the passage of time.

Truth may be only one of many possible elements in the pursuit of reconciliation.

Thus, truth may be only one of many possible elements in the pursuit of reconciliation. Transitions in places such as Spain and Mozambique suggest that a substantial degree of national reconciliation can sometimes occur even in the absence of a formal truth-seeking process. Whether reconciliation in

* The International Center for Transitional Justice is a nongovernmental organization based in New York which provides technical assistance to countries in transition. The authors can be reached at the ICTJ at 20 Exchange Place, 3rd Floor, New York, NY 10005; 917-438-9300; phayner@ictj.org or mfreeman@ictj.org

these and other cases can or will be as genuine or as sustainable as in places where truth commissions were instituted remains very much an open question.

8.2 Instruments of Truth-Seeking

One of the most popular transitional mechanisms in recent years is what has come to be known, in its generic form, as the truth commission. Section 8.3 is entirely devoted to this major instrument for dealing with a painful past. Although truth commissions were developed only recently, their potential contribution has been widely recognized, to the extent that transitional societies today are almost certain to consider establishing them. In recent years two major truth commissions, in Guatemala and South Africa, have brought considerable attention to the subject of official truth-seeking. They are examined in the case study at the end of this chapter. New commissions are under way or very recently concluded, as of mid-2002, in places such as Panama, Uruguay, the Federal Republic of Yugoslavia (FRY), Nigeria, East Timor and Peru, and are in the process of formation in Sierra Leone and Ghana.

Because truth commissions deal with many events that could also be the subject of judicial trial, many observers confuse truth commissions with courts, but truth commissions should not be equated with judicial bodies, nor should they be considered to be a replacement for judicial trials. Truth commissions are non-judicial bodies and as such clearly have fewer powers than do courts. They have no power to put anyone in prison, they cannot enforce their recommendations and most have not even had the power to compel anyone to come forward to answer questions.

While this chapter focuses largely on the experience and challenges of truth commissions, the importance of other truth-seeking mechanisms should not be overlooked. There are at least three other kinds of truth-seeking inquiries into human rights violations that can be contrasted with truth commissions. All are important forms of inquiry in their own right. In addition, in some contexts they may constitute the only available mechanism for truth-seeking, or perhaps the most appropriate one.

In some countries, governments have established "historical commissions". These are present-day inquiries into state abuses that took place and ended many years, or even decades, ago. In contrast to truth commissions, historical commissions are not established as part of a political transition and may not even pertain to today's political leadership or practices. Instead, they serve to clarify historical truths and pay respect to previously unrecognized victims or their descendants. Another distinction is that, in contrast to truth commissions, historical commissions have generally not investigated instances of widespread political repression but have instead focused on practices that may have affected specific ethnic, racial or other groups. Examples include the US Commission on Wartime Relocation and Internment of Civilians, and the Canadian Royal Commission on Aboriginal Peoples.

A number of examples of official or semi-official inquiries into past human rights violations share the main characteristics of truth commissions but are distinguishable by the fact that they are less independent of political processes, or more limited in scope or authority, or undertaken only as a precursor to a fully-fledged truth commission. Examples of such commissions include the various parliamentary inquiries and congressional investigative committees established by legislatures around the world, the inquiry undertaken by the National Commissioner for the Protection of Human Rights in Honduras in 1993 regarding disappearances in that country, the investigations carried out by the Northern Ireland Victims Commissioner in the late 1990s, or the various event-specific tribunals of inquiry that are commonly established in Commonwealth countries and elsewhere. Other forms of official or semi-official inquiry that overlap with truth commissions include a variety of international inquiries, often sponsored by the UN or by regional organizations, which investigate and report on war victims or national cases of severe repression. Examples of these inquiries include the Organization of African Unity (OAU, now the African Union), International Panel of Eminent Personalities to Investigate the 1994 Genocide in Rwanda and the Surrounding Events, and the various war crimes commissions and bodies established by the UN to look into violations committed in places such as East Timor, Rwanda and the former Yugoslavia. Generally speaking, these inquiries have the advantage of being relatively easy to establish in comparison to a truth commission, and of being more official and powerful than a purely non-governmental project. At the same time they may head off calls for a more independent, comprehensive or robust inquiry, notwithstanding the fact that limitations in their independence, scope or authority will often result in a less than complete picture of the past.

There have been a great number of non-governmental projects which, like truth commissions, have documented violations and patterns of abuse of a previous regime - generally at great personal risk. These projects are usually undertaken by national human rights organizations, sometimes with church backing, and have sometimes produced remarkable results. Prominent examples include the work of organizations such as the Service for Peace and Justice in Latin America (Servicio Paz y Justicia en América Latina, SERPAJ) in Uruguay in the 1980s and the Inter-Diocesan Project for the Recovery of the Historical Memory (Proyecto Interdiocesano para la Recuperación de la Memoria Histórica, REMHI) in Guatemala in the 1990s. In contexts where official truth-seeking is not possible, non-governmental projects are particularly important because they may provide the only reliable documented record of victims and past violations. At the same time, non-governmental projects lack the very important attributes of many modern truth commissions such as powers of investigation, guaranteed access to government records, personal immunity for commissioners and the benefit of a state obligation to implement or at least report on the implementation of final recommendations.

8.3 Understanding Truth Commissions

The purpose of this section is not to survey or examine all or even most of the past and current truth commissions in the world. Instead it seeks to explain in practical terms what a truth commission is, how it operates and what it can potentially achieve for a country in the process of democratic transition.

The section is divided into six subsections. Subsection 8.3.1 defines what a truth commission is and then distinguishes commissions from other truth-seeking mechanisms. Subsection 8.3.2 explores the potential benefits, as well as the potential risks, of having a truth commission. Subsection 8.3.3 provides a brief review of the various constraining and enabling factors that can affect the establishment and operation of a truth commission. Subsection 8.3.4 briefly explains how a truth commission typically is sponsored while subsection 8.3.5 provides a review of the principal design concerns in establishing a truth commission. Subsection 8.3.6 takes a close look at how truth commissions operate and explores a few of the more difficult issues that they must confront. The chapter concludes with a comparative examination of the truth commissions of South Africa and Guatemala.

8.3.1 What is a Truth Commission?

Generally, the term "truth commission" refers to bodies that share the following characteristics.
At least 25 official truth commissions have been established around the world since 1974, though

Truth commissions generally:

• are temporary bodies, usually in operation from one to two years;

• are officially sanctioned, authorized or empowered by the state and, in some cases, by the armed opposition as well as in a peace accord;

• are non-judicial bodies that enjoy a measure of de jure independence;

• are usually created at a point of political transition, either from war to peace or from authoritarian rule to democracy;

• focus on the past;

• investigate patterns of abuses and specific violations committed over a period of time, not just a single specific event;

• complete their work with the submission of a final report that contains conclusions and recommendations; and

• focus on violations of human rights and sometimes of humanitarian norms as well.

they have gone by many different names. There have been "commissions on the disappeared" in Argentina, Uganda and Sri Lanka; "truth and justice commissions" in Haiti and Ecuador; "truth and reconciliation commissions" in Chile, South Africa, Sierra Leone and now the Federal Republic of Yugoslavia; and most recently a "commission for reception, truth and reconciliation" in East Timor. Although these commissions all fit within the definition above, it should

At least 25 official truth commissions have been established around the world since 1974.

be noted that some of them did not at the time of their operation consider themselves to be truth commissions, nor were they understood to be such by the wider public.

8.3.2 Potential Benefits and Risks
Potential Benefits

Although truth commissions may not be appropriate in every context, they have the potential to generate many benefits for societies in transition. The following list of potential benefits may assist in initial reflections on the role and focus of a truth commission while a new commission is in development:

Commissions can help establish the truth about the past. They can establish a record of the past that is accurate, detailed, impartial and official. This record can serve to counter the fictitious or exaggerated accounts of the past that were propagated by the previous regime (or other parties to a past conflict) and bring the true scale and impact of a violent past to the public consciousness. In addition, commissions can locate the whereabouts of missing victims who may have been forcibly "disappeared" or buried clandestinely.

Truth commissions can promote the accountability of perpetrators of human

A truth commission can:

• help establish the truth about the past;

• promote the accountability of perpetrators of human rights violations;

• provide a public platform for victims;

• inform and catalyse public debate;

• recommend victim reparation;

• recommend necessary legal and institutional reforms;

• promote social reconciliation; and

• help to consolidate a democratic transition.

rights violations. They can complement the work of criminal prosecutors by gathering, organizing and preserving evidence that can be used in prosecutions. They can also build a case for and recommend forms of accountability short of criminal sanction, such as civil liability, removal from office, restitution or community service schemes.

Commissions can provide a public platform for victims. They can put victims - long ignored and forgotten by the public - at the forefront and centre of the transition process. This can help to make victims whole again, both individually and as a group, and give them a sense of personal vindication. In addition, by providing a public platform for victims to speak in their own voices, commissions can help to educate the public about the individual human impact of past crimes and thereby build support for further victim-centred transitional justice initiatives such as reparation programmes.

Commissions can inform and catalyse public debate. They can help stimulate public deliberation on the complex array of moral, political and legal issues that must be addressed during a transition process. This can be achieved by engaging with the public through commission activities and encouraging broad media coverage. In addition, truth commissions can themselves serve as a model for the public, as the public begins to take up again the critical practice of discussing controversial political subjects without fear of recrimination or resort to violence. Commissions can also serve as independent, impartial and public arbiters if and when members of the previous regime grossly misrepresent or distort events of the past.

Commissions can recommend victim reparation. They can build a case for reparation as a necessary form of compensation for past abuses and for ongoing psychological, physical and economic injuries experienced by victims. They can also establish fair and effective definitions and categories of "victim" for the purpose of financial reparation or benefits to follow. In addition, commissions can help to repair the moral dignity of victims by carrying out their work in a manner that is both sensitive to and acknowledges the harm suffered by them. Commissions can also make creative and appropriate suggestions regarding symbolic forms of reparation for victims, such as memorials, reburials and commemorative ceremonies.

Commissions can recommend necessary legal and institutional reforms. Through their investigations they can provide clear evidence of how particular institutions individually and collectively failed to uphold human rights protection in the past. In addition, commissions can identify and recommend specific legal and institutional reforms that will enable the country to achieve the long-term social, economic and political objectives that are essential to ensuring a better future. Such reforms

> Truth commissions can promote reconciliation by providing a safe and impartial forum for direct restorative justice processes.

may include, for example, strengthened civilian oversight of intelligence agencies and the military; new appointment, tenure and disciplinary rules for the judiciary; the establishment of an independent and well-financed prosecutor's office; redesign of the electoral and political system; land reform; and new human rights training programmes for the police and armed forces.

Commissions can promote reconciliation. They can promote tolerance and understanding by allowing conflicting parties to hear each other's grievances and suffering. This may help build empathy, thereby deterring acts of vengeance and countering the rivalries and hatreds arising from past events. Commissions can also provide a safe and impartial forum for direct restorative justice processes in which the victim, the offender and/or other individual or community members can actively participate in the mediation and resolution of past grievances of a less serious nature. In addition, commissions can recommend practical and fair measures for the necessary reintegration of certain categories of offenders back into society.

Commissions can help to consolidate a democratic transition. By all the above means, they can signal a formal break with a dark and violent past, and the transition to a more open, peaceful and democratic future. If they are successful, truth commissions can have the effect of weakening anti-democratic actors who might otherwise continue to pursue their goals outside the democratic process.

Reasons Why Truth Commissions Are Not Always Used

Just as truth commissions have the potential to generate many benefits for societies in transition, they also have the potential to produce certain harms. In fact, precisely to avoid specific harms, in transitional contexts ranging from Spain in the 1970s and Cambodia in the 1980s to Mozambique in the 1990s, civil society and democratic political leaders have sometimes consciously opted against any attempt at formally establishing the truth about the past. The hesitation to engage in official truth-seeking initiatives in these and other cases generally appears to be based on one or more of the following considerations:

Fear of ongoing or renewed violence or war. There is a perception that violence would increase, war could return or the current violence or war would not end if old crimes were revisited.

Ongoing conflict. The utility of a truth commission in a context where an intense armed conflict is ongoing is particularly dubious because it would be virtually impossible to achieve the appearance of neutrality, or to ensure victim and witness participation and security. In addition, geographical access as well as access to key information is likely to be severely limited in such a context. At the same time, even in the middle of a conflict, it may be useful to begin to deliberate and plan some form of official truth-seeking to take place following the ending of the conflict and the beginning of a transition.

Lack of political interest. There is little or no interest on the part of the political leadership in truth-seeking and a lack of pressure from significant non-governmental actors.

Other urgent priorities. The government and public want to focus on survival and rebuilding in the aftermath of extensive destruction.

Insufficient capacity. There is a lack of resources or basic institutional structures to support a formal truth-seeking process.

Alternative mechanisms or preferences. The indigenous national culture is one that eschews confronting past crimes, or there are existing community-based mechanisms that can better respond to the recent violence.

These all appear to be reasons why societies in transition forgo official truth-seeking and why it may be preferable or necessary to focus instead on non-governmental truth-seeking mechanisms. It will, however, often be a difficult decision, particularly if a number of victims are calling for a truth commission. Certainly, one should treat with considerable scepticism any decision to forgo official truth-seeking that is taken with little or no public consultation, or by parties who have an interest in preventing investigation of the past.

Potential Risks

Improper motives. Even where a truth commission is established, there is no certainty that it has been established with the proper motives or that it will achieve the many potential benefits discussed above. For example, it is possible that a government may perceive a truth commission as a vehicle for the indirect pursuit of political vendettas or as a way to delegate responsibility to others for difficult tasks that it is not willing to carry out itself. It may also make the commission deliberately weak and thereby make it easier to challenge or reject the results later. Cynical governments may also establish truth commissions to try to insulate themselves against criticism from victims that not enough has been done to redress the human rights abuses of the past.

Bias. In addition, commissioners themselves may approach commission work with a bias that would make an objective and complete account of the past impossible.

Unrealistic expectations. On a different level, commissions must also be careful not to foster unrealistic expectations on the part of victims and the public generally, which can lead to renewed frustrations and further distress for victims.

In fact, experience to date shows that few past commissions have suffered from the first two possible risks listed above. In particular, where there are a strong civil society and vocal and independent media in a given country, many of these risks can be mitigated through public pressure. None of these risks is unavoidable. However, in many transitional contexts neither civil society nor the media will be particularly strong. As a consequence, these risks must be understood in advance by those who would, in good faith, advocate the use of a truth commission.

8.3.3 The Political Context

Because truth commissions are created at points of political transition, there are a variety of constraining factors and enabling factors that can affect their establishment and operation.

Constraining Factors

Constraining factors tend to be greatest where the transition process is relatively non-consensual, although they may be present to greater or lesser degrees in more consensual processes.

Many political transitions are the result of bitter negotiation and may depend on the opposition conceding amnesties or "reserve domains" of power to the outgoing regime as the price of obtaining formal control of the state. It is also typical for there to be widespread destruction of evidence of crimes by the outgoing regime. There may be ongoing and legitimate public fears about testifying (and even private intimidation and threats against witnesses) that can significantly hamper the ability of a truth commission to get to the truth and force the commission to become a private and in some cases confidential process, rather than an open and public process. Weakness or corruption in the administration of justice and lack of cooperation from the police or army can make a truth commission something of a paper tiger, since commissions must rely to some extent on support and cooperation from key actors in the principal institutions responsible for the administration of justice. Finally, the establishment and operation of a commission can be undermined where there is widespread social identification with the perpetrators, rather than the victims, or when there are widespread concerns about scuttling a fragile process of demobilization, disarmament and reintegration.

Enabling Factors

Enabling factors tend to be strongest where the transition process is relatively free and consensual, although they may be present to greater or lesser degrees in constrained transitions as well. The following factors are particularly important:
• public support for the establishment of a truth commission; the presence of a vigorous and engaged civil society (and in particular of strong victims' groups, human rights groups, religious leaders and intellectuals);
• widespread social identification with the victims of the abuses; vocal and independent media; and
• persistent international attention and pressure.

In the absence of these factors, a truth commission may not be useful, desirable or effective. Indeed, public "ownership" and the active participation of certain key social sectors (both national and international) are critical ingredients in ensuring a successful commission.

8.3.4 Sponsorship

Truth commissions tend to be created in one of the following ways:
• the executive branch of government passes a decree establishing the commission;
• the legislative branch of government passes legislation establishing the commission; or
• the government and armed opposition sign an agreement authorizing the establishment of a commission (and there may or may not be a subsequent decree or legislation).

In many countries, the way in which a truth commission is created will have a direct effect on what its powers can be. For example, in democratic countries with presidential or semi-presidential forms of governance, the executive branch of government usually cannot, on its own, confer search and seizure or even subpoena powers; that tends to be the exclusive preserve of the legislative branch. The same may also be true in respect of powers of reporting, including the question of whether the commission can make binding recommendations. Similarly, who establishes the commission can affect the allocation of funding, since one branch of government may have greater access to resources and a greater commitment to the commission's work.

8.3.5 Design

Some of the principal issues involved in establishing a truth commission are:
• the process of selection for and ultimate composition of the commission;
• the design of the commission's mandate and powers; and
• decisions about material and human resources.

Composition

Perhaps more than any other single factor, the persons selected to manage a truth commission will determine its ultimate success or failure. In fact, several commissions have run into serious problems that were clearly rooted in weak management by commissioners. Although commissioners are generally not involved in the day-to-day administration of a commission, they usually direct investigations, shape commission policy and have the last word regarding what will go into the final report. As the public face of the commission, the commissioners' personal and political authority can also be critical in dealing with recalcitrant authorities.

The members of most truth commissions have been appointed through procedures that relied on the good judgement of the appointing authority, with little to no consultation of civil society. This was the case, for example, in Argentina, Chad, Chile, Haiti and Uganda. In more recent years, however, the selection of commissioners has increasingly been conducted through more creative and consultative processes. The key lesson from past truth commissions is that a commission will generally garner greater public and international support where its members are selected through a consultative process and where an honest attempt is made to ensure a fair balance in the representation of political views, ethnic or religious groups and gender.

A powerful example of the consultative approach to commissioner selection is that of the South African TRC. A selection committee was formed that included representatives of human rights organizations. The committee called for nominations from the public and ultimately received some 300 nominations, which it then trimmed down to 50 people to be interviewed. The interviews took place in public session and were closely followed by the press. The selection committee eventually narrowed the finalists to a list of 25 candidates, which it sent to President Nelson Mandela for final selection. To provide geographical and political balance, Mandela added two members who did not go through the full selection process.

> A commission will generally garner greater public and international support where its members are selected through a consultative process and where an honest attempt is made to ensure a fair balance.

Another good example comes from Sierra Leone. There, the statute establishing the truth commission designated the Special Representative of the UN Secretary-General as selection coordinator and directed him to call for nominations from the public. At the same time, a selection panel was formed with representatives appointed by the former armed opposition, the president, the governmental human rights commission, the non-governmental inter-religious council and a coalition of human rights groups. This panel interviewed the finalists, ranked and commented on each and submitted the evaluations to the selection coordinator, who then selected the final four national candidates (the three international members of the commission were selected by the UN High Commissioner for Human Rights (UNHCHR). The lists of both national and international commissioners recommended were then submitted to the president of Sierra Leone for appointment. The commissioners were appointed in May 2002.

A similar consultative selection process was also employed in East Timor in establishing its truth commission.

Mandate and Powers

Every truth commission to date has been unique, differing in important ways from commissions in other countries. Truth commissions are inherently flexible and each new one can be crafted to respond to the specific needs and circumstances of the country in which it will work. While much can be learned from prior experience, including from the specific language used in the truth commission legislation of other countries, it is essential that any new truth commission be derived from an indigenous process of strategic planning and reflection on the needs and opportunities of the particular country.

In recent years, it has become clear that truth commissions enjoy greater legitimacy where the

> Truth commissions enjoy greater legitimacy where the process of defining their powers and mandate includes active involvement from many different sectors of society.

process of defining their powers and mandate includes active involvement from many different sectors of society. Although there is often a need to move quickly at a point of transition, it is important to attempt to build a broad base of support for the commission among several important constituencies. In some countries where the government has established a truth commission with virtually no consultation with civil society, the commissions have suffered as a result. For example, in Guatemala it took time and considerable effort for the truth commission to gain the backing of the religious and advocacy groups on which it depended to undertake its work.

In terms of the actual content of a commission's mandate, the sponsors of the commission - whether the executive or legislative branch of government or the parties to an armed conflict - will typically give consideration to a number of key issues. Among the most important will be the following:

Objectives. The terms of reference of the commission should generally set out its main objectives. These might include, for example, establishing the truth about the past, contributing to national reconciliation, making recommendations to help victims and preventing a relapse into war or authoritarian rule. The objectives will serve as the guide for the commission's work and the yardstick against which it will be assessed.

Period of operation. The terms of reference will also need to establish start and end dates for the operation of the commission. These dates can be flexible, allowing for one or more possible short-term extensions. However, the total possible period of operation must be fixed, otherwise the commission can go on for too long, lose focus and ultimately cease to interest the public. Past experience indicates that a time frame of 1–2 years of operation is generally desirable.

Types of violation under investigation. The terms of reference should set out what types of violation the commission is to examine. Human rights violations, of course, tend to be the focus of truth commission work; however, there are many different types of human rights violations and often too many for a single commission to tackle meaningfully in such a short period of time. Accordingly, the commission might be restricted to examining or prioritizing those violations that were most prevalent or considered to have been most serious or pernicious in that particular society. Such prioritization can, however, create understandable frustration on the part of victims of those violations that are excluded from the commission's mandate. When that is the case, it is essential that other public policies and mechanisms be implemented to assist those persons.

Period of time under consideration. The specific span of time the commission is to inquire into should be clear from the start. This is often a controversial aspect of a com mission's mandate, particularly where there is a sense of victimization on the part of both or all sides of a past conflict. Some commissions have examined violations that took place over a 30-year period, while others have examined violations that occurred over much shorter periods of time. The particular span of time will generally be chosen on the basis of those periods in the nation's history when the worst or the greatest number of violations took place, and accordingly will often correspond to periods of civil war or authoritarian rule. To avoid the appearance of bias, it is generally important for the time span chosen to be consecutive and not broken up to focus only on selected periods in a nation's history.

Functions of the commission. The key functions of the commission through which it will pursue its objectives should also be indicated in the terms of reference. Normally these include publicizing its mandate, carrying out research and investigation, and submitting a final report setting out its findings and recommendations. Some commissions have also been directed to identify the individuals responsible for specific violations; in other cases commissioners have either been precluded from "naming names" or left with the discretion to decide for themselves. Truth commissions are also increasingly being authorized to hold public hearings, inspired in large measure by the power of the TRC experience in South Africa. In a few cases, truth commissions have also been asked to provide some form of emotional support or counselling to victims and witnesses, who may experience trauma in the course of recounting their stories.

Powers. The powers to be given to a commission will help to determine its strength and reach. At a minimum, commissions generally need to be able to interview anyone who can provide relevant information, receive the cooperation of public authorities and carry out any necessary on-site visits (ideally unannounced). Increasingly, however, commissions are being given powers that extend well beyond those just mentioned to include powers of subpoena, search and seizure powers, and in some cases even witness protection. The conferral of such powers must be carefully balanced against the need to preserve the non-judicial character of the commission process. Each addition of such powers moves the process further away from that of a truth commission towards a court process.

Sanctions. The commission should generally be given sufficient power to ensure that sanctions - perhaps fines, imprisonment or both - can be brought against anyone who improperly interferes with or knowingly provides false information to it, or fails to respond to a subpoena without appropriate justification.

Follow-up. The terms of reference should ideally set out what obligations, if any, the government will have both to publicize the commission's final report and to implement its recommendations. Consideration will also have to be given to the auditing, safekeeping and general subsequent use to be made of the commission's files and records after it has ceased its operations.

Resource Issues

Even the best-designed mandate will not ensure a successful truth commission if it lacks adequate material and human resources. This is not to suggest that truth commissions are expensive undertakings. In fact, with the exception of the truth commissions in South Africa and Guatemala (which both had multimillion dollar budgets), truth commission budgets have all been less than USD 5 million and frequently less than USD 1 million. However, as the terms of reference of truth commissions become increasingly sophisticated and as the international community takes an increasing interest in these bodies, the average budget of new commissions has risen to USD 5–10 million. This is true of several of the commissions now in operation or being set up, including those in Peru, East Timor, Ghana and Sierra Leone. In terms of the source of funds, the trend is to combine national government funds with funds received from donor states and private foundations, where available. Office space and equipment are generally provided directly by the national government.

> The average budget of new commissions has risen to USD 5–10 million.

The truth commissions in South Africa and Guatemala hired more staff than previous commissions - over 200 multidisciplinary staff each, including both nationals and non-nationals. Current commissions have followed a similar approach to staffing, although budget constraints may limit the numbers of persons hired. In those cases, greater reliance may be placed on staff seconded from the government.

8.3.6 Truth Commissions in Operation
The Preparatory Phase

It is generally a good idea for truth commission members to try to devote their first weeks after inauguration to essential preparatory tasks. These may include:
• developing a staffing plan and hiring staff;
• drafting internal regulations and policies;
• adopting a work plan;
• designing and installing an effective database for the storage, organization and retrieval of records and data;
• preliminary background research;
• collecting existing documentation from national and international NGOs, the UN, foreign governments and other sources;

- designing a public education campaign; and
- fund-raising and budget preparation.

Undertaking these preparatory activities in a timely manner can serve the commission extremely well in both the short and the long term. Indeed, past experience suggests that a commission that does not get off to a good start will lose precious time and political capital in the first year of its life.

Principal Activities Of A Truth Commission During Its Lifetime

Outreach

Public outreach by a truth commission is critically important. The nature and the extent of a commission's outreach efforts will profoundly affect its access to information, its effectiveness in addressing the needs of victims, its ability to manage public expectations and its general reputation in the eyes of the public. Some of these efforts can be carried out directly by the commission through holding public information meetings and through the preparation, publication and dissemination of pamphlets, videos and publications in popular form about the role and mandate of the commission. The commission can also achieve its outreach goals by engagement with and effective use of NGOs, local grass-roots organizations and the media. Relations with civil society and the media can, however, be complicated by the fact that they will often play a dual role vis-à-vis the commission, working simultaneously as partner to it and as critical watchdog of its procedures and actions.

> *Public outreach by a truth commission is critically important.*

Statement-Taking

Most truth commissions collect most of their information through private, closed-door meetings, usually by commission staff taking testimony from individual victims in one-to-one encounters. This process is referred to as "statement-taking" and typically involves both a meeting and the filling out of a statement form by the deponent. Statement-taking is important in at least two ways: it furthers the goal of establishing the truth about the past; and it provides an opportunity for victims to come forward and recount their traumatic experiences in a sympathetic and generally safe environment.

Because of the sensitive nature of the process and the often horrific character of the information involved, statement-taking requires staff to exhibit concentration, respect and emotional control, and should generally involve intensive training before it is undertaken. Statement-takers need to know when and how to listen and how to respect the often unexpected rhythm and logic of a person's memory. Although there can be a tension between the desire to focus only on the specific type of information being sought by the commission and the need to allow the deponent to tell the story in his or her own way, a statement-taker must find a way to strike the right balance.

For most victims and witnesses, a statement-taker will be the only personal contact they have with the commission, and as a result the impressions they leave on deponents and communities are especially significant and enduring.

Research and Investigation

Research units and police-like investigation units are increasingly becoming a part of the structure of truth commissions. Such units, however, tend to form only part of commissions with large budgets and robust mandates, such as the TRC in South Africa. Research units tend to be relatively small but staffed by persons with strong research skills and familiarity with national think tanks, NGOs, local archives and other key sources of information. In contrast, investigative units may include people with legal backgrounds or even experience in law enforcement. Many truth commissions combine research and investigation into one department, which has many advantages.

Data Processing

Truth commissions have to deal with enormous volumes of information which must be organized and systematized. This requires, among other things, an effective database for the storage, organization and retrieval of records and data. Generally speaking, commissions which do rigorous data collection and analysis will be better able to defend their findings on scientific grounds. A strong data management system will help arrive at a "big picture" analysis of historical patterns that can show, for example, the exact ratio of violations committed by one side to those committed by the other. In terms of staffing, commissions should hire a programmer to write and maintain the basic software and to extract the data in formats appropriate for the analysts. They will also need professional statisticians (or social scientists fluent in statistical methods) to review the data before it is published, and a team of data processors to input all the information received by the commission.

Public Hearings

Most past truth commissions have not held public hearings. There is, however, an increasing trend to give commissions a mandate to do this. This is the case for the new commissions in Peru, East Timor and Sierra Leone, to name only a few.

There are persuasive reasons for a commission to hold public hearings. By giving victims and survivors a chance to tell their story before a public audience - particularly where the hearings are aired on television or the radio - a commission can formally acknowledge past wrongs, encourage public understanding and sympathy for victims, reduce the likelihood of certain sectors of society continuing to deny the truth, and enhance the transparency of its work. Public hearings can also help to shift a truth commission's focus from product (i.e., its final report) to process, by engaging the public as audience, encouraging press coverage of its issues over a longer period of time and generally stimulating an authentic national discourse about the past.

The truth commissions in Uganda, Sri Lanka and Nigeria have all held public hearings, but it was the public hearings of the South African TRC that had the greatest international impact. Not only were there hundreds of days of public hearings; there was also a unique diversity in the types of hearing held, including victim hearings, amnesty hearings, special thematic hearings (e.g., on women and children), special event hearings (e.g., on the 1976 Soweto student uprising), institutional hearings (e.g., with the legal and health sectors) and political party hearings. Lured by the powerful example of South Africa, a number of analysts have recommended that all truth commissions should hold proceedings in public.

There may, however, be legitimate reasons not to do so, including security risks for commissioners and victims, time and resource constraints, and concerns about "judicializing" commission proceedings. At the same time, public "truth" proceedings are potentially powerful enough to at least warrant consideration by all commissions.

Emotional Support

Truth commissions seem to satisfy a clear need on the part of some victims to tell their stories, be listened to and ultimately be healed in some way. For others, however, the process can lead to re-traumatization, which may in some cases have severe after-effects.

Past truth commissions have not generally given this issue enough attention, but this is starting to change. For example, in South Africa, the TRC hired four mental health professionals, provided training in trauma counselling for staff and hired "briefers" who had the job of providing constant support to those giving testimony at public hearings. It is worth noting that commission staff can themselves be traumatized by the process and require emotional support. In many societies, however, standard psychological counselling may not be the appropriate model for helping victims, for cultural reasons or because of resource constraints. The ideal source of support in some places, therefore, may be collaboration with community organizations, traditional healers, religious institutions or self-help support groups.

> *Truth commissions can lead to re-traumatization. Past truth commissions have not generally given this issue enough attention.*

Final Reports

Often the defining moment for a truth commission is the completion and publication of its final report. Final reports have often constituted the enduring legacy of commissions and have also been used as a resource for human rights education or for subsequent prosecutions. If they are well documented and methodologically sound, final reports can serve as a critical guard against revisionism. In many ways, however, the impact of a final report may depend less on its content than on a variety of surrounding factors, including when and how the report is publicized, how widely it is distributed, how much coverage it receives in the media and whether there are both traditional and alternative presentations of the findings.

Although the content and format of reports will vary, final reports usually contain a section on findings and a section on recommendations. The findings section will typically identify the causes and patterns of past violations, as well as the victims of those violations. In some cases, individual and/or institutional responsibility for violations may also be reported - a practice which is examined in greater detail in the subsection on *Naming Names and Due Process* below. There may sometimes be a tension within a commission between a preference for a legal or empirical approach and an emphasis on a narrative, historical account.

In addition to reporting findings, truth commissions usually make recommendations, aimed variously at providing assistance or redress to victims, making necessary constitutional, legal and institutional reforms in order to prevent future relapse into war or authoritarian rule, and facilitating the consolidation of democracy and the rule of law. In many cases, commissions have also made recommendations for follow-up measures to ensure their timely and effective implementation. Unfortunately, the record on implementation of commission recommendations is not encouraging.

Naming Names and Due Process

A number of truth commissions have had the power to publicly name those individuals found to be responsible for human rights crimes. These include the commissions in El Salvador, Chad and South Africa. Others have not been expressly granted this power but have been creative in finding indirect ways of naming individuals. For example, some commissions have effectively identified individual perpetrators by printing (unchallenged) direct quotations of witnesses or victims that mention the perpetrators' names, or by identifying those who headed particular units or regions where particular violations took place, thereby making perpetrator identities easily discoverable. In other cases, attribution of individual responsibility has been effected through deliberate or unintentional press leaks by the commission.

Few of the issues surrounding truth commissions have attracted as much controversy as this question of "naming names", and the issue remains a point of tension for those crafting new bodies. The disagreement is between two contradictory principles, both of which can be strongly argued by rights advocates. The first is that due process requires that individuals accused of crimes be allowed to defend themselves before being pronounced guilty. Due process is violated if a commission, which is different from a court of law and does not have the same strict procedures, names individuals responsible for certain crimes. The second principle is that telling the full truth requires naming persons responsible for human rights crimes when there is clear evidence of their culpability.

The question therefore becomes: What standards and procedures of due process should apply to individuals who may be named in a report? Should they be informed of the allegations against them and told that the commission intends to name them in a public report? Should they be given the opportunity to respond to the evidence against them and offer a defence? Should the commission be obligated to state clearly that its own conclusions about individual responsibility do not amount to criminal guilt? These are the sorts of issue that commissions must grapple with.

Past experience seems to suggest that the best practice is to allow commissions to name names but ultimately to leave it at their discretion whether or not to do so. This is because there may be a range of legitimate reasons for not naming names. For example, there may be real security risks for commissioners, victims or witnesses, or there may be due process problems such as a lack of sufficient evidence to publicly condemn an individual, or an inability to afford proper notice or procedural safeguards for those accused of violations.

> Few of the issues surrounding truth commissions have attracted as much controversy as the question of "naming names".

If a commission decides not to name perpetrators, it should at least be required to set out its reasons for not doing so, and these reasons must be politically, morally and legally defensible. Where a commission does decide to name names, it must clearly state that its findings do not amount to a finding of legal or criminal guilt. As to the due process entitlements that should apply, it seems that at a minimum persons who might be named should be (a) informed without undue delay of the allegations against them and of the intention to name them in a public report, and (b) given the opportunity to respond to the evidence against them and offer a defence, but not necessarily through an oral hearing. Additional due process entitlements, such as the right to counsel or the right to cross-examine witnesses, should be offered only in very exceptional circumstances.

As a general rule, it is both unnecessary and undesirable to burden truth commissions with due process requirements equivalent to those of a court. Burdening a commission in this way would seriously undermine its ability to carry out its most essential duties by considerably slowing down the investigation and hearing process, stifling its capacity to gather facts and evidence, and generally over-judicializing commission procedures.

This is not to say that commissions ought to sacrifice the rights of perpetrators in the name of the victims. It is simply to emphasize that a rational balance must always be found between the dual interests of fairness and efficiency.

The Challenge of Engaging Perpetrators in the Process

One of the greatest shortcomings of past truth commissions has been their inability to secure meaningful cooperation from perpetrators, whether in the police, the military, the intelligence agencies or elsewhere. The one significant (and controversial) exception is the TRC in South Africa, which had the power to grant individual amnesty to perpetrators of politically motivated crimes. Amnesty was granted to those who fully confessed to their involvement in past crimes and showed them to be politically motivated. For particularly serious crimes, the applicant was required to appear in a public hearing to answer questions. Several thousand perpetrators came forward to the commission to disclose their involvement in and knowledge of past human rights violations under this process.

Of course, the use of a "truth-for-amnesty" formula as a means to secure perpetrator cooperation raises difficult moral, legal and political issues. Amnesties generally violate the right of victims to redress and will generally be inconsistent with a state's obligation under international law to punish perpetrators of serious human rights crimes. They can also subvert the rule of law by allowing only certain groups of perpetrators to escape liability. They can undermine both specific and general deterrence, and promote cynicism and disillusionment among victims of human rights abuses, which in turn could cause them to take the law into their own hands and embark on acts of private vengeance. On the other hand, a "truth-for-amnesty" arrangement can be more defensible where: (a) the commission's power has been given reasonably democratically; (b) amnesty is given on an individual, not class, basis; (c) a form of public procedure is imposed on its recipients; (d) victims are given an opportunity to question and challenge an individual's claim to amnesty; and (e) reparation payments are made to victims. An amnesty's scope can also be narrowed by making the grant of amnesty reversible following the commission of a new and similarly grave offence.

> One of the greatest short-comings of past truth commissions has been their inability to secure meaningful cooperation from perpetrators.

To date, only South Africa has used the "truth-for-amnesty" formula. The example should be copied only with the greatest caution, and only where there are similarly compelling circumstances. First, in the absence of a credible threat of prosecution (a factor which is rarely present in transitional contexts), it is unlikely that perpetrators will feel compelled to apply for an amnesty. They are more likely to prefer to remain silent, thereby avoiding any risk of public shame or social ostracism. Second, a range of mechanisms to encourage perpetrators to come forward may be available that are more principled and practical than the granting of amnesty and could better serve the causes of truth and reconciliation. For example, commissions might offer mechanisms for testimony to be provided on an anonymous or confidential basis; they might use a subpoena power; or they might be able to offer a witness protection/relocation service. Another possibility is that truth commission sponsors could create a new punishable offence of failure by witnesses (other than victims) to come forward to the commission with information about past crimes.

None of these alternative approaches will necessarily lead to extensive cooperation from perpetrators and reluctant witnesses. Without them, however, cooperation may be virtually non-existent.

Follow-Up Efforts

Once a truth commission submits its final report, archives its files and is formally dissolved, the task of carrying out its recommendations will naturally fall to others. Unfortunately, the implementation of recommendations has frequently been a major shortcoming for truth commissions, even where there has been a legal obligation on the part of government to implement them (as there was in El Salvador, for example).

> The implementation of recommendations has frequently been a major shortcoming of truth commissions.

One of the main causes of non-implementation appears to be lack of political will; but even when sufficient political will is present, there may not be sufficient institutional capacity or funds. Whichever the case, it is critically important for truth commissions to suggest mechanisms that can ensure proper monitoring and follow-up. Sometimes truth commissions are fortunate in that a plan of follow-up is built into the mandate, as is the case in Sierra Leone. For most, however, a system of follow-up must be recommended. In Chile, the commission recommended the creation of a public commission to continue some of its own work and to facilitate compliance with reparation measures. In Guatemala, the commission recommended the creation of a follow-up institution (the Foundation for Peace and Harmony, Fundación por la Paz y la Concordia, to be made up of government and civil society representatives) to implement some recommendations directly and monitor the implementation of others.

8.4 Concluding Remarks

This chapter has sought to explain in practical terms what a truth commission is, how it operates and what it can potentially achieve for a country in transition.

Scepticism has been expressed here as to the universal utility of truth commissions and as to the strength of the contribution truth-seeking can be expected to make to reconciliation, but it is nevertheless important to appreciate the sometimes remarkable but little-known contributions that truth commissions have occasionally made. For example, in Chile, almost entirely on the basis of the commission's findings, the state initiated a broad reparation programme for many victims of the Pinochet era. Critical judicial reforms were put in place in El Salvador following the truth commission investigations there. In South Africa, very few people will now defend or try to justify the system of apartheid or question the fact that brutal practices were used to keep apartheid in place.

A truth commission is, however, only one of the many mechanisms available to countries in transition that are seeking to consolidate democracy, human rights and the rule of law. Other possible components of a full programme of transitional justice could include trials, vetting programmes, legal reform, victim reparation, and restitution and reintegration measures. There appears to be a new trend towards the integration or synthesis of these different elements of transitional justice. This can be seen in places ranging from Sierra Leone (where a truth commission and a hybrid national–international criminal court will operate alongside one another) to Rwanda (where the new *gacaca* system is seeking to merge prosecutorial goals with the pursuit of truth and community reintegration) to East Timor (where a truth commission will serve as a facilitator of refugee return, the prosecution of serious crime, and restitution and reintegration for less serious offences). There are many challenges and complications in trying to integrate transitional goals and mechanisms in this way, generating creative and original solutions. Clearly the full story about truth commissions has yet to be written.

References and Further Reading

Main Sources

Hayner, Priscilla B. *Unspeakable Truths: Confronting State Terror and Atrocity.* New York: Routledge, 2001 (paperback edition, published as Hayner, Priscilla B. *Unspeakable Truths: Facing the Challenge of Truth Commissions.* New York and London: Routledge, 2002).

Truth Commissions: A Comparative Assessment. An Interdisciplinary Discussion Held at Harvard Law School in May 1996. Cambridge, Mass.: Harvard Law School Human Rights Program, 1996.

International Center for Transitional Justice, http://www.ictj.org

Centre for the Study of Violence and Reconciliation, http://www.wits.ac.za/csvr

Truth Commissions Project, http://www.truthcommission.org

United States Institute of Peace Library, http://www.usip.org/library/truth.html

Other Sources

Kritz, Neil (editor), *Transitional Justice: How Emerging Democracies Reckon with Former Regimes, Vol. I-III.* Washington, DC: United States Institute of Peace Press, 1995.

Nunca Mas: The Report of the Argentine National Commission on the Disappeared. New York: Farrar Straus Giroux, 1986.

Report of the Chilean National Commission on Truth and Reconciliation (translated by Phillip E. Berryman; introduction by José Zalaquett), Notre Dame: University of Notre Dame Press, 1993.

From Madness to Hope: the 12-year War in El Salvador: Report of the Commission on the Truth for El Salvador. New York: United Nations, 1993.

Informe de la Comision de la Verdad de Panama, 2002. (Panama Truth Commission Report).

Biggar, Nigel (editor), *Burying the Past: Making Peace and Doing Justice After Civil Conflict,* Washington, D.C.: Georgetown University Press, 2001.

Internet Sources

Report of the Truth Commission on El Salvador, http://www.derechos.org/nizkor/salvador/informes/truth.html

Commission for Reception, Truth and Reconciliation in East Timor, http://www.easttimor-reconciliation.org

Peru Reconciliation Commission, http://www.cverdad.org.pe/

Sierra Leone Truth and Reconciliation Commission, http://www.sierra-leone.org/trc.html

The Truth Commissions of South Africa and Guatemala

MARK FREEMAN AND PRISCILLA B. HAYNER
INTERNATIONAL CENTER FOR TRANSITIONAL JUSTICE

The truth commissions of South Africa and Guatemala were two of the largest and most prominent of recently-completed commissions. This case study is divided into two parts: a broad overview of the context and work of each commission; and a brief review of the main similarities and differences between them.

South Africa

During 45 years of apartheid and almost 30 years of armed resistance by the African National Congress (ANC) and others, tens of thousands of South Africans suffered serious human rights violations and war crimes. The greatest number of deaths took place in the conflict between the ANC and the government-backed Inkatha Freedom Party.

Serious discussions about the idea of a truth commission began after Nelson Mandela was elected president in 1994. After considerable input from civil society and hundreds of hours of hearings, in 1995 the South African Parliament passed the Promotion of National Unity and Reconciliation Act establishing the Truth and Reconciliation Commission (TRC). Following a public nomination and selection process, 17 commissioners were appointed. The act provided the most complex and sophisticated mandate for any truth commission to date. It gave the TRC the power to grant individualized amnesty, search premises and seize evidence, subpoena witnesses and run a sophisticated witness protection programme. With a staff of up to 350, a budget of some USD 18 million each year for two-and-a-half years (plus an additional, smaller budget for another three years) and four large offices around the country, the TRC dwarfed previous truth commissions in its size and reach.

The Promotion of National Unity and Reconciliation Act designed the TRC to work in three interconnected committees. The Human Rights Violations Committee was responsible for collecting statements from victims and witnesses and recording the extent of violations; the Amnesty Committee processed and decided on individual applications for amnesty; and the Reparations and Rehabilitation Committee (RRC) designed and put forward recommendations for a reparation programme.

The TRC took testimony from 23,000 victims and witnesses, 2,000 of whom appeared in public hearings. Media coverage was intense: most newspapers ran a number of stories on it every day, and radio and television news often led with a story on the latest hearings. The TRC also held special hearings focused on sectors or key institutions of society and their response to or participation in abusive practices. Other special hearings looked at important thematic issues, while still others focused on uniquely significant events in the country's history.

The greatest innovation of the TRC, and the most controversial of its powers, was its ability to grant individual amnesty for politically motivated crimes. The amnesty-granting power was the subject of an unsuccessful constitutional challenge early in the life of the TRC, as well as of numerous subsequent court battles. The TRC received over 7,000 applications for amnesty, most of which were ultimately refused. Amnesty was granted only to those who fully confessed to their involvement in past crimes and showed them to be politically motivated. For particularly serious crimes, the applicant was required to appear in a public hearing to answer questions from the TRC, from legal counsel representing the victims and their families, and from victims themselves. The Amnesty Committee considered a number of factors in determining whether the applicant satisfied the terms for amnesty, including, for example, whether there was proportionality between the crime committed and the political objective pursued. Neither an apology nor any sign of remorse was necessary for amnesty to be granted. However, crimes committed for personal gain or out of personal malice, ill will or spite were not eligible for amnesty.

Given the detailed public disclosure that was required to gain amnesty, it was clear that this "truth-for-amnesty" offer would only be taken up by those who reasonably feared prosecution. It was hoped that a number of early trials would increase the perceived threat of prosecution. A few high-profile trials for apartheid-era crimes did successfully result in convictions and long sentences, which spurred an increase in amnesty applications. However, when another important trial (that of former minister Magnus Malan and 19 others) ended in acquittal, it was clear that the threat of prosecution would not be strong enough to persuade many senior-level perpetrators to apply for amnesty. The TRC then tried to increase the pressure on perpetrators to come forward by holding some investigative hearings behind closed doors. In the end, however, many former perpetrators took the risk not to apply, particularly political leaders of the apartheid government and senior officers of the army.

The TRC's five-volume final report was released in October 1998 and sparked intense controversy, including an attempt by the ANC to block its release. It was formally considered in parliament several months later, but the government made no commitment to implementing the TRC's many recommendations, including - most controversially - the recommendations on victim reparation. The Amnesty Committee, which was not able to conclude its review of all amnesty applications by the appointed deadline, continued to hold amnesty hearings for another two years. The full TRC was expected to reconvene in late 2002 to release an addendum to the final report that will incorporate the final investigations and amnesty hearings.

Looking back at the TRC experience, it is difficult not to marvel at its level of ambition and originality. For all the criticisms against it, the TRC marked a decisive turning point in South African history by "narrowing the range of permissible lies". Like no other commission before it, the TRC had a truly international impact, leading to great interest in this kind of mechanism all around the world. Although the legacy of apartheid continues to haunt South Africa, this cannot be attributed to particular failures of the TRC. Such a legacy cannot be fully addressed, nor the damage rectified, in a few short years. New initiatives - possibly including long-overdue prosecutions of persons implicated by the TRC - will probably be required to fully consolidate democracy and human rights in the new South Africa.

Guatemala

The civil war in Guatemala, fought between anti-communist government forces and leftist rebels Guatemalan National Revolutionary Unit (Unidad Revolucionaria Nacional Guatemalteca, URNG), lasted over 30 years and resulted in some 200,000 deaths and disappearances. Among the most controversial issues on the table during the peace negotiations was the question of how past human rights violations and war crimes would be addressed during the transition to peace. This was resolved in June 1994 when the government and the URNG agreed to establish a Commission for Historical Clarification (Comisión para el Esclarecimiento Histórico, CEH). It would, however, be another three years until the final peace accords were signed and the CEH would begin its work.

The idea of a truth commission attracted intense interest from civil society and victims' groups in Guatemala, which lobbied negotiators hard during the talks. Their main concern was with the short time period the CEH was given (six months, with the possibility of extension for another six months) and with the stipulation that the CEH would be precluded from naming names of perpetrators. Although there was considerable anger that the URNG agreed to these limitations, civil society gradually came to support the commission after the commissioners were appointed and the CEH hired an impressive team of staff. In the end, the CEH was able to operate for a total of 18 months.

The chair of the CEH was a non-national appointed by the UN Secretary-General, while the other two commissioners were nationals selected by the chair with the agreement of the two parties. The CEH operated in several phases, with staff size ranging from 200 at its peak (with 14 field offices) to fewer than 100 for the months of analysis, investigation and report writing. Its staff included both nationals and non-nationals. Its total budget was approximately USD 11 million. The CEH received less than USD1 million from the Guatemalan Government; the remainder of the funding came from the US, Norwegian, Dutch, Swedish, Danish and Japanese governments. The mandate of the commission was to "clarify" the human rights violations and acts of violence committed between 1962 and 1996 and connected with the armed conflict. It was required to prepare a final report based on its investigations, containing conclusions as well as recommendations to encourage peace, democracy and human rights, and to preserve the memory of the victims. The commission's proceedings were required to be confidential; however, it was obligated to publicize its establishment and mandate, and to invite interested parties to offer testimony.

Many Guatemalan villages are very isolated, and CEH staff sometimes had to trek by back roads to reach scattered communities, in some cases walking for six or eight hours through the mountains before arriving at a village to take testimonies. Upon arrival in some locations, staff sometimes discovered that the community was not even aware that the civil war was over, and more than once the commission staff were assumed to be guerrillas themselves. Despite these challenges, CEH staff were ultimately able to visit almost 2,000 communities and register 7,338 testimonies, including 500 collective testimonies.

The CEH also requested the declassification of files from the US Government with the help of the US National Security Archive. This resulted in the successful declassification of thousands of documents. Considerably less information was forthcoming from the Guatemalan armed forces themselves, which claimed to have no records on the events under investigation. The CEH also incorporated the data from two national NGOs, in particular two projects that were established as alternative truth efforts several years before the start of the CEH. Both projects had collected thousands of testimonies, many of them audiotaped and transcribed, leaving behind a detailed database of cases and even published reports.

The CEH completed its lengthy and hard-hitting report in February 1999, releasing it to the public in an emotional ceremony attended by thousands. The report described acts of extreme cruelty and noted that a "climate of terror" permeated the country as a result of these atrocities. The CEH also analysed the economic costs of the armed conflict, concluding that costs of the war, including the loss of production due to death, equalled 121 per cent of the 1990 gross domestic product (GDP). Ninety-three per cent of the violations documented were attributed to the military or state-backed paramilitary forces; three per cent were attributed to the URNG. Perhaps the CEH's strongest conclusion, however, was that, on the basis of the patterns of violence in the four regions of the country worst affected by it, agents of the state committed acts of genocide in the years 1981–1983 against groups of Mayan people. Although the CEH was precluded from naming those responsible, it did report that the majority of human rights violations occurred "with the knowledge or by order of the highest authorities of the State". The CEH also submitted a long chapter on recommendations.

Three weeks after the release of the final report, the government responded with a statement that suggested that it considered all relevant matters in the CEH's recommendations to be sufficiently addressed in the peace accord. However, as a result of persistent pressure from civil society, some of the key recommendations may yet be implemented. For example, the CEH had recommended the establishment of a joint government–civil society council to oversee the follow-up process, and a decree has now been passed authorizing its establishment (although progress on implementing the decree has been very slow). As to the recommendations concerning accountability for the worst abusers, it is also encouraging to note that there have been some judicial investigations into gross human rights violations, albeit at the initiative of victims and human rights groups, not the state.

Despite these minor advances, the realities of life in Guatemala remain largely unchanged. There has not been a renewal of conflict, but most of the root causes of the conflict persist, including pervasive insecurity, lack of justice, racism, and extreme and widespread poverty. Moreover, there has been limited dissemination of the CEH's final report, so that many of the communities that suffered the worst abuses often know little about the commission's work.

Similarities and Differences

The differences between the Guatemalan and South African truth commissions are striking. Indeed, there are a number of important features of the South African TRC which stand out in comparison to most other truth commissions to date (such as the unique "truth-for-amnesty" arrangement, its extensive media coverage and its significant powers of investigation).

Table 8A.1 illustrates the differences between the two. The points of similarity were:
- Both had large, multidisciplinary staffs.
- Both had relatively large budgets.
- There was strong involvement of civil society in both.
- Both presented detailed and comprehensive final reports.
- The periods of time they investigated spanned more than 30 years.
- Both received funds from government and from foreign sources.
- The recommendations in their final reports were not binding.
- Both took thousands of statements from survivors and witnesses.
- The selection of commissioners in both cases involved a consultation process.
- Staff travelled long distances to remote areas to take statements from victims.
- Both relied on prior investigative reports done by local NGOs.

Guatemala	South Africa
No public hearings	Hundreds of public hearings
Limited media coverage until final report	Extensive media coverage throughout
Mixed national and international commissioners	All commissioners national
Reconciliation not an explicit part of mandate	Reconciliation an explicit part of mandate
Recommendations as to reparation not an explicit part of mandate	Explicit mandate to recommend reparation
3 commissioners	17 commissioners
No amnesty-granting power	Amnesty-granting power
Did not name individual perpetrators	Did name individual perpetrators
Significant UN role	No UN role
Operated for 1.5 years	Operated for 2.5 years plus 3.5 more
100 cases investigated in depth	Corroborated all victim statements
Primarily a "vertical" conflict	Both a "vertical" and a "horizontal" conflict
No simultaneous high-level prosecutions	Some simultaneous high-level prosecutions
Created as part of a peace accord	Set up by legislation
Not subjected to legal challenges	Subjected to several legal challenges
No significant powers of investigation	Powers of subpoena and search and seizure
No formal witness protection programme	An advanced witness protection programme
Working in a context of:	
A weak and corrupt judicial system	A relatively robust judicial system
Over 200,000 persons killed or disappeared	ca 25,000 persons killed or disappeared

References and Further Reading
Main Sources

Guatemalan Historical Clarification Commission. *Guatemala: Memory of Silence, Report of the Commission for Historical Clarification: Conclusions and Recommendations*, CEH, 1999.

Truth and Reconciliation Commission, *"Truth and Reconciliation Commission of South Africa Report."* Cape Town: Juta and Company Ltd; New York: Grove's Dictionaries, Inc., March 1999.

van der Merwe, Hugo. *The South African Truth and Reconciliation Commission and Community Reconciliation: A Case Study of Duduza*. Johannesburg: Centre for the Study of Violence and Reconciliation, 1998.

Villa-Vicencio, Charles & Verwoerd, Wilhelm, eds., *Looking Back Reaching Forward: Reflections on the Truth and Reconciliation Commission of South Africa*. Cape Town: Univ. of Cape Town Press, and London: Zed Books, 2000.

Other Sources

Boraine, Alex. *A Country Unmasked: South Africa's Truth and Reconciliation Commission*: Cape Town; Oxford, UK: Oxford University Press, 2001.

Internet Sources

South African Truth and Reconciliation Commission, http://www.doj.gov.za/trc/index.html

Guatemalan Historical Clarification Commission, http://shr.aaas.org/guatemala/ceh/

CHAPTER 9

Reparation

STEF VANDEGINSTE

9.1 Introduction

The concept of political transition in a post-conflict state and the notion of reparation are in their very essence interrelated and interdependent. On the one hand, reparation is a key element of any true transitional justice and reconciliation process. A transition must go beyond the introduction or reform of norms, institutions and procedures to mandate elected representatives if it is to eliminate discrimination and imbalances. This also involves the recognition and protection of individual rights and freedoms, and the state is under a corresponding obligation to provide redress if there have been abuses of these fundamental rights by state actors or former armed insurgents. On the other hand, transitional justice in practice has reshaped the notion of reparation. The concept has long been oriented to compensation and to the past. Today, however, reparative measures taken in the context of actual political transitions have broadened the very definition of reparation, which today includes important symbolic and future-oriented measures.

> *Reparation is a key element of any true transitional justice and reconciliation process.*

9.2 What is Reparation?

9.2.1 Clarification of the Terminology

In international and national norms and case law, and in the political and historical literature, different terms are used to express sometimes identical or similar concepts - reparation, restitution, compensation, rehabilitation, satisfaction and redress. This chapter will use the term "reparation" as the most comprehensive notion, including all these concepts and covering a wide range of measures that are taken to redress past wrongs which may or may not qualify as human rights violations and/or as criminal offences. It will therefore not limit the use of the term reparation to the international law of state responsibility.

Traditionally in international law, "restitution" (or "re-establishment of the situation which existed before the wrongful act was committed") was the main and preferred form of reparation, and was therefore often considered almost synonymous with "reparation". It remains an important component of reparation as it relates to essential "belongings", such as the return of property, the restoration of liberty, citizenship and other legal rights, the return to place of residence and the restoration of employment.

"Compensation" is the payment of money as a recognition of the wrong done and to make good the losses suffered. A distinction can be made between nominal damages (a small amount of money symbolizing the vindication of rights), pecuniary damages (intended to represent the closest possible financial equivalent of the loss or harm suffered), moral damages (relating to immaterial harm, such as fear, humiliation, mental distress or harm to a person's reputation or dignity) and punitive damages (which are of a different nature, and intended rather to punish or deter than to make up for the loss suffered).

"Rehabilitation" can be defined as the restoration of a victim's physical and psychological health. Including rehabilitation in a full reparation programme will normally require an initiative on the part of the state and its active involvement in the provision of medical and psychological care and of legal and social services. (The mere reimbursement of medical and other related expenses can be considered a form of compensation.)

The term "satisfaction" applies to those types of redress that do not aim to make good specific individual losses or harm. The main forms of satisfaction are: (a) the verification of the facts and the disclosure of the truth; (b) an apology; (c) sanctions against individual perpetrators; and (d) commemorations of and tributes to the victims.

All reparation measures have some minimal deterrent effect. Guarantees of non-repetition are specifically and purely preventive: they include structural reforms relating to the independence of the judiciary, civilian control of military and security forces, and the protection of those who defend human rights.

9.2.2 The Nature and Types of Reparation

The terminological clarification above has shown that reparation is an evolving concept and one that is becoming broader. Policy makers and victim support groups designing or advocating a reparation programme need to be aware of the different types of reparation measures:
- reparation rights and reparation politics;
- individual and collective measures;
- financial and non-financial measures; and
- commemorative and reform measures.

Reparation Rights and Reparation Policies

Some forms of reparation may find a legal basis in domestic law or in international human rights law, while other forms are a matter of policies and priorities. For instance, the right to compensation for victims of torture is an individual subjective right in most domestic legal systems and is justiciable in criminal, civil, administrative or other proceedings, depending on the national legal setting. In addition, after domestic remedies have been exhausted, international complaints procedures may be available, as a result of which an international judicial body, such as the Inter-American Commission on Human Rights or the European Court of Human Rights, can order a state to pay compensation in cases where the court finds that a violation has occurred.

There is no individual subjective right to other reparation measures, such as reform of the judiciary or the commemoration of torture victims. Even so, the impact of these elements of reparation may be much more important at a structural level, and they must therefore logically be included in a reparation policy. The work of international reporting mechanisms (such as the UN Committee Against Torture) may be helpful for civil society groups when designing proposals or lobbying for such structural reparation measures.

It is nevertheless important to stress the interaction between the enforcement of reparation rights and the adoption of reparation policies. In Argentina, for instance, proceedings instituted by victims before the Inter-American Commission on Human Rights were an essential incentive for the adoption of a national reparation policy, which included, among other things, the issuing of "certificates of forced disappearance". This allowed the relatives of those forcibly "disappeared", for instance, to deal with questions of inheritance.

Individual and Collective Measures

Irrespective of the legal or exclusively political nature of a specific form of reparation (see above), reparation measures can be taken individually or collectively. Transitional justice schemes will often need to deal with large numbers of violations committed under a previous regime. In such a context, almost paradoxically, the provision of purely individual reparation measures will often be insufficient and may be impossible. They will be insufficient because individual reparation measures are unlikely to truly remedy situations that have resulted from a long-standing practice of oppression. They should therefore, ideally, be supplemented by collective measures, such as access to medical services, education and employment for specific disadvantaged ethnic, religious or other groups or minorities. However, this combination of individual and collective approaches will often raise questions of logistical feasibility, financial constraints, and political and financial priority setting.

Financial and Non-Financial Reparation Measures

Some of the individual, non-financial reparation measures which can be considered for inclusion in a reparation programme are the restoration of citizenship, the issuing of death certificates of those who have been "made" to disappear, the facilitation of exhumations and reburials, and the expunging of criminal records. When designing a reparation programme it should be taken into account that a balanced package, including both financial and non-financial elements, is most likely to meet victims' expectations and needs.

Commemorative and Reform Measures

Fairly recently there has been an increase in the incidence of claims for reparation related to injustices committed a long time ago, such as the Holocaust or the transatlantic slave trade. In this context, the US historian John Torpey distinguishes between two types of reparation claim. The first type is based on commemorative projects which call attention to the barbarity and humiliation associated with the past oppression. These claims are largely backward-looking, built on a perception - both internal (among the victims) and external (among the general public) - of victimhood, and not related to any current economic damage suffered as a result of past oppression. A second type of claim is rooted in a continuing economic disadvantage which is the result of a past oppressive system. These claims are forward-looking and non-systemic, tactical instruments used as part of larger projects of social transformation which seek to fundamentally alter the social and economic conditions of disadvantaged groups.

9.3 Why Reparation?

The close link between reparation, on the one hand, and post-conflict reconciliation and democratization, on the other hand, and the importance of including a reparation component in transitional politics and law can be shown from different perspectives.

A new post-conflict state, which commits itself to upholding the rule of law should guarantee the individual rights of all its citizens. If the state is responsible for acts of torture or other human rights violations committed under a previous regime, it should immediately show the seriousness of that commitment by living up to its obligation to provide reparation to the victims. In international legal terms, the responsibility of a successor regime or government for abuses committed by the previous regime is beyond any doubt. Honouring this commitment from the very start will shape the new political identity.

Reconciliation aims to break a cycle of violence and promote peaceful coexistence. In order to achieve this, acts of revenge by victims of past oppression should be stopped - or, putting it more positively, victims' legitimate hunger for justice should be accommodated. This entails public recognition of their status as victims, public recognition of their suffering and the damage they have sustained, and a serious public effort to repair at least symbolically the harm done. It is a crucial instrument in allowing a society to get on with life.

Acknowledging and repairing the suffering of victims is a way of recognizing them as human beings, as equals, with their own human and civic dignity. In order to get on with life individually and to be able to function properly in the new society, each victim needs a renewed self-confidence. For the restoration of his or her psychological health and dignity, reparation - not only in its immaterial but also in its material, financial dimension - is an important tool. Moreover, continued preoccupation with their own distress cannot but hinder people's ability to be reconciled with others. The actual psychological impact of receiving reparation can differ greatly between people. For some victims reparation may mean the end of a personal healing process; for others it may be just the start of it.

Reparation gives victims a role in the transitional justice process. Theoretically, a political transition could limit itself to legal and institutional reforms (of the army, the judiciary, the constitution and so on) and to sanctioning perpetrators, leaving the victims out of the picture; but victims are likely to be better integrated into the transitional process if a reparation component is included. As a consequence, the confrontation between victims and perpetrators and the issue of reconciliation become much more immediately relevant. The Guatemalan Commission for Historical Clarification (Comisión para el Esclarecimiento Histórico, CEH), for instance, recommended in particular that collective (as opposed to individual) reparation measures be implemented in such a way as to facilitate reconciliation between victims and perpetrators, without stigmatizing either.

> The responsibility of a successor regime or government for abuses committed by the previous regime is beyond any doubt.

Reparation, in the context of political transition, acts as a bridge between the past and the future. It combines the backward-looking objective of compensating victims with the forward-looking objectives of political reform. Thus, it also helps the new state in reconciling itself with its past.

In some cases, reparation can function as a compromise. In some post-conflict societies, systematic criminal prosecution of all those involved in the past oppression may threaten political stability and undermine democratic consolidation. On the other hand, requests by members of the previous regime that the past be simply forgotten are equally unacceptable. Reparation, which necessarily includes a form of sanctioning and honouring of victims' rights, is therefore in itself a useful instrument of compromise. This is all the more true in those cases where an amnesty law denies victims the right to institute civil claims against perpetrators: a state reparation programme may counter, to some extent, the effects of the amnesty legislation.

9.4 Sources of Reparation

Claims for reparation are most often based on two different types of source:
• Fundamental feelings that justice needs to be done and that harm needs to be undone may provide a strong moral basis.
• International (human rights) law and national legislation may provide a solid legal basis.
In many cases the two will be mutually reinforcing.

9.4.1 The Ethics and Politics of Reparation

Reparation is not an exclusively legal notion, and sources in international law are only one perspective from which to look at the recent, global practice of reparation.

The ever-increasing trend of attempts to repair historical injustices has led some observers to conclude that a new moral order is emerging in world politics and a critical shift taking place in political and economic bargaining. According to Elazar Barkan, a historian at Claremont Graduate University, USA: "The discourse of restitution encourages governments to admit that their policies were unjust and discriminatory and to negotiate with their victims over morally right and politically feasible options". Looking at it from this perspective, reparation is primarily a matter of ethics and politics, and both national and international law will necessarily be framed according to the desired political end.

Roy Brooks distinguishes four mainly political and ethical conditions that need to be fulfilled for any demands for reparation to be successful: (a) claims for redress must be addressed to legislators rather than to judges: they must reach the hearts and minds of lawmakers and citizens; (b) strong political pressure is needed (which, according to Barkan, can be most effectively based on a system of "public shame"); (c) they will need strong and unquestioned internal support from the victims; and, critically important, (d) claims must be meritorious: showing that a well-documented human injustice has been committed, with lasting harmful effects for a distinct group of victims.

9.4.2 Reparation in Human Rights Law
International Human Rights Law

Under international law, any conduct which is attributable to the state and which constitutes a breach of an international obligation of the state is an international wrongful act. An international wrongful act entails a corresponding responsibility on the part of the state. The legal consequences of this international responsibility are (a) the obligation to cease the wrongful conduct and (b) the obligation to make adequate reparation. In strictly legal terms, reparation may be defined as the various ways in which a state can redress an international wrong and, in doing so, discharge itself from state responsibility towards injured state parties and individuals or groups of victims for a breach of an international (human rights) obligation.

These general principles of public international law, laid down in the UN draft Articles on State Responsibility of the International Law Commission, are firmly embodied in a large number of international and regional human rights conventions. The obligation on states to provide reparation to victims of human rights violations has been further refined by the jurisprudence of a large number of international and regional courts, as well as other treaty bodies and complaints mechanisms. International human rights law has thus created a wide range of remedies, which include declaratory judgements with findings of violations, awards of (importantly, differentiated amounts of) compensatory damages, and orders for specific state action.

At the universal level, the UN Commission on Human Rights (UNCHR) has created various monitoring mechanisms dealing with particular human rights issues and remedies for human rights violations, outside the context of specific human rights treaties. In addition, UN treaty bodies monitor state compliance with specific human rights conventions. These conventions generally include provisions on reparation which have often been further defined and refined by treaty bodies.

Both these extra-conventional and conventional mechanisms may receive petitions or communications by or on behalf of victims within their specific jurisdictional limits. The procedural issues are not dealt with in detail here. Reference can be made, for instance, to the UN Working Group on

Disappearances, the Human Rights Committee and the Committee Against Torture. Although their findings and recommendations are not binding, the work of these mechanisms can usefully inspire policy makers, as well as victims, their relatives and their representatives, in their attempts to obtain reparation from the responsible state authorities.

At the regional level, international norms and mechanisms have been established by the Organization of American States (OAS), the Council of Europe and the Organization of African Unity (OAU, now the African Union). The jurisprudence of these mechanisms can be found on the websites listed in the Annex to this Handbook.

The above deals with state responsibility for reparation. As far as the responsibility of individuals is concerned, there is no international mechanism for bringing an international civil action against an individual perpetrator. The two ad hoc international criminal tribunals for the former Yugoslavia (the ICTY) and for Rwanda (the ICTR) do not allow victims to participate in the criminal trials as civil claimants. While the statutes and rules of procedure and evidence of both tribunals do contain some provisions on reparation, in practice these have yielded little or no result so far. More importantly, the 1998 Rome Statute on the establishment of a permanent International Criminal Court (ICC), which entered into force on 1 July 2002, deals more extensively with reparation. It provides for the establishment of a Trust Fund for the benefit of victims which could fill an important gap, although the ICC's actual role remains uncertain.

> There is no international mechanism for bringing an international civil action against an individual perpetrator.

The most recent, still ongoing effort to bring together various reparation rights and components is the draft UN Basic Principles and Guidelines on the Right to Reparation for Victims of Violations of Human Rights and International Humanitarian Law by special rapporteurs van Boven and Bassiouni. Although a number of important issues remain to be resolved, such as the distinction between violations and gross violations, they are nevertheless already being used as an authoritative source of inspiration, including by the ICC's Preparatory Commission and some national legislators.

Reparation under National Law

It is important to conclude that international norms and mechanisms primarily deal with the responsibility of the state for violations and with the state's obligation to provide redress to victims. Furthermore, most of the international mechanisms cannot themselves issue binding reparation judgements. These conventions primarily oblige states to adopt and implement national legislation. This legislation will necessarily deal with, inter alia, the criminal prosecution of suspected perpetrators, the right to compensation for victims and so on.

It is, for obvious reasons, not possible to provide an overview of all national norms and mechanisms. However, generally speaking, at the national level a distinction can be made between judicial and non-judicial reparation mechanisms.

The judicial mechanisms can again be subdivided into (a) reparation proceedings which are closely associated with the criminal prosecution of individual perpetrators, with victims participating and seeking reparation as civil claimants (*constitution de partie civile*), and (b) tort proceedings which may allow victims to claim compensation independently of the criminal prosecution of the perpetrator. Examples of the latter type are the US Alien Tort Claims Act and Torture Victims Protection Act.

A wide variety of mechanisms are non-judicial, that is, they do not operate in the context of formal court proceedings. They range from state-administered compensation funds for victims of violent crime and abuse of power, to mediation programmes which involve both offender and victim, to traditional means of conflict resolution based on a restorative justice approach. (See chapter 7 on restorative justice.)

These judicial and non-judicial mechanisms and programmes may be specifically designed to deal with reparation for victims of particular forms of human rights violations (for instance, a fund for the rehabilitation of victims of torture) or may deal with victims of crime in general. The 1985 UN Declaration of the Basic Principles of Justice for Victims of Crime and Abuse of Power calls upon states to guarantee certain rights to victims of criminal offences and of human rights violations relating to access to justice and fair treatment, restitution, compensation and (material, medical, psychological and social) assistance. The UN Commission on Crime Prevention and Criminal Justice has drafted a *Guide for Policymakers on the Implementation of the 1985 UN Declaration* and a *Handbook on Justice for Victims on the Use and Application of the 1985 UN Declaration.*

9.5 How to Develop and Run a Reparation Programme

Decisions on the establishment of a reparation programme will depend on a set of factors which also shape the overall political transition. These include the nature and the popular support of the previous regime, the type of transition, the democratic or other nature of the new political regime, and the extent of support from the international community. It is therefore extremely difficult to prescribe a particular model. Nevertheless, this section tries to identify the dilemmas and constraints likely to be faced by all governments and civil society groups seeking to create a reparations programme.

As far as possible, recommendations are formulated to help in responding to these difficulties. However, they should be considered as suggestions which may need to be adapted to the particular circumstances, not as guaranteed solutions.

9.5.1 A Major Strategic Choice: Taking the Best from both Judicial and Non-Judicial Approaches

In the context of political transitions, reparation cannot be provided effectively to a large number of victims through an exclusively judicial approach. Access to justice and legal remedies is obviously extremely important for victims seeking redress for the harm they have suffered. The developments in international law and in many national legal systems mentioned above, which strengthen victims' rights, are therefore encouraging for victims. However, there are certain restrictions associated with approaching reparations solely as the outcome of a successful judicial exercise. A victim may lack legal skills, solid evidence or financial resources, and amnesty legislation may have been passed. All these factors can make access to judicial mechanisms extremely difficult for the victim, if not impossible, but they should not deprive him or her of the exercise of his or her right to reparation and should not discharge the state of its obligation to provide redress. At the same time, if a non-judicial approach to reparation is chosen, policy makers need to try to incorporate the strengths of a judicial approach. For instance, the value of a judicial precedent in determining standards of compensation or in recognizing certain categories of people as victims should be reflected in the reparation programme.

> In the context of political transitions, reparation cannot be provided effectively to a large number of victims through an exclusively judicial approach.

This section presents some of the advantages and risks of a judicial approach. These may apply to both criminal and civil proceedings, although some inherent distinctions between the two need to be borne in mind.

The Judicial Approach: Limitations and Merits
Limitations

1. A judicial approach presupposes the existence of a properly functioning system of justice. However, in post-conflict societies the justice system itself may have been a victim of past oppression. Neither the legislation, the personnel nor the infrastructure are likely to be adequate.

2. Criminal justice systems are not designed to deal with large numbers of violations or of perpetrators, or to accommodate such subtleties as the differences between direct and indirect victims. Rendering justice and providing reparation to victims within a reasonable period of time is therefore likely to be beyond the capacity of any system.

3. A judicial approach will in most cases be designed to deal with individual guilt or civil responsibility and individual harm and redress. In a transitional context, the issue of responsibility (of the leaders, the "ordinary" perpetrators or the beneficiaries of past offences) is likely to be much more complex than it is in normal situations and requires a broader approach. Also, the total amount of reparation needed is likely to add up to more than the sum of individual needs. A judicial approach is unlikely to be able to respond fully to needs which have a strong collective dimension.

4. In a judicial approach, procedural guarantees and conditions of legitimacy should be carefully taken into consideration in order not to impose (criminal) sanctions and reparative payments on suspected perpetrators and/or beneficiaries in an unsubstantiated or arbitrary manner. In a judicial process the human rights of suspected perpetrators must be respected. This contrasts with an administrative procedure before a compensation commission, where obtaining reparation is not linked to establishing the guilt or civil responsibility of an individual.

5. As a result of these guarantees, the standards of evidence required under a judicial procedure may be too high for the victim. He may be able to provide sufficient evidence that he has suffered damage as a result of the abuse, but it may be much more difficult to prove "beyond all reasonable doubt" the responsibility of an individual. A non-judicial body can give the "benefit of the doubt" to claimants in awarding reparation, which is not possible in a judicial procedure.

6. Asking beneficiaries (see chapter 5) - offenders who, legally speaking, are not responsible for the violations - to contribute to reparation is normally impossible through a judicial approach. Only when beneficiaries can be shown to be directly or indirectly complicit does this become a potential avenue. It may be easier to involve beneficiaries through a non-judicial mechanism, thus giving them the opportunity to acknowledge the benefit they have enjoyed from past oppression or abuse, to express solidarity with the victims and to contribute to reparation schemes. This may be an important factor in a wider effort to promote reconciliation and unity.

7. Judicial proceedings against suspected perpetrators may in practice not be an option, for example, because of amnesty legislation, temporary immunities granted within the framework of a peace agreement or statutes of limitation. Although such legislation may, if contested, be found to be contrary to international law (as it certainly is in the case of international crimes), in practice the safest strategy for victims and their representatives may be to advocate the use of non-judicial mechanisms.

8. Irrespective of the particular domestic legislation, access to a judicial process may not be more than a theoretical option for the poorest victims: they will often lack the information, legal assistance or financial means needed to initiate civil claims against perpetrators, to travel to a court or to participate as civil claimants in criminal proceedings. This is all the more likely in countries where international or national support groups have limited capacity. A relevant question in this context relates to the admissibility of class actions under the relevant national legislation.

Merits

Despite these limitations, judicial approaches set important precedents, both at a symbolic and at a practical level.

1. A judicial decision sends a very strong signal that a certain practice will not be tolerated and that victims of that practice are entitled to redress. This in itself may provide victims with a certain degree of satisfaction, despite the fact that criminal trials are usually more focused on perpetrators than on victims. The judicial decision also confirms the validity and the binding nature of the norms that were violated.

2. At a practical level, a successful legal claim may be the most convincing argument for a government to acknowledge the suffering of victims and to adopt reparation legislation and establish other, non-judicial reparation mechanisms. For instance, the decision by the Japanese Government to seriously consider the issue of reparation for around 20,000 so-called comfort women, abused as sex slaves during World War II, was prompted by the legal action undertaken by one individual victim. It should be noted that, in cases where domestic legal action is not an option, proceedings before an international human rights body or before national judiciaries in other states may have a similar effect.

3. Even if non-judicial mechanisms are created, the judicial enforcement of the right to reparation should preferably remain an option for those victims who are not satisfied with the non-judicial approach. Reparation should indeed remain an individual, justiciable right, whatever supplementary reparation policies are developed.

Illustrations of a Non-Judicial Approach

Several bodies have been established to deal with reparation for past abuses at the international and at the national level. This section will briefly present three different types of non-judicial bodies, looking at specific examples:
• the United Nations Compensation Commission (UNCC);
• truth commissions; and
• national administrative bodies.

The UN Compensation Commission

The UNCC was created in 1991 as a subsidiary organ of the UN Security Council. Its mandate is to process claims and pay compensation for losses and damages suffered as a direct result of Iraq's unlawful invasion and occupation of Kuwait in August 1990. The funds are raised through a tax on Iraqi oil exports. The UNCC's approach to reparation is strictly limited to compensation.

Claims which are broader that just damage resulting from gross human rights violations must be submitted through standard forms to the UNCC Secretariat and have been classified into six categories. Type A claims concern individuals who were forced to leave Iraq or Kuwait as a result of the invasion; type B claims concern serious personal injury or death; type C claims concern other cases of personal injury, including mental pain and anguish, and losses of property or other interests; type D claims concern losses over USD 100,000 and are paid after A, B and C claims have been compensated; type E covers corporate claims; and type F concerns claims by governments and international organizations. As of July 2001, most of the 2.6 million claims filed with the commission had been processed. The compensation awarded against the claims processed so far amounts to USD 35.4 billion; the 10,000 claims yet to be resolved represent requests for over USD 200 billion in compensation.

The UNCC sets an important precedent which shows that, if only there is sufficient political interest, it is possible to process a large number of individual compensation claims, even at the highest international level: the normative framework has been created, a secretariat established and a funding mechanism found. The UNCC experience offers inspiration for the processing of claims on a very large scale - the use of standard submission procedures, classification into different categories, the use of fixed sums for certain types of injury and the use of compensation ceilings. Such procedures may be of use for the management of other reparation mechanisms.

However, the UNCC has also highlighted the way in which the objectives of reparation and reconciliation can remain completely disconnected. In the UNCC case, reparation has been reduced to a technical, financial operation that is exclusively backward-looking. Moreover, it operates one-sidedly, deliberately excluding the suffering of Iraqi nationals as a result of the military operations of their own government or of the US Government and its allies. Finally, the financing mechanism of the UNCC raises serious questions given that it is intimately linked to a wider sanctions regime which has been denounced for its impact on human rights.

Truth Commissions

The work of a truth commission, when properly done, automatically leads to some form of reparation, as understood in the broader sense defined above. (Their work is the subject of chapter 8.) Allowing victims to speak out and be heard, investigating and establishing the truth about violations, public acknowledgements (possibly combined with apologies or expressions of regret), memorials to victims and recommendations to reform public institutions - all are important aspects of a full reparation package. Other reparation needs of victims are at least partly dependent on some form of payment: analysis of a representative sample of statements before the South African Truth and Reconciliation Commission (TRC) revealed that deponents' prime expectation of the TRC was financial assistance. The second most common request was for investigation of violations.

The Reparation and Rehabilitation Committee (RRC) of the TRC recommended a reparation and rehabilitation policy consisting of five components: (a) urgent interim reparation payments for people in urgent need, to enable them to access services and facilities; (b) individual reparation grants for each victim of a gross human rights violation paid over a period of six years; (c) symbolic, legal and administrative reparation measures; (d) community rehabilitation programmes; and (e) institutional reforms. The TRC Act provided for the establishment of a President's Fund to administer the individual reparation grant system. Contributions to the fund would come from the national budget, international and local donations, and interest earned on the fund. The TRC report recommended that each of the approximately 22,000 victims registered should receive between ZAR 17,000 and ZAR 23,000 (ca USD 1,678–2,270), with the total budget amounting to some ZAR 2.8 billion (USD 0.28 billion) over six years.

The TRC sets an important example through its holistic approach to reparation as both a backward- and a forward-looking concept, which goes beyond financial compensation and is thoroughly embedded in a wider search for truth, justice and reconciliation. Reparation should indeed be linked to truth and justice: if compensation is used merely to buy the victims' silence in the absence of truth, their psychological rehabilitation is likely to be impeded. On the other hand, the RRC's power was limited to formulating recommendations: it

> Reparation should indeed be linked to truth and justice.

did not have the same decision-making powers as the Human Rights Violations Committee and the Amnesty Committee. Three years after the publication of the TRC's report, the South African Government is coming in for strong criticism both for failing to pay out reparation grants and for adding insult to injury by paying no more than token amounts.

National Administrative Bodies (Trust Funds, Compensation Commissions)

Several countries have enacted legislation and established reparation funds or commissions to compensate victims of human rights abuses committed under a previous regime. The creation of such administrative bodies may be the direct or indirect result of a truth commission, or they may be established independently. Some examples follow:

1. Brazil in 1995 established by law a Reparations Commission to compensate the relatives of 135 members of an armed rebel movement who disappeared under Brazil's military rule.

2. A 1991 Hungarian law established a National Damage Claims Settlement Office to remedy the harm unlawfully caused by the state seizure of property through the payment of lump-sum compensations.

3. Prompted in part by the friendly settlement procedure of the Inter-American Commission on Human Rights, Argentina in 1991 adopted reparation legislation to compensate victims of specific human rights violations, focusing especially on disappearances. The government Human Rights Office was the implementing body.

4. In 1992, the Chilean legislature established the National Corporation for Reparation and Rehabilitation which was mandated to implement the Chilean Truth Commission's recommendations on reparations.

5. In 1997, in Australia, the report of the National Inquiry into the Separation of Aboriginal and Torres Strait Islander Children from their Families recommended the payment of compensation to people affected by forcible removal through a National Compensation Fund.

9.5.2 Other Strategic Issues

This section presents some of the strategic choices that arise within judicial and non-judicial approaches, as well as a number of dilemmas and constraints that governments and/or civil society groups may face when developing, advocating and/or running a reparation programme. As far as possible, recommendations are formulated to assist in responding to these difficulties. The strategic issues are divided into five categories on the basis of the following questions:
• Who will qualify as a beneficiary of the reparation measures?
• Which reparation measures will be provided for?

- How does reparation relate to other developmental or humanitarian needs?
- How will the reparation programme be funded?
- What are common logistical issues?

It should be noted at the outset that, in many countries, reparation has been and continues to be the subject of a long process of campaigning, with the actual end result remaining uncertain. This process towards a "negotiated justice", when it is sufficiently inclusive and "owned" by the victims, may well be important in itself. It allows people to become actively involved, to have their experiences recognized by and shared with others, and to regain a sense of dignity. This process is valuable. However, this should not be used as an excuse by the state to forget about the end result.

The Beneficiaries of Reparation

If an integrated approach is adopted to deal with issues of justice, reparation and reconciliation, the range of potential beneficiaries of a reparation programme must logically be defined taking into account the notion of victim that is used under other justice and reconciliation mechanisms. It is likely that the criminal justice mechanism will deal only with a limited range of violations. Truth commissions and mediation programmes may deal with other consequences of past oppression. Any reparation programme should take into account how victims are to be approached under all the instruments being used in the transition and then decide how to select them. Two examples may clarify this dilemma.

First, reparation should not be seen as a "reward" for testifying in a criminal case or before a truth commission, so the link between testifying and reparation must be correctly conceived.

Second, victims of practices which have not been included in criminal justice or truth commission mandates or in mediation programmes may have valid and unmet reparation needs. To exclude them from a reparation programme may be perceived as unjust and create feelings of resentment. The example of Chilean torture victims, who are not covered by the mandate of the Corporation for Reparation and Reconciliation, is a clear illustration of this dilemma.

It is extremely important to provide adequate information and avoid creating unrealistic expectations.

Reparation programmes should avoid strengthening existing or creating new discriminatory practices. Reparation should not be perceived as a form of revenge in the hands of the new regime. Victims of torture, whether at the hand of agents of the past regime or of former rebels, should in principle be given access to the same reparation regime. Politically biased or one-sided reparation will make reconciliation more difficult and should be avoided at all costs.

Similarly, attention should be paid to instances of victim competition. Some categories of victim may, as a result of experience, good organization or political affiliation, be able to make themselves heard better than others. Policy makers must be aware of the strength of, and competition between, victim support groups and design their programmes accordingly.

The above issues also have an impact on victim registration. The registration of victims as beneficiaries of reparation can, in part, build on the work of a truth commission or the criminal justice system, but should ideally go beyond that threshold. In any case, it should be depoliticized and non-discriminatory. Further, the threshold for reparation for all victims who meet the criteria should be sufficiently low. For example, victims living in remote areas should not be excluded in practice because they are geographically isolated.

Should victims be categorized in terms of their suffering, with priority given to those who are judged to have suffered the most? This raises the question whether it is possible to quantify and compare suffering. Should reparation, rather, be prioritized in accordance with victims' current needs? Or should all victims who meet the criteria and who are eligible as beneficiaries receive equal compensation?

In the case of wrongful death or disappearance, a range of indirect victims (see chapter 4) may claim reparation. The reparation programme should consider carefully who to accept as indirect victims - only spouses, children and parents, or other relatives and dependants as well? Furthermore, will these indirect victims receive compensation for the suffering of the direct victim only, or also for their own mental suffering and financial damage as a result of the wrongful death or disappearance of their relative? Victim support groups may find arguments in international human rights law which clearly affirm a state's obligation to repair an indirect victim's own suffering as well.

Whichever categories of victim are in the end eligible for reparation, it is extremely important to provide adequate information and avoid creating unrealistic expectations. This applies both to the range of reparation measures and amounts of compensation and to the role of the various transitional mechanisms: victims may well testify before a court or a truth commission, but it should be made absolutely clear what the powers of the court or the commission, if any, might be in awarding compensation.

The Range of Reparation Measures

Crucial decisions need to be taken on the nature of the reparation and as to whether to offer cash or services to those who suffered or a combination. The South African RRC identified a number of disadvantages of a "services package" - a package of access to health, housing, education and other basic services. These included higher administrative and logistical costs, less flexibility to adapt to victims' changing needs, the potential for tensions within a community as a result of a select group of individuals having preferential access to services, and (less predictably) budget implications. The committee therefore chose to give the recipients some freedom of choice and recommended financial reparations at a level which would enable reasonable access to essential basic services, thus generating the opportunity for people to achieve a dignified standard of living within the particular socio-economic context.

The determining argument for the RRC was the expectations of the victims themselves. It is important to design a reparation package consisting of a considered balance of services and financial reparation. The package should consider all the practical and financial factors affecting victims' ability to access basic services as well as the preferences expressed by victims and their support groups or other representatives.

This approach obviously presupposes that basic services are available to all concerned.

Careful consideration should be given to the different kinds of compensatory damages to be included - nominal, pecuniary, moral and/or punitive (see section 9.2.1).

The financial element of a compensation package is quite important. At the very least, adding insult to injury should be avoided. It may not be realistic to aim to provide financial compensation that is proportionate to the suffering of each individual victim, but any payment made should be enough at least to make some difference. Pecuniary awards may be either determined on a strictly individual basis - i.e., in accordance with the actual loss and suffering of an individual victim - or determined on the basis of fixed compensation schemes, with statutory or administrative regulations laying down certain amounts of damages for each type of injury, for example, one day of unlawful imprisonment, the loss of a thumb, or one day in hospital.

As noted above, full individual reparation to all victims after mass victimization will be neither sufficient (because of the structural damage) nor possible (because of the number of people who were victimized). Collective measures will be necessary to deal with past abuses adequately. In order to be effective, the threshold for collective reparation measures will necessarily be low, which in itself will make them more attractive. Thus collective measures have the advantage of reaching a larger number of victims. There is also less risk of an artificial and arbitrary limitation on the range of beneficiaries. Furthermore, they seem better suited to offer a remedy for a past which has, in actual fact or in people's perceptions, collectively victimized certain groups, beyond the violations suffered by individual members of the group.

The beneficiaries of a collective reparations programme should ideally have ownership over its design. The Guatemalan CEH, for instance, highlighted the need for the Mayan population to be involved in defining the priorities of the collective reparation process.

This said, the extent to which collective measures can replace or supplement individual reparation measures should be carefully considered. As far as possible, individual reparation rights should be respected and existing judicial mechanisms should remain available to deal with individual reparation claims. In many cases, as illustrated by the South African situation, the threshold (particularly in financial terms) to access these mechanisms will in any case be excessively high for the "average" victim. Ideally, some combination and integration of the individual and the collective dimensions should be achieved. Providing better and more easily accessible health services to previously oppressed minorities in remote areas, for instance, is likely to be a useful collective reparation measure. However, for this to be psychologically restorative at the individual level, it may need to be personalized: for those members of the target group who have been tortured, for instance, specific personalized and free counselling services may also be organized.

> It is important to maintain some link between the material reparation awarded to victims and acknowledgement of wrongdoing and responsibility.

Generally, it is important to maintain some link between the material reparation awarded to victims and acknowledgement of wrongdoing and responsibility. Japan's financial compensation for the "comfort women" through the establishment of the Asian Women's Fund was criticized for being a welfare-oriented system based on gender and development needs rather than on acceptance of responsibility for wrongdoing and an obligation to provide reparation. The risk of this kind of response is certainly greater where exclusively collective reparation measures are used.

International legal scholars generally award primacy to restitution as a preferred form of reparation. This theoretical debate is not without practical repercussions: primacy should not rule out a certain flexibility when designing reparation schemes under transitional justice mechanisms. Ideally, even when full restitution remains materially possible, victims may wish to opt for financial compensation. On the other hand, reparation programmes should not allow the responsible state to renounce some of its obligations at its own discretion: for instance, the payment of compensatory damages should not be used as a substitute for returning citizenship to members of a formerly oppressed minority.

Victims' expectations and perceptions of reparation may vary widely. The variables which affect their view of reparation include their cultural background, their post-conflict socio-economic position, whether they are in exile or not, gender, and the passage of time since the violations suffered. It is therefore highly unlikely that it will be possible to meet all expectations of all victims on an individual basis. Generally, it seems advisable to have a balanced package of individual and collective, pecuniary and non-pecuniary, and commemorative and reformative reparation measures.

Reparation versus Other Development or Humanitarian Needs

Any serious reparation programme will have important budget consequences. Although it will be difficult to tell at exactly what point the state has exhausted its financial resources for reparation, this logically raises the issue of priorities. One of the main arguments of the South African Government against the immediate full-scale implementation of the RRC recommendations was the need to budget for other development needs (housing, education, health infrastructure). Striking the right balance between reparation and other needs is a difficult exercise.

Some comments may help to give guidance in addressing this issue:

1.   A successful reparation claim before a judicial body, resulting in the state's being obliged to provide compensation to victims, is an important lever for victim support groups. These awards will normally - i.e., under the rule of law - outweigh other policy needs - in fact, judicial awards have to be implemented irrespective of other needs. Although a purely judicial approach may not be feasible for a large number of claims (see above), the mere possibility of this avenue may be an important lever when negotiating a programme.

2.   One way for the government to express its sincere commitment to providing reparation to victims is for it to review its overall policy goals in the light of victims' collective reparation needs. As a consequence, budget allocations to the justice, health, education and housing sectors will logically take priority, for example, over defence budgets and income tax reductions. This should also be part of the public political debate: policy decisions, for instance, dealing with public infrastructure, should be explicitly motivated from a reparation perspective.

3.   To distinguish between urgent humanitarian and other reparation needs, a two-track approach, similar to the one adopted - at least theoretically - in Rwanda may be interesting. Rwanda, on the one hand, established a National Fund for Assistance to Survivors of the Genocide and Massacres, and, on the other hand, intends to establish a Compensation Fund for Victims. The latter will deal with the implementation of judicial awards in favour of survivors or relatives of victims. The aim of the former is of a more humanitarian nature: the most economically disadvantaged victims of the genocide are eligible for assistance with housing, education, health and social reintegration, irrespective of judicial recognition of their right to reparation.

Financing a Reparation Programme

As a rule (although this might often leave a bitter taste), state responsibility for injustices committed under a previous regime lies with the new regime. In most cases, however, there will already be other enormous political challenges which go well beyond the state's financial resources. How, then, can additional funds be found for a reparation programme?

1.   Civil responsibility should lie with former leaders and other perpetrators individually. However, a victim's right to reparation should not be dependent on the availability or accessibility of perpetrators' individual resources. It is the responsibility of the state to secure reimbursement from perpetrators for reparation payments made to victims.

There is an important role in this regard for the governments of foreign countries where perpetrators have assets. In October 2001, a US Federal District Court in New York ruled that President Robert Mugabe in his capacity as leader of the Zimbabwe African Nationalist Union-Patriotic Front

(ZANU-PF) party was liable to pay compensation to various victims of human rights violations by members of this party. The Marcos litigation in the USA is another example. Both cases present interesting illustrations not only of innovative procedures being used to deal with large numbers of claims in a judicial context but also of the role which foreign assets and governments can play in financing part of a reparation programme.

2.   It is highly unlikely that this source of financing will be enough. A further contribution may come from a "reparations tax", although this will be highly unpopular if it is designed in such a way as to cause victims to suffer a second time. Careful thought should be given to designing a tax scheme which targets primarily the least vulnerable (while, obviously, at the same time not financially "chasing" them out of the country).

3.   National and international law deals with the responsibility of perpetrators. A legal approach pays little or no attention to the different types and hierarchies of guilt. Under national or international law primary perpetrators carry legal criminal guilt and legal civil responsibility. In the case of indirect offenders, guilt is of a political and/or moral nature (see chapter 5). Their offence is caused by the direct or indirect advantages they enjoyed during the pre-transitional period (as "beneficiaries"), by their inaction when witnessing human rights violations (as "bystanders and onlookers") or by unintentional harmful action. When designing a reparations process, the inclusion of indirect offenders among those who bear responsibility should be one of the core issues considered.

Financially speaking, some of the most interesting indirect offenders are companies which have benefited from the abusive policies of the past. Careful attention should be given to the question whether corporate conduct under the former regime qualifies as corporate complicity in past abuses and therefore leads to legal responsibility on the part of the company. Another option is to advocate indirect offenders' financial involvement through voluntary contribution schemes.

4.   An additional problem - that of "intergenerational justice" - arises when a period of time passes before a reparations programme is established. Can successor generations of perpetrators and beneficiaries be expected to pay for the wrongs perpetrated by regimes long gone to successor generations of victims who may (or may not) suffer from the continuing effects of the past injustices?

Legally speaking, there is no such thing as succeeding generations' personal responsibility. However, the continuing moral and political duty of the state to provide redress to the victims or their succeeding generations may lead to the adoption of a fiscal policy which obliges them to pay. In such cases, their duty to contribute might be more easily conceived and presented as primarily linked to their citizenship (and their general status as taxpayers) rather than based on some sort of inherited "perpetratorship". It is also likely that, in this context, reparation will take a collective form as social redistribution policies or affirmative action-type programmes.

5.   To ease some of the immediate budget constraints, a system of compensatory payments through yearly or other periodic instalments, possibly pension plans, might be an option, instead of immediate payments of the full amount.

6.   One delicate question relates to contributions from foreign governments. Although in some cases the political and even legal responsibility of foreign states may be unquestionable, it may be highly problematic for a newly democratic state to claim compensation from other states through legal

proceedings. This is notably the case for Rwanda, which could, theoretically and probably success-fully, initiate reparation claims against the UN, Belgium and possibly other states. For primarily diplomatic reasons, no such initiative has been taken so far.

The contribution of foreign states can also, obviously, be other than merely financial: any truth-telling exercise may require information to be provided by third countries or former allies of the past regime.

> *The inclusion of indirect offend-ers among those who bear responsibility should be one of the core issues considered.*

Logistics

Even in the case of large-scale victimization, the decision to recognize a victim's right to reparation and to award reparation can to some extent be carried through by the regular transitional justice mechanism, be it a classical criminal tribunal or a truth commission. However, the actual implemen-tation of a reparation programme will be better done by a separate reparation body. Some examples have been mentioned above. The operational requirements in terms of logistics alone are completely different from those required of institutions dealing with truth-telling or criminal prosecution. Also, the other transitional justice mechanisms may necessarily be of limited duration - the end of their term symbolizing a return to "normality" - whereas a reparation body may require a much longer period of activity.

The different components of a reparation programme may require partly similar, but also largely different, approaches in terms of organization, personnel and skills. Some of the issues that may arise include the following:

• Listing the victims who meet the criteria of beneficiaries of the reparation programme is generally a first logistical challenge. Part of this work may be based on the activities of the courts, a truth commission or other transitional justice mechanisms, but the reparation programme should prefer-ably also be open to those who do not wish to participate in such mechanisms. Listing the victims presupposes nationwide information campaigns and easily accessible registration mechanisms.

• Statement takers need to be recruited and trained in registering victims' reparation needs and in explaining the limitations of the reparation programme.

• Awarding compensation requires a preliminary assessment of damages or, if lump-sum amounts are to be used, at least a verification that the damage has been suffered as a result of the past oppression. This requires effective corroboration of victim statements, which is a very time-consuming exercise. Otherwise false statements are likely to jeopardize the whole operation.

• Sufficient time and personnel are needed to undertake the administrative processing of claims. To give just one example, the award of reparation in response to multiple claims by several indirect victims for the suffering of the same person should be avoided.

• Appropriate payments procedures need to be developed, in particular for people who do not have bank accounts.

9.6 Concluding Remarks

Reparation is an essential item on any post-conflict agenda: it should be solidly integrated into a wider approach to truth, justice and reconciliation. This chapter has shown how reparation has recently been shaped and redefined in the light of the legitimate expectations of victims of grave abuses. Their right to reparation is finding an increasingly solid basis in international human rights law. However, bridging the gap between theory and practice remains an enormous challenge, particularly in the case of large-scale victimization. Several strategic choices need to be made and a whole range of dilemmas and constraints need to be dealt with, at a time when few examples of "best practice" are available.

As a general rule, when designing and implementing a reparation programme, great attention should be paid to inclusiveness, appropriateness and effectiveness as guiding principles. Inclusiveness should inspire the accurate definition, identification and involvement of all relevant players in the reparations process, victims as well as perpetrators, including, ideally, beneficiaries of past abuses. In so doing, "ownership" and links between reparation and responsibility can be achieved. Appropriateness should guide decisions on the range of reparation measures and assist in striking the right balance between financial and immaterial measures as well as between reparation and other post-conflict challenges. Effectiveness goes hand in hand with the treatment of reparation as an individual legal right while at the same time seeking to overcome the important limitations of classical judicial enforcement methods. Effectiveness as a guiding principle should guarantee access and delivery.

> When designing and implementing a reparation programme, great attention should be paid to inclusiveness, appropriateness and effectiveness as guiding principles.

References and Further Reading
Main Sources

Barkan, Elazar. *The Guilt of Nations: Restitution and Negotiating Historical Injustices*. New York: Norton, 2000.

Redress. *Torture Survivors' Perceptions of Reparation: A Preliminary Survey*. London: Redress, 2001.

Shelton, Dinah. *Remedies in International Human Rights Law*. New York: Oxford University Press, 1999.

Teitel, Ruti G. *Transitional Justice*. New York: Oxford University Press, 2000.

Other References

Brooks, Roy. *When Sorry Isn't Enough: The Controversy over Apologies and Reparations for Human Injustice*. New York: New York University Press, 1999.

Torpey, John. "'Making Whole What Has Been Smashed': Reflections on Reparations." *Journal of Modern History* 73(2) June 2001:333–358.

Internet Sources

Organization of American States, http://www.oas.org

Inter-American Court of Human Rights, http://www.corteidh.or.cr

Council of Europe, http://www.coe.int

European Court of Human Rights, http://www.echr.coe.int

Organization of African Unity, http://www.oau-oua.org (a compilation of the decisions on communications of the African Commission on Human and People's Rights, on the basis of the commission's activity reports, was published by the Institute for Human Rights and Development, based in Banjul, in 1999: see http://www.africaninstitute.org)

International Criminal Court: http://www.un.org/law/icc/index.html_

United Nations Compensation Commission, http://www.unog.ch/uncc (the *Handbook on Justice for Victims on the Use and Application of the 1985 UN Declaration* and the *Guide for Policymakers* can be downloaded from http://www.uncjin.org)

South African TRC, http://www.truth.org.za

CHAPTER 10

The International Community

LUC HUYSE

In the chapters on healing, justice, truth and reparation, brief references were made to the interventions of third parties, such as UN agencies and foreign NGOs, in these areas. This chapter now takes a closer look at the potential role and the limits of outside attempts to foster lasting reconciliation. Two questions will be raised here:
• What should be the "canon" of international engagement?
• In what reconciliation areas can third party support be useful?

10.1 Rules of Engagement

Reconciliation in post-conflict societies cannot be imported from the outside. Foreign actors must see their role as one of support and facilitation of domestic policies. Several, more practical, imperatives follow from this critical engagement perspective.

10.1.1 A Cautious and Restrained Approach

Caution from the side of the international community implies:

> Reconciliation in post-conflict societies cannot be imported from the outside.

• awareness of the specific political, cultural and historic forces in a transitional society;
• accepting that the process must be locally "owned"; and
• being sensitive to such issues as appropriate timing and tempo.

Assessing the Particular Context of a Post-Conflict Situation

Recently, trials and truth commissions have become increasingly popular with international donor communities and NGOs. Rama Mani, a consultant for the Centre for Humanitarian Dialogue in Geneva, writes that this has created "an implicit obligation for countries newly emergent from conflict to adopt one or both". This commitment has sometimes been written into internationally brokered peace agreements, as in Guatemala, Sierra Leone and Burundi. Mani concludes: "There are forceful arguments in favor of both options. However proponents of trials and truth commissions afford less attention to the difficulties of applying these two mechanisms in low-income post-conflict societies, and to their shortcomings in these politically and materially constrained contexts".

The international community must avoid such a one-sided approach. Each transition from violence to peace is indeed almost unavoidably unique. Earlier in the Handbook attention was drawn to the impact of such factors as the nature, scale and degree of violence, the intensity of division in society, and the previous and post-transition balance of power. In addition, the strength of the political will to tackle the question of reconciliation may vary considerably. So do capacities and resources, both inside the political leadership and in civil society.

Accepting the Local "Ownership" of the Reconciliation Process

Durable reconciliation must be home-grown. Pain, misery and discrimination can only be known and acknowledged by those who suffered and those who caused the injustice. Only the victims and the perpetrators can reconcile themselves with one another. From this it follows that the international community must facilitate instead of impose, empower the people instead of "picking the fruits of sorrow", support local initiatives instead of drowning the post-conflict society in a sea of foreign projects (as happened in Kosovo), and choose capacity building above importing experts.

Sometimes societies coming out of a violent and long-lasting conflict will be so weak that external support must be much more extensive and far-reaching. But even then so-called mixed projects, where domestic and foreign agencies and NGOs jointly take responsibility (as in the case of the Guatemalan truth commission), are preferable.

A Cautious Time Frame

International peacemakers and facilitators tend to advocate a rushed approach to reconciliation. This is often a reflection of their own short-term interests and/or based on the unfounded conviction that

> *International peacemakers and facilitators tend to advocate a rushed approach to reconciliation. Such a perspective is more often than not counterproductive.*

the success of a transition depends on a rapid move towards national unity. At several points in this Handbook it is argued that such a perspective is more often than not counterproductive. Reconciliation as a process is a difficult, long and unpredictable voyage, involving various steps and stages. Its timescale must be measured not in months or years but in generations. Where unhurried reconciliation activities may seem at first glance to be a hindrance to establishing a working democracy, in fact they are a necessary requirement for the survival of that democracy.

An adequate time frame also involves foreign actors, governmental and non-governmental, ensuring a long-term engagement, with a continuous evaluation of past international projects and interventions.

10.1.2 Protecting the Prospects of Enduring Reconciliation

International agencies (particularly in the form of the World Bank and the International Monetary Fund) are inclined to suggest - even force - transitional societies to give priority to political and economic reforms at the expense of reconciliation programmes. It remains essential that care be taken not to damage the prospects of long-term reconciliation by establishing inappropriate political and economic structures.

10.2 Areas Where International Support Can Be Useful

Justice is the domain where the international community is directly involved in processes that have a reconciliation potential. This is firmly demonstrated by the ad hoc tribunals in The Hague and Arusha, the International Criminal Court (ICC), the UN-initiated tribunals in Cambodia and Sierra Leone, and the implementation of the principle of universal jurisdiction. Truth-telling is another field where foreign agencies and NGOs are prominent. Examples are the UN-sponsored commissions in El Salvador, Guatemala and East Timor.

Other forms of support aim at:
• generating opportunities; and/or
• creating favourable conditions for reconciliation processes.

10.2.1 Generating Opportunities

The amount of available information on healing, truth-seeking, justice and reparation programmes has grown considerably. Information networks (for example, the New York-based International Center for Transitional Justice and the Cape Town-based Institute for Justice and Reconciliation) have been created. They offer professional expertise and organize regional workshops where local decision makers can exchange information and advice. Several international NGOs sustain reconciliation activities in post-conflict countries. Avocats Sans Frontières, for example, produced the manual that has been used to train the *gacaca* judges in Rwanda.

> Lack of coordination between donor countries and NGOs has often curtailed the efficacy of international support.

Most societies emerging from brutal conflict are totally impoverished. They lack the material and technical resources to set up healing projects, truth commissions and reparation programmes. This is where outside support is badly needed and extremely useful. It may take the form of:
• assisting truth commissions with forensic experts to identify victims in mass graves or supporting the publication (in various indigenous languages) of the commission's reports;
• creating or financially backing funds for restitution to the victims;
• providing for witness protection; and
• assisting claimants in civil suits against torturers, as has been done by Redress, a UK-based NGO.

Lack of coordination and networking between donor countries and NGOs has, however, often curtailed the efficacy of international support. The need for coordination is clearly visible in the context of Kosovo today, where more than 300 international agencies have been registered.

Another problem is the one-sided preoccupation of the international community with the material consequences of a violent conflict. This reflects the priority it gives to easing the *effects* of civil war and oppression. Much less attention goes to targeting the *roots* of human rights violations.

10.2.2 Creating Favourable Conditions

The international community is often a party in the processes that lead to the end of a civil war. It has, consequently, the opportunity to negotiate reconciliation programmes into peace agreements. It also may help in the drafting of suitable domestic legislation and provide protection for those, such as the members of a truth commission, who will be locally responsible for the implementation of such programmes and legislation. Outside actors can put pressure on those groups in a post-conflict society that are ready to renew a civil war or stage a coup. In cases where trials are a crucial step towards reconciliation foreign states may facilitate the extradition of notorious murderers and torturers.

Transnational NGOs and official agencies have an important role to play in drafting international guidelines that may strengthen local political and civil society leaders. Examples are the UN guidelines on the fight against impunity, the right to truth and the right to restitution for victims of gross human rights violations.

International reporting and monitoring mechanisms are most useful instruments. Examples include the Organization of African States' International Panel of Eminent Personalities to Investigate the 1994 Genocide in Rwanda and the Surrounding Events, and the various war crimes commissions and bodies established by the UN to look into violations committed in places such as the former Yugoslavia, Rwanda and East Timor. Another illustration is the work of UN Committee against Torture, which may be helpful for civil society groups when designing proposals or lobbying for reparation measures. Human Rights Watch published testimonies on atrocities in Bosnia. The Genocide Studies Program at the University of Yale, USA, compiled databases on the Cambodian genocide. In countries where criminal proceedings are partly based on unwritten evidence outside agencies may support the computerized storage of evidence. The US Agency for International Development (USAID) has offered such assistance to the Ethiopian Special Prosecutor's Office in its preparation of the trials of pre-1991 human rights violations.

It is, however, clear that third-party states must be ready to facilitate the transfer of significant information stored in their government and secret service archives. The international truth commission of El Salvador was refused access to 12,000 very relevant documents which the US Government had collected on the civil war in El Salvador. The Guatemalan truth commission, on the other hand, successfully requested the declassification of thousands of US documents - with the help of the National Security Archive, a US-based NGO.

References and Further Reading

Mani, Rama. *Beyond Retribution: Seeking Justice in the Shadows of War*. Cambridge and Malden, Mass: Polity Press and Blackwell, 2002.

Conclusion

DAVID BLOOMFIELD

The material in this Handbook represents most of the accumulated wisdom so far on reconciliation. Reconciliation is a relatively new addition to the post-conflict scene, and thus there are still large gaps in our knowledge and serious imperfections in our practice. But contained in these pages are the expertise and experience in the field as it currently stands. Much of that valuable information boils down to a few points, simply expressed but still immensely challenging to put into practice. Here, we focus on just three.

First, there is no one road to reconciliation. There is no right answer that has been worked out, no perfect model from South Africa or Peru or Rwanda or Cambodia that others can simply import and imitate. Nor will any single tool solve the whole problem: neither truth-telling alone, nor healing, nor justice, nor forgiveness. In every new context, a new and multi-stranded individual process must be designed. But this is not a handicap by any means. On the contrary, it should give those faced with the challenge of designing their own process the confidence to realize that they are the experts on their own situation, to trust their own judgement about what will work and what will not in their context, and to use, adapt, alter or replace ideas from elsewhere.

Second, it is not sensible to judge an entire reconciliation process as a success or a failure. Each process consists of many small successes and failures. The work is not easy, and the challenges of the overall process can occasionally seem overwhelming. But it is important to see the progress and successes, small and large, where and when they appear. Every step forward is a success - indeed, as one practitioner commented, "every silence that is broken is a victory for reconciliation". A reconciliation process consists of a multitude of initiatives, steps and stages, where progress is an accumulation of small steps. Success happens at the individual level, as well as the collective level. Sensitively and appropriately designed, reconciliation will bring these small successes. And the small victories accumulate to form the bigger ones.

Third, reconciliation is necessarily a long-term process. It is pointless to plan to "do" reconciliation first and then move on to justice, or economic reform, or constitutional reform. But reconciliation is also a pressing need, and one which does not ease simply with time. Quite the reverse: the collective and individual hurt, pain, frustration and anger that are the legacy of violence will only grow, not diminish, if left unaddressed. So it is equally counterproductive to leave reconciliation until after those other priorities have been achieved.

How then can these opposing pressures be resolved? Quite simply, it is necessary to view reconciliation as a part of peace-building and democratization, just as integral to the post-conflict solution as constitutional reform or any other key element. Reconciliation must be implemented in parallel with and as a constitutive part of those other activities of reform or reconstruction. This is precisely because reconciliation underpins all those other strands of rebuilding - the rebuilding of relationships underpins, and must run concurrently with, rebuilding all the other structures and processes. It must be done not before, not after, but at the same time.

This Handbook points to some methods for doing this. The crucial actors (victims and offenders) must be understood. The crucial procedures (healing, justice, truth and reparation) must be undergone. And the habits and patterns of the past must be undone. Those are the crucial patterns of attitude and behaviour that produced and sustained the violence. If they remain unchanged, they will eventually produce the same outcome again.

As the saying goes, those who ignore their history are condemned to repeat it. We must examine our past history, not only for its own sake and that of its victims, but in order to build a strategy - a reconciliation process - that guarantees a secure future. However painful that history has been, it has vital lessons for the future, and indeed it is the starting point for our journey into the future.

This is not simply a moral argument about doing the right thing, even though reconciliation can contain strong moral elements, such as justice, respect and equality. It is much more than that. Put bluntly, good democratic politics - even the best politics - only works when relationships between the various actors are positive enough to permit basic trust, respect and cooperation. Bad relationships - those still built on distrust, suspicion, fear, accusation, even ignorance - will effectively and eventually destroy any political system based on respect for human rights and democratic structures. Reconciliation is the means to change relationships.

A democracy is built on respect for the human rights of all concerned. Unreconciled people, still driven by fear or suspicion, do not afford each other's human rights the same respect. If human rights are not upheld widely and collectively, the basis for democracy is fatally flawed.

The work of building democracy is never finished, never perfect. It has to be constantly tended and mended, refined and re-tuned. So with reconciliation - the commitment must be for the long term, for the widest and deepest possible process, and it must be seen as an integral part of, not some addition to, overall reform and reconstruction.

The good news is that it can be done. Never perfectly, perhaps, but often effectively: this is the message from many of the examples we have examined in this book. Other examples show how it can go wrong, go backwards, even fail. But - and here we end where we began - the most conspicuous examples are those where reconciliation was ignored or treated superficially: in every case, it has come back to haunt the society. Only by building reconciliation in as a vital, equally important, piece of the jigsaw, along with economics, politics, justice and the other parts of the peace-building puzzle, can a society truly move with confidence from a divided past to a shared future.

Relevant Institutions and Web Sites

Amnesty International (international NGO), http://www.amnesty.org

Avocats Sans Frontières (ASF) (international NGO):
—— *Belgium: http://www.asf.be/*
—— *France: http://asffrance.multimania.com*
—— *Lawyers Without Borders, http://lawyerswithoutborders.gobizgo.com/*

Centre for the Study of Violence and Reconciliation (CSVR), South Africa,
http://www.wits.ac.za/csvr

Coalition for an International Criminal Court (CICC) (international NGO),
http://www.igc.org/icc/
—— CICC web page on the Rome Treaty Conference,
http://www.igc.org/icc/rome/index.html

Coalition to Stop the Use of Child Soldiers (international NGO),
http://child-soldiers.org

Council for Aboriginal Reconciliation, Australia (governmental),
http://reconciliation.org.au

Creative Associates International (CAII) (USA, private international consulting firm),
http://www.caii-dc.com/
—— Conflict Prevention: A Guide,
http://www.caii-dc.com/ghai/outline.htm
—— War Crimes Tribunals/Truth Commissions (Commissions of Inquiry),
http://www.caii-dc.com/ghai/toolbox23.htm

Fédération Internationale des Ligues des Droits de l'Homme (FIDH) (international NGO),
http://www.fidh.org/

Human Rights Watch,
http://www.hrw.org

Initiative on Conflict Resolution and Ethnicity (INCORE), University of Ulster and United Nations
University (academic),
http://www.incore.ulst.ac.uk/
—— Guide to Internet sources on Truth and Reconciliation,
http://www.incore.ulst.ac.uk/cds/themes/truth.html
—— Dealing with the Past, Conference Papers, 8–9 June 1998,
http://www.incore.ulst.ac.uk/home/publication/conference/thepast/index.html

International Center for Transitional Justice (ICTJ), USA (NGO),
http://www.ictj.org

International Commission of Jurists (international NGO),
http://www.icj.org/

International Committee of the Red Cross (ICRC) (UN-mandated),
http://www.icrc.org/

International Court of Justice (ICJ) (United Nations),
http://www.icj-cij.org/

International Criminal Court,
http://www.un.org/law/icc/index.html

International Criminal Tribunal for the Former Yugoslavia (ICTY) (United Nations),
http://www.un.org/icty/

International Criminal Tribunal for Rwanda (ICTR) (United Nations),
http://www.ictr.org/

International Crisis Group (ICG), (international NGO),
http://www.intl-crisis-group.org/

International Internet Bibliography on Transitional Justice (Gunnar Theissen,
Free University, Berlin) (academic),
http://userpage.fu-berlin.de/~theissen/biblio/index.html

No Peace Without Justice (NPWJ) International Committee of Parliamentarians,
Mayors and Citizens,
http://www.agora.stm.it/npwj/frame.html

Penal Reform International (PRI) (international NGO), http://penalreform.org

Project on Justice in Times of Transition, Harvard University (academic),
http://www.ksg.harvard.edu/justiceproject/

Redress. Seeking Reparation for Torture Survivors (international NGO),
http://redress.org

Transitional Justice Project, University of the Western Cape and the Humboldt University of Berlin
(academic),
http://www.uwc.ac.za/law/tjp/

Truth Commissions Project, Harvard Law School – Search for Common Ground (academic–NGO),
http://www.truthcommission.org

Truth and Reconciliation Commission (TRC), South Africa (governmental),
http://www.truth.org.za/
—— Report of the South African TRC,
http://www.polity.org.za/govdocs/commissions/1998/trc/index.htm

United States Institute of Peace (USIP) (independent federal institution), http://www.usip.org/
—— Truth Commissions and Commissions of Inquiry,
http://www.usip.org/library/truth.html

Carter Center (associated with Emory University),
http://www.cartercenter.org/hr.html

Contributors

David Bloomfield is Senior Executive for Democracy, Dialogue and Conflict Management with IDEA. Born in Belfast, he ran reconciliation projects in Northern Ireland in the 1980s, and has been a trainer in conflict resolution skills in Ireland and elsewhere around the world. With an MA in peace studies and a PhD in conflict resolution, he has researched and taught at the universities of Harvard, Bradford and Ulster, and published three books on the Irish peace process.

Noreen Callaghan holds a M. Phil. in International Peace Studies from Trinity College, Dublin. She devised, co-ordinates and teaches a Diploma in Reconciliation Practice at the National University of Ireland, Galway's Community Education Centre. She teaches groupwork and reconciliation courses at the PRONI Institute of Social Education and Leadership in Croatia and Bosnia. She is the author of *Building Peace: A Guide for Community Groups.*

Vannath Chea has extensive experience working with governments and national and international non-governmental organizations both in Cambodia and in USA. She served in the special missions of the United Nations Transitional Authority in Cambodia (UNTAC) 1992-1993 and is currently the president of the Cambodian Center for Social Development (CSD), a non-governmental organization, advocating good governance through the institutionalization of democratic values and principles. Chea's articles have been nationally and internationally published in reviews and magazines.

Mark Freeman currently works as a Senior Associate at the International Center for Transitional Justice. He previously worked as a human rights officer at the UN Office of the High Commissioner for Human Rights in New York, and as a commercial lawyer at a large private firm in Canada. He has participated in a wide range of human rights projects in Canada and internationally over the past decade, including as a consultant to the Office of former Vice President Hugo Cardenas in Bolivia. He has published a number of law journal articles on human rights and transitional justice, and has forthcoming chapters in three books.

Brandon Hamber was born in South Africa and is a clinical psychologist. He works in Belfast as an associate of the think-tank, Democratic Dialogue. He is an honorary fellow at the School of Psychology at Queen's University in Belfast. Formerly, he coordinated the Transition and Reconciliation Unit at the Centre for the Study of Violence and Reconciliation, South Africa. He has published widely and has worked with various projects in different countries focusing on dealing with the past in post-conflict societies. He edited the book *Past Imperfect: Dealing with the Past in Northern Ireland and Societies in Transition.*

Priscilla Hayner is a co-founder of the International Center for Transitional Justice and directs its work on Sierra Leone, Peru, Ghana, and a number of other countries. An expert on truth commissions and transitional justice initiatives around the world, she has written widely on the subject of official truth-seeking in political transitions. She is the author of *Unspeakable Truths* (Routledge, 2001), which explores the work of over 20 truth commissions worldwide. Prior to joining the ICTJ, she was a consultant to the Ford Foundation, the UN High Commissioner for Human Rights, and numerous other organizations. Priscilla Hayner was previously a program officer on international human rights and world security for the Joyce Mertz-Gilmore Foundation in New York. She holds degrees from Earlham College and the School of International and Public Affairs at Columbia University.

Luc Huyse was, until his retirement in 2000, professor of sociology and sociology of law at the Leuven University Law School (Belgium). He has written extensively on the consolidation of young democracies. His current research is on the role of retributive justice after violent conflict. He has been a consultant to governments and NGOs in Burundi and Ethiopia.

Peter Uvin is the Henry J. Leir Chair of International Humanitarian Studies and Director of the Institute for Human Security at the Fletcher School of Law and Diplomacy at Tufts University. He has worked and consulted extensively in Africa for a variety of donor agencies. His numerous publications deal with development aid, NGO scaling up, hunger and food aid, and genocide in the African Great Lakes region. His most recent book *Aiding Violence. The Development Enterprise in Rwanda* (Kumarian Press, 1998) received the African Studies Association's Herskowits award for the most outstanding book on Africa in 1998. Lately, he has worked with the OECD, the UNDP, and the Belgian Secretary of State for Development Cooperation on post-conflict issues in Rwanda.

Stef Vandeginste has an M.A. in law (Catholic University of Leuven, 1990). He did research on the human rights situation in the Central African Great Lakes region for Amnesty International and worked for the United Nations Development Programme in Rwanda. He is currently doing research on the international right to reparation for victims of gross and systematic human rights violations at the University of Antwerp.

Ian White is presently Chief Executive of the Glencree Centre for Reconciliation. He studied Youth and Community Work at the University of Ulster, Jordanstown, before becoming a Youth Worker in East Belfast. He has worked in youth, community work and community relations for the past 20 years and is a former manager with International Voluntary Service and Co-Operation Ireland. He is currently a member of the advisory committee of the Travellers Mediation Project and is the Treasurer of the Irish Peace and Reconciliation Platform. Ian White is also a member of the advisory committee of the American based Peace Initiatives Institute.

Index

INDEX